Treasury of Great American Sayings

Also by the Authors:

Instant Almanac of Events, Anniversaries, Observances, Quotations and Birthdays for Every Day of the Year, 1972—Parker Publishing Company, Inc.

Treasury of Great American Sayings

Compiled by

Leonard and Thelma Spinrad

Parker Publishing Company, Inc. West Nyack, New York

Library of Congress Cataloging in Publication Data

Spinrad, Leonard, comp.
Treasury of great American sayings.

Includes indexes.
1. Quotations, American. I. Spinrad, Thelma, joint comp. II. Title.
PN6081.S7234 818'.02 75-1098
ISBN 0-13-930560-2

Printed in the United States of America

To each other, in each's conviction
that the other has the last word.

INTRODUCTION

Most of the books of quotations that have been put together have drawn upon the wisdom and history of all the known world, from the Bible and the ancient Greek sages to Shakespeare and Voltaire and Winston Churchill. *Treasury of Great American Sayings* sticks closer to home.

To begin with, it is a selection confined exclusively to American quotations. It spans less than 400 years, and it is a selection rather than a collection. These sayings have been culled and chosen, not merely collected, with an eye toward their pertinence in our own times.

Our criteria have been simple. The quotations are intended for the use of speakers, writers and others concerned with material applicable to the present day rather than as an encyclopaedic reference for scholars. Another criterion is that the sayings should generally be constructive, even if they illuminate weaknesses and foibles. Finally, and most important, the sayings should be interesting.

Even though, in a sense, *Treasury of Great American Sayings* is also a form of history, its quotations from the 1600's on through the 1970's are presented with the thought of relating their own times and historical settings with our own.

We have been interested not only in what was said and who said it when, but also in the story behind the quotation (when there is such a story). Not every saying in this volume has a story worth telling beyond the attribution and the date; many are simply cogent lines picked up from works of fiction, songs, plays and other sources. And some extremely interesting quotations of modern vintage are not included because the people who own the copyrights have chosen to impose restrictions. But since our effort was to be discriminating, rather than all-inclusive, we have found an ample supply of quotes from which to choose.

To make the best use of *Treasury of Great American Sayings*, read the section entitled "How to Use This Book," beginning on this page. As with so many American products today, the first thing you have to do is read the directions.

HOW TO USE THIS BOOK

Suppose you are preparing a speech or writing an article. *Treasury of Great American Sayings* offers three ways of finding appropriate quotations for your purpose. The first section of the book lists quotations by subject. The second section is a key word index. The third is an index by authors' names.

Subject Section. Under the subject headings, which are arranged alphabetically, groups of sayings referring to a particular subject can be found, as well as cross references to other related topics. For example, if you look for sayings about *Accomplishments* to use as a literary peg or as the theme of a speech, you will find various comments under that subject heading, listed in the alphabetical order of their authors' last names, with anonymous quotations last. (Where there are several quotations from the same author, the earliest sayings are listed first.) But if you can't find exactly what you want under *Accomplishments,* you will be able to consult a whole list of cross references to other subject headings such as *Business, Success* and *Work.* And you may find other subject headings connected with the particular theme you are trying to cite.

Key Word Index. A second way of finding quotations on a particular subject is to consult the key word index section. There you will find, for example, every quotation in which "accomplishment" or "accomplishing" or "accomplishes" is an important part of the saying. You will also find quotations in which synonyms for accomplishment may be the key words, such as "deeds" or "achievement" or "success." The key word index is an alphabetical listing of these words, with an indication of the gist of the quotation and its number. (All quotations are numbered for ease in locating them.)

Author Index. The last section of *Treasury of Great American Sayings* is an alphabetical listing of the names of all the authors quoted in the book, with a brief biographical identification and the number of each quotation from the particular author. In most cases, the year of birth and the occupation of the author are included.

The Right Heading. Speakers, writers and teachers often have several different words for the same subject—and anyone using a quotation book should be mindful of the fact that subject headings may vary. In this book you won't find any sayings at all under the heading *Flying,* but you will find the subject you are looking for under *Airplanes.* You won't find *Liberty* in the subject headings because those sayings are included under *Freedom;* but if you specifically want sayings using the word "liberty," you can find them under L in the key word index.

Numbering. The sayings are numbered serially in each subject heading. But you may find a gap in the numbering between subjects. That is because with every new subject heading we start a new numbered sequence. *Accomplishments* has quotations numbered from one to nine; the next heading, *Advertising,* begins a new sequence with the number 11. Every subject heading starts its own series. *Atomic Energy,* for example, is the series beginning with number 141, *Colleges* with 361.

Duplicates. Most quotations appear in the book only once, under a single subject heading, but there are a few cases where the same saying appears under the several different subject headings to which it applies. In some instances, rather than reprint the whole saying in different sections, we divide it into its pertinent subjects. At the 1964 Republican convention, Senator Barry Goldwater said: "I would remind you that extremism in the defense of liberty is no vice! And let me remind you also that moderation in the pursuit of justice is no virtue." We put the first sentence under *Freedom,* the second under *Justice;* and you will also find them indexed in the key word section under "extremism," "liberty" and "moderation" as well.

Dates. In the context of contemporary reference to a great saying, it is very often helpful to know the date and circumstances of the quotation. Was it from a book or a speech or a poem, and when was it spoken or published? So we have tried to provide this information. When available, we give the exact date of quotations, and the office, if any, that the author of the quotation may have held at the time. In the case of quotations from books, it is worth pointing out that the year in which the book was published is not always the same year in which the saying was created. Some books, such as Thoreau's journals, carefully date each entry. But Emerson, for example, drew many of his published observations from lectures he had given in previous years and polished with each use.

Conflicts. There are some instances where conflicting versions of a quotation, a date or even an author's name have previously been published. In those cases, we have checked available sources and either made a judgment as to which is correct or indicated that a conflict exists.

Contexts. People say things in different circumstances at different times in their lives. We have identified the authors of quotations in the context of the particular time. Those quotations of Daniel Webster when he was in the United States Senate refer to him as Senator Webster; those when he was a private citizen give him no title; those when he was Secretary of State identify him with that Cabinet title.

Treasury of Great American Sayings includes the words of a few people such as William Penn, Thomas Paine and George Santayana, who were either not Americans or removed from the American scene. In these cases, however, we have felt that the connection with America was so strong and clear that their inclusion was justified—Penn as the founder of a great American commonwealth, Paine as a voice of the American Revolutionary War (we have quoted only what he wrote when he was in this country) and Santayana during the period when he was an American college professor. We believe that their words in these circumstances are part of American history.

Above all, we have tried, in the following pages, to capture the spirit, the wit, the wisdom and the varied outlooks of Americans. Some of these quotations will seem very familiar. Some merely deserve to be more familiar than they are. We commend them all to your attention.

Leonard and Thelma Spinrad

ACKNOWLEDGMENTS

We wish to acknowledge with thanks the permissions to quote received from the following:

Brooks Atkinson, for "Once Around the Sun," copyright 1951 by Brooks Atkinson.

Audubon Films, "Collected Speeches of Spiro Agnew," copyright 1971 by Audubon Films and published by Audubon Books.

Lewis Berg, "Molly and Me," by Gertrude Berg with Cherney Berg, copyright 1961 by Cherney Berg and published by McGraw-Hill Book Company, Inc.

Blue Seas Music, Inc. and Jac Music Co., Inc., "What the World Needs Now Is Love," by Burt Bacharach and Hal David, © copyright 1965 by Blue Seas Music, Inc. and Jac Music Co., Inc. All rights reserved.

Brandt & Brandt, "John Brown's Body," by Stephen Vincent Benet.

John Ciardi, "This Strangest Everything," by John Ciardi.

Thomas Y. Crowell Company, Inc., publisher, "Crime: Its Cause and Treatment" by Clarence Darrow. Copyright 1950, 1922 by Thomas Y. Crowell Co., Inc.

The Dial Press, publisher, "The Fire Next Time," by James Baldwin, copyright 1963 by James Baldwin.

Doubleday & Company, Inc., publisher, "Amy Vanderbilt's Everyday Etiquette," copyright © 1952, 1954, 1956; "The Sheltered Life," by Ellen Glasgow, copyright 1932 by Ellen Glasgow; "Declaration of Conscience," by Margaret Chase Smith, copyright 1972 by Margaret Chase Smith; "The Final Diagnosis," by Arthur Hailey, copyright © 1959 by Arthur Hailey.

Grosset & Dunlap, Inc., publisher, "Survey of Broadcast Journalism (1968–69)," edited by Marvin Barrett, copyright © 1969 by the Trustees of Columbia University in the City of New York.

Harcourt Brace Jovanovich, Inc., publisher, "Crapshooters" from "Smoke and Steel," by Carl Sandburg.

Harper & Row, Publishers, Inc., "The House of Intellect," by Jacques Barzun; "Yet Do I Marvel" from "On These I Stand," by Countee Cullen; "The Case for Modern Man," by Charles Frankel; "The Art of Loving," by Erich Fromm; "Profiles in Courage" by John F. Kennedy; "The Future of American Politics," by Samuel Lubell; "The Lawyers," by Martin Mayer; "Anything Can Happen," by George and Helen Papashvily; "The Second Tree from the Corner," by E. B. White; "Our Town," by Thornton Wilder.

Holt, Rinehart and Winston, Inc., publisher, "The National Football Lottery," by Larry Merchant.

Houghton Mifflin Company, publisher, "The Affluent Society," by John K. Galbraith.

Intext Press, "My Several Worlds," by Pearl S. Buck, copyright 1954, published by The John Day Company.

Little, Brown and Company, publishers, "The Age of Jackson," by Arthur M. Schlesinger, Jr.

Macmillan Publishing Co., Inc., "The Autobiography of William Allen White," copyright 1946 by Macmillan Publishing Co., Inc., renewed 1974 by Macmilian Publishing Co., Inc., and W. L. White.

Eric Sevareid, "This Is Eric Sevareid," copyright 1964 by Eric Sevareid, reprinted by permission of The Harold Matson Company.

McGraw-Hill Book Company, publisher, "Soul on Ice," by Eldridge Cleaver, copyright 1968 by Eldridge Cleaver, used with permission of McGraw-Hill Book Company.

The New American Library, Inc., publisher, "The Negro Revolt," by Louis E. Lomax.

G. P. Putnam's Sons, publisher, "Getting High in Government Circles," by Art Buchwald, copyright 1968, 1970, 1971 by Art Buchwald; "Counting Sheep," by Art Buchwald (line from "Sheep on the Runway"), copyright 1970 by Art Buchwald; "The Quest for Certainty," by John Dewey, copyright 1929 by John Dewey; "The Presidential Papers," by Norman Mailer, copyright 1963 by Norman Mailer; "Alumnus Football" from "The Sportlights of 1923" by Grantland Rice, copyright 1923, 1924 by Grantland Rice; "Never Go Anywhere Without a Pencil," by Harriet Van Horne, copyright 1972 by Harriet Van Horne.

Random House, Inc. and Alfred A. Knopf, Inc., publishers, "The Immense Journey," by Loren Eiseley, copyright 1946, 1950, 1951, 1953, 1956, 1957 by Loren Eiseley; "Growing Up Absurd," by Paul Goodman, copyright © 1956, 1957, 1958, 1959, 1960 by Paul Goodman; Four Plays by S. N. Behrman, copyright 1925, 1932, 1934, 1936, 1952 by S. N. Behrman; "Watch on the Rhine," by Lillian Hellman, copyright 1941 by Lillian Hellman; "Gideon's Trumpet," by Anthony Lewis, © copyright 1964 by Anthony Lewis; "Middle of the Night," by Paddy Chayevsky, © copyright 1957 by Paddy Chayevsky; "Lonesome Cities," by Rod McKuen, copyright 1965, 1967, 1968 by Rod McKuen; "The Magic Christian," by Terry Southern, copyright 1960 by Terry Southern; "Up the Organization," by Robert Townsend, copyright 1970 by Robert Townsend; "Pigeon Feathers and Other Stories," by John Updike, copyright © 1962 by John Updike; "The Glass Menagerie," by Tennessee Williams, copyright 1945 by Tennessee Williams; "Future Shock," by Alvin Toffler, copyright 1970 by Alvin Toffler.

Saturday Review Press, Publisher, "The Feminine Eye," by Shana Alexander, copyright © 1964, 1965, 1966, 1967, 1968, 1969 by Time Inc., copyright © 1970 by Shana Alexander.

Schroder Music Company and Malvina Reynolds "Little Boxes," words and music by Malvina Reynolds, © copyright 1962 by Schroder Music Co. (ASCAP). Used by permission.

Charles Scribner's Sons, Publishers, "Death in the Afternoon," by Ernest Hemingway, copyright 1932.

We also acknowledge the permissions and cooperation extended by United Air Lines, Mayor Wes Uhlman, Lee Trevino Enterprises, Inc., Stanley J. Goodman, Carl Stokes, Cornelia Otis Skinner, John D. Rockefeller 3rd, Bayard Rustin, Governor Ronald Reagan, Senator Edmund S. Muskie, Dr. Billy

Graham, Professor Irving Kristol, Clark Kerr, Senator Hubert H. Humphrey, George Gallup, Jr., Senator Sam J. Ervin, Jr., Dr. Erik H. Erikson, Eastern Airlines, Will Durant, The Honorable Emanuel Celler, Dr. Edward Bloustein.

L. S. and T. S.

CONTENTS

ACCOMPLISHMENTS

(See also Business, Success, Work)

---

1. The American system is the greatest engine of change and progress the world has ever seen. The American system has produced more goods, more widely distributed than any other system, any time, any place. It has given more people more true freedom—in the sense not only of political freedom, but in the sense of freedom to work at jobs of their own choosing—than any other system, any time, any place. And it provides the best means yet devised by man of directing progress not toward the ends that some arbitrary authority might choose, but toward the ends that the people themselves choose.

• Vice President Spiro T. Agnew, speech at the annual convention of the American Legion in Portland, Oregon, September 2, 1970, on the eve of a Congressional and state election campaign and on the heels of a period of campus unrest and dissatisfaction over the continuance of the Vietnam war.

2. . . . great men have done great things here, and will again, and we can make America what America must become.

• James Baldwin, *The Fire Next Time,* "Letter to My Nephew," 1963. This was the period of the flowering of black aspirations in America. Baldwin was at the height of his impact as a black writer.

3. America's factories are making more than the American people can use; American soil is producing more than they can consume. Fate has written our policy for us; we must get an ever-increasing portion of foreign trade.

• Albert J. Beveridge, speech in Boston, April 27, 1898. Elected to the U. S. Senate from Indiana the following year, Beveridge was a Theodore Roosevelt Republican who foresaw what would still be a challenge three-quarters of a century later, foreign trade, but could never have dreamed of this country running short of raw materials.

4. I also learned that it is easier to do evil than it is to do good.

• Eldridge Cleaver, *Soul on Ice,* 1968. Cleaver, a fugitive from American justice, did not share the same definitions of what or who was evil that most of his fellow Americans accepted; as a revolutionary, his solutions were equally partisan.*

5. . . . there are no gains without pains.

• Adlai Stevenson, speech accepting the Democratic nomination for President, in Chicago, July 26, 1952. He was to face a Republican candidate named Dwight D. Eisenhower. First said by Benjamin Franklin in 1750's.

6. The difficult we do immediately; the impossible takes a little longer.

• Original authorship unknown; gained popularity during World War II as the motto of both armed forces units and factory and civic groups.

7. They said it couldn't be done, but we did it.

• Anonymous, early 20th century, when not even the sky was the limit for American pride and optimism.

8. Those who dare, do; those who dare not, do not.

• Anonymous, probably late 18th century.

9. While it is an accomplishment to fill a need, it is a greater accomplishment to create a need.

• Anonymous, early 20th century, often cited in the 1920's as an aphorism about the importance of advertising.

ADVERTISING

(See also Broadcasting, Business, Newspapers)

---

11. The advertisements in a newspaper are more full of knowledge in respect to what is going on in a state or community than the editorial columns are.

• Henry Ward Beecher, *Proverbs from Plymouth Pulpit,* 1887. The Reverend Dr. Beecher was not only minister of Plymouth Church in Brooklyn, N.Y. but also an editor. He had begun his journalistic work at 23 on the *Cincinnati Journal* and founded the weekly *Christian Union,* later known as the *Outlook.*

12. Advertisements contain the only truths to be relied on in a newspaper.

• Thomas Jefferson, letter to Nathaniel Macon, U.S. Senator from North Carolina, 1819. Jefferson, whose opinion of newspapers varied widely (he fought for freedom of the press perhaps more than any man in our history, but he also wrote that "Nothing can be believed which is seen in a newspaper" in an 1807 letter) repeated this view of advertising in an 1820 letter to Charles Pickering: "I read but one newspaper . . . more for its advertisements than its news."

13. Advertising moves the goods.

• American advertising is one of our most eloquent forms of expression. But it hasn't created too much eloquence in its own behalf. This anonymous explanation of the function of advertising cannot be accused, however, of being wordy. Believed to have originated in first decade of 20th century.

14. It pays to advertise.

• Anonymous; one of the best known and most effective business slogans in American history. Gained popularity after World War I.

15. Madison Avenue.

• Synonymous with the advertising business, in the same way that Wall Street means stocks and bonds. It came into general use after World War II, when novels like *The Hucksters* (1947) turned public attention to the geographical and cultural world of advertising agencies.

16. The first explorations of space and time were not by the astronauts but by advertising. Advertising men were selling space and time and reaching for the moon before we had an astronaut.

• Anonymous, early 1960's, common saying in U.S. advertising circles.

17. We are merchants of dreams.

• Popular phrase used by advertising men in the 1920's and 1930's—the era of advertising's spectacular growth.

AGE

(See also Death, Longevity, Youth)

21. . . . when you reach forty you can't do anything every day.

• Henry "Hank" Aaron, home-run hitter of baseball, just before celebrating his 40th birthday on February 5, 1974, in Atlanta.

22. To me, old age is always fifteen years older than I am.

• Bernard M. Baruch, whose peak of public service came after he reached 70, first said this some time before 1949 (and on other occasions thereafter). Mr. Baruch was 95 when he died, in 1965.

23. . . . it is easier to run the risk of being killed (or fired) in action if before long you are going to be dead anyway. This freedom seems to me the chief consolation of old age.

• Elmer Davis, *But We Were Born Free,* copyright 1952, 1953, 1954 by Elmer Davis, reprinted by permission of the publisher, The Bobbs-Merrill Company, Inc. Journalist Davis was one of broadcasting's most fearless and successful newsmen.

24. If I don't open my mouth they may take it for the wisdom of age.

• Erik H. Erikson, psychoanalyst, remark at a professional conference in New York, April 25, 1971, when he was 69.

25. At twenty years of age, the will reigns; at thirty the wit; at forty the judgment.

• Benjamin Franklin, *Poor Richard's Almanac,* 1741, when he was 35.

26. We do not count a man's years until he has nothing else to count.

• Oliver Wendell Holmes, *The Autocrat of the Breakfast-Table,* 1858. At age 49 Dr. Holmes had a great deal else to count.

27. The riders in a race do not stop short when they reach the goal. There is a little finishing canter before coming to a standstill. There is time to hear the kind voices of friends and to say to one's self: "The work is done."

• Oliver Wendell Holmes, Jr., speech on his 91st birthday in Washington, D.C., March 8, 1932. He had resigned from the Supreme Court two months earlier.

28. Tranquility is the old man's milk.

• Thomas Jefferson, letter to Edward Rutledge, June 24, 1797. Jefferson was 54 when he wrote this letter to a younger fellow-signer of the Declaration of Independence.

29. My only fear is that I may live too long. This would be a subject of dread to me.

• Thomas Jefferson, letter to his friend Philip Mazzei, March 1801. Jefferson, just beginning his Presidency at 57, was to live another quarter of a century.

30. . . . age is opportunity no less / Than youth itself, though in another dress.

• Henry Wadsworth Longfellow, "Morituri Salutamus," read in 1875 at the 50th anniversary of the Class of 1825 of Bowdoin College. Longfellow was a member of that Class.

AIRPLANES

31. Bandits at three o'clock!

• Anonymous, popularized during World War II as a means of describing the location of enemy aircraft. The relative position of the enemy was described in terms of the circular face of a clock.

32. Bombs away!

• World War II aerial bombing communication signifying release of bombs.

33. Coming in on a wing and a prayer.

• Expression of 1930's that gained popularity during World War II as a means of describing battle-damaged plane returning to its home base.

34. Fly now, pay later.

• Used by U.S. airlines in 1950's and thereafter as inducement to travelers.

35. Fly the friendly skies . . .

• United Air Lines, 1960's. (Originally "Fly the friendly skies of United." Later it became "Fly the friendly skies of your land.")

36. . . . the wild blue yonder.

• Probably originated in the 1920's, it ultimately became a phrase in the Army Air Corps song, describing the area where U.S. planes operated.

37. The wings of man.

• Eastern Airlines motto, from the 1960's.

AMBITION
(See also Aspiration)

---

41. My ambition is to be critic-at-large of things-as-they-are.

• S. N. Berhman, *Biography,* Act II, 1932.

42. Ambition: An overmastering desire to be vilified by enemies while living and made ridiculous by friends when dead.

• Ambrose Bierce, *The Devil's Dictionary,* 1906.

43. Whatever America hopes to bring to pass in the world must first come to pass in the hearts of America.

• President Dwight D. Eisenhower, Inaugural Address, January 20, 1953. He was speaking to a nation awaiting the solution of the Korean War.

44. Hitch your wagon to a star.

• Ralph Waldo Emerson, *Society and Solitude:* Civilization, 1870. The simile from the horse-and-buggy days is just as applicable in the era of space exploration.

45. The traditional goals of earning a great deal of money and making one's mark in the world have lost some of their charm.

• George Gallup, Jr., President of the Gallup Poll, remarks at a career guidance conference in Virginia, November 16, 1973.

46. Nothing is so commonplace as to wish to be remarkable.

• Oliver Wendell Holmes, *The Autocrat of the Breakfast-Table,* 1858.

47. Most people would succeed in small things if they were not troubled with great ambitions.

• Henry Wadsworth Longfellow, *Driftwood:* Table Talk, 1857.

48. Not failure, but low aim, is crime.

• James Russell Lowell, *Under the Willows and Other Poems:* For an Autograph, 1868. It is probably not accidental that so many of our quotations on Ambition are from New England poet philosophers, whose heritage was intellectual, revolutionary and optimistic.

49. Ambition is hard work.

• Anonymous.

50. Ambition lubricates the mind.

• Anonymous, believed to be of 18th century origin.

AMERICANISM

(See also Attitudes, Democracy, Flag, Freedom, Patriotism)

---

51. America! America! / God shed His grace on thee / And crown thy good with brotherhood / From sea to shining sea!

• Katherine Lee Bates, "America the Beautiful," 1895. The poem was set to music later.

52. To me the fundamental premise of our American civilization, the premise of Catholic, Protestant and Jew alike, is a belief in the dignity of the individual.

• James B. Conant, testimony before Senate Foreign Relations Committee in support of Lend Lease Bill, February 11, 1941. The Bill was designed to provide aid to England, before we entered World War II, in that nation's fight against Nazi Germany.

53. My God! How little do my countrymen know what precious blessings they are in possession of, and which no other people on earth enjoy.

• Thomas Jefferson, letter to James Monroe, June 17, 1785. This letter from one future President to another was written in Paris.

54. . . . the land of the free and the home of the brave.

• Francis Scott Key, "The Star-Spangled Banner," September 14, 1814. Written as Key watched the Battle of Fort McHenry off Baltimore in the War of 1812.

55. If a man is going to be an American at all let him be so without any qualifying adjectives; and if he is going to be something else, let him drop the word American from his personal description.

• Henry Cabot Lodge, Forefather's Day address, to the New England Society of Brooklyn, December 21, 1888. Then a member of the House of Representatives, Lodge went on to a career in the Senate which was capped by his leadership of the fight to keep the United States out of the League of Nations. (See the heading *Immigrants* for some other views.)

56. I believe in the United States of America as a government of the people, by the people, for the people, whose just powers are derived from the consent of the governed; a democracy in a republic; a sovereign nation of many sovereign states; a perfect union, one and inseparable; established upon those principles of freedom, equality, justice and humanity for which American patriots sacrificed their lives and their fortunes. I therefore believe it is my duty to my country to love it, to support its Constitution, to obey its laws, to respect its flag and to defend it against all enemies.

• William Tyler Page, "The American's Creed," adopted by the U.S. House of Representatives, April 3, 1918. He was a member of the staff of the House for half a century.

57. America is a country where anything, anything at all can happen.

• George and Helen Papashvily, *Anything Can Happen,* 1945. These were his sentiments 20 years before as he immigrated to the U.S. from Russian Georgia.

58. We are a nation of many nationalities, many races, many religions—bound together by a single unity, the unity of freedom and equality. Whoever seeks to set one nationality against another, seeks to degrade all nationalities. Whoever seeks to set one race against another seeks to enslave all races. Whoever seeks to set one religion against another seeks to destroy all religions.

• President Franklin D. Roosevelt, speech in New York City, November 1, 1940. He spoke at a time when, once again, ethnic prejudices of a Europe at war were finding disturbing echoes in this country.

59. There can be no fifty-fifty Americanism in this country. There is room here for only 100% Americanism, only for those who are Americans and nothing else.

• Theodore Roosevelt, speech at Saratoga, N.Y., July 19, 1918. (See the heading *Immigrants* for some other views.)

60. The driving force behind our progress is our faith in our democratic institutions. That faith is embodied in the promise of equal rights and equal opportunities which the founders of our Republic proclaimed to their countrymen and to the whole world.

• President Harry S Truman, State of the Union message, January 5, 1949.

61. Liberty and Union, now and forever, one and inseparable.

• Senator Daniel Webster of Massachusetts, speech in Senate, January 26, 1830, defending the idea of national government against the doctrine of nullification and states' rights espoused by Senator Robert Y. Hayne of South Carolina.

62. I was born an American; I will live an American; I shall die an American.

• Senator Daniel Webster of Massachusetts, speaking in support of the Compromise of 1850 in the Senate, July 17, 1850. Webster's stand in support of the Compromise was extremely unpopular with many of his abolitionist constituents, since the Compromise provided for recognizing the rights of territories to decide for themselves whether they wished to be slaveholding or free.

ANCESTRY

(See also Animals, Posterity)

---

71. The pride of ancestry increases in the ratio of distance.

• George W. Curtis, *Prue and I,* 1856.

72. Here in America we are descended in blood and in spirit from revolutionists and rebels . . .

• President Dwight D. Eisenhower, speech in New York City, May 31, 1954, to a bi-centennial dinner of Columbia University, where he had also served a term as president.

73. A child's education should begin at least one hundred years before he was born.

• Oliver Wendell Holmes, *The Autocrat of the Breakfast-Table,* 1858.

74. . . . virtue is not hereditary.

• Thomas Paine, *Common Sense,* 1776.

75. Nor honored less than he who heirs / Is he who founds a line.

• John Greenleaf Whittier, "Amy Wentworth," 1862.

76. A family tree is the only tree nobody wants to be shady.

• Anonymous.

ANIMALS

81. The Democratic Party is like a mule. It has neither pride of ancestry nor hope of posterity.

• Ignatius Donnelly, speech to the Minnesota legislature, September 13, 1863. The remark has not particularly endured as a description of the Democratic Party, although the symbol has, but it is a much quoted comment on the animal.

82. I wish the Bald Eagle had not been chosen as the Representative of our Country; he is a Bird of bad moral Character . . . generally poor, and often very lousy. The Turkey is a much more respectable Bird, and withal a true original Native of America.

• Benjamin Franklin, letter to his daughter, Sarah Bache, January 26, 1784.

83. The one absolutely unselfish friend that man can have in this selfish world, the one that never deserts him, the one that never proves ungrateful or treacherous, is his dog. A man's dog stands by him in prosperity and in poverty, in health and in sickness. He will sleep on the cold ground, where the wintry winds blow and the snow drives fiercely, if only he can be near his master's side. He will kiss the hand that has no food to offer, he will lick the wounds and sores that come in encounter with the roughness of the world. He guards the sleep of his pauper master as if he were a prince. When all other friends desert, he remains. When riches take wings and reputation falls to pieces, he is as constant in his love as the sun in its journey through the heavens.

• George G. Vest, address to a jury in Warrensburg, Missouri, September 23, 1870. Vest's eloquent eulogy of the dog won the case for his client. He later served as U.S. senator from Missouri, 1879–1903.

84. They say a reasonable amount o' fleas is good fer a dog —keeps him from broodin' over *bein'* a dog, mebbe.

• Edward N. Westcott, *David Harum,* 1898.

85. The old gray mare she ain't what she used to be, many long years ago.

• Folksong.

ARISTOCRACY

91. The aristocrat is the democrat ripe and gone to seed.

• Ralph Waldo Emerson, *Representative Men;* Napoleon, 1850.

92. All communities divide themselves into the few and the many.

• Alexander Hamilton, at the Constitution Conventional in Philadelphia, 1787. One of many statements by Hamilton in favor of the idea of a privileged aristocracy.

93. He comes of the Brahmin caste of New England. This is the harmless, inoffensive, untitled aristocracy.

• Oliver Wendell Holmes, *The Atlantic Monthly,* January 1860.

94. . . . I agree with you that there is a natural aristocracy among men. The grounds of this are virtue and talents . . . There is also an artificial aristocracy, founded on wealth and birth, without either virtue or talents; for with these it would belong to the first class.

• Thomas Jefferson, letter to John Adams, October 28, 1813. In this same letter Jefferson went on to say "An insurrection has consequently begun, of science, talents, and courage, against rank and birth, which have fallen into contempt." He referred to what was happening in Europe.

95. Aristocracy is always cruel.

• Wendell Phillips, "Toussaint L'Ouverture," 1861.

96. It is an interesting question how far men would retain their relative rank if they were divested of their clothes.

• Henry D. Thoreau, *Walden,* 1854.

ARMED FORCES

(See also Airplanes, Army, Navy, Marine Corps)

101. In the councils of Government, we must guard against the acquisition of unwarranted influence, whether sought or unsought, by the military-industrial complex.

• President Dwight D. Eisenhower, farewell address, January 17, 1961. This warning was particularly interesting because it was voiced by one of the great generals of American history.

102. The military establishment has often been the pioneer that blazed the trail toward the solution of great social problems.

• Secretary of Defense Melvin R. Laird, speech at U.S. Military Academy commencement, West Point, N.Y., June 9, 1971. Secretary Laird spoke at a time when the Army, like the rest of the country, was being challenged to cope with drug addiction during the Vietnam War.

103. The army and navy are the sword and the shield which this nation must carry if she is to do her duty among the nations of the earth . . .

• Governor Theodore Roosevelt of New York, speech in Chicago, April 10, 1899. Teddy Roosevelt had served as Assistant Secretary of the Navy and then as a leader of the Army's Rough Riders in the Spanish-American War. The army and navy were both close to his heart.

104. The Army and Navy forever, / Three cheers for the red, white and blue.

• Adapted as "Columbia, the Gem of the Ocean," a rousing patriotic song, from "Britannia, the Pride of the Ocean," a British song of 1843 by David T. Shaw.

105. "Thrice is he armed that hath his quarrel just"— / And four times he who gets his fist in fust.

• Artemus Ward (Charles Farrar Browne), "Shakespeare Up to Date," mid-19th century.

106. To be prepared for war is one of the most effectual means of preserving peace.

• President George Washington, message to Congress, January 8, 1790.

107. Nervous in the service.

• Anonymous, used to describe the attitude of members of the armed forces in general and conscripts in particular in World War II and thereafter.

108. Uncle Sam wants *you.*

• Motto on recruiting posters of World War I.

ARMY, U.S.
(See also Armed Forces)

---

111. I am convinced that the best service a retired general can perform is to turn in his tongue along with his suit, and to mothball his opinions.

• General of the Army Omar N. Bradley, Armed Forces Day address, May 16, 1959. General Bradley had been perhaps the most reticent and certainly the least flamboyant of the great American generals of World War II. He practiced what he preached.

112. No nation ever had an army large enough to guarantee it against attack in time of peace or insure it victory in time of war.

• President Calvin Coolidge, speech on October 6, 1925. After the large drafted army of World War I, the U.S. had gone back to the idea of a small professional peacetime force.

113. There is a kind of valorous spleen which, like wind, is apt to grow unruly in the stomachs of newly made soldiers, compelling them to box-lobby brawls and brokenheaded quarrels, unless there can be found some more harmless way to give it vent.

• Washington Irving, *A History of New York by Diedrich Knickerbocker,* 1809.

114. . . . like the old soldier of that ballad, I now close my military career and just fade away.

• General of the Army Douglas MacArthur, address to joint session of Congress, April 19, 1951. He was paraphrasing "one of the most popular barracks ballads" of his days at West Point "which proclaimed most proudly that old soldiers never die; they just fade away."

115. . . . the soldier above all other people prays for peace, for he must suffer and bear the deepest wounds, and scars of war . . .

• General of the Army Douglas MacArthur, speech at West Point, N.Y., May 12, 1962, acknowledging the Sylvanus Thayer medal, an alumni award of the U.S. Military Academy.

116. . . . in the evening of my memory I come back to West Point. Always there echoes and re-echoes: duty, honor, country.

• General of the Army Douglas MacArthur, speech at West Point, N.Y., May 12, 1962. See note for quotation 115.

117. When we assumed the soldier, we did not lay aside the citizen.

• George Washington, speech in New York, June 26, 1775, when he was about to take command of the Continental Army and give up the civilian life of a Virginia planter.

ART
(See also Culture)

---

121. For many people art, displacing religion, has become the justification of life, whether as the saving grace of an ugly civilization or as the pattern of the only noble career.

• Jacques Barzun, *The House of Intellect,* 1959.

122. New arts destroy the old.

• Ralph Waldo Emerson, *Essays, First Series:* Circles, 1841. In the golden age of New England, art was a popular topic for the region's literary men—and a hundred years later it occupied the attention of another New Englander. (See Kennedy quotation below.)

123. Art is a jealous mistress.

• Ralph Waldo Emerson, *The Conduct of Life:* Wealth, 1860.

124. Artists and bohemians have always gravitated to the bottom of the income pyramid. It is cheaper there. There is less timetable.

• Paul Goodman, *Growing Up Absurd,* 1960.

125. We must never forget that art is not a form of propaganda; it is a form of truth.

• President John F. Kennedy, speech at Amherst College, Amherst, Mass., October 26, 1963. In his time in the White House, he played host to more representatives of the arts than most of his predecessors.

126. In free society art is not a weapon.

• President John F. Kennedy, speech at Amherst College, Amherst, Mass., October 26, 1963.

127. Art is long and Time is fleeting.

• Henry Wadsworth Longfellow, "A Psalm of Life," 1838.

128. Art's perfect forms no moral need / And beauty is its own excuse . . .

• John Greenleaf Whittier, *Songs of Labor:* Dedication, 1850.

ASPIRATION
(See also Ambition)

---

131. Bring me men to match my mountains, / Bring me men to match my plains, / Men with empires in their purpose, / And new eras in their brains.

• Sam Walter Foss, "The Coming American," read at an Independence Day celebration in Woodstock, Connecticut, July 4, 1894.

132. The traditional goals of earning a great deal of money and making one's mark in the world have lost some of their charm.

• Public opinion researcher George Gallup, Jr., remarks at Virginia Polytechnic Institute, November 16, 1973.

133. Build thee more stately mansions, O my soul.

• Oliver Wendell Holmes, "The Chambered Nautilus," 1858. Using a sea shell as his theme, Dr. Holmes penned one of the outstanding poetic expressions of a philosophy of meaningful life.

134. If you would hit the mark, you must aim a little above it.

• Henry Wadsworth Longfellow, "Elegiac Verse," 1881.

135. Be ashamed to die until you have won some victory for humanity.

• Horace Mann, commencement address, Antioch College, Yellow Springs, Ohio, 1859. The famous educator was the first President of Antioch.

136. *The Status Seekers.*

• Vance Packard, title of best-selling book, 1959.

137. . . . if one advances confidently in the direction of his dreams, and endeavors to live the life which he has imagined, he will meet with a success unexpected in common hours.

• Henry D. Thoreau, *Walden,* 1854. Success was not used by Thoreau in its normal worldly meaning.

138. While there's hope there's life.

• The humorous magazine, *Life,* in the 1930's used a rejection slip that read "While there's Life there's hope." In the latter days of the publication, which ultimately sold its title to a new picture magazine later in the decade, the uncertainty of the magazine's future led to the remark that "While there's hope there's Life." It seemed to make sense as a general observation long after both magazines named *Life* had given up the ghost.

ATOMIC ENERGY

141. We are here to make a choice between the quick and the dead.

• Bernard M. Baruch, speech at United Nations Atomic Energy Commission meeting, New York, June 14, 1946.

142. We are now facing a problem more of ethics than physics.

• Bernard M. Baruch, speech at United Nations Atomic Energy Commission meeting, New York, June 14, 1946. The atom bomb, developed by the United States, was very fresh in the minds of the UN delegates less than a year after its awesome power had been demonstrated at Hiroshima and Nagasaki.

143. The United States would seek more than the mere reduction or elimination of atomic materials available for military purposes. It is not enough just to take this weapon out of the hands of the soldiers. It must be put into the hands of those who will know how to strip its military casing and adapt it to the arts of peace.

• President Dwight D. Eisenhower, speech to United Nations General Assembly, December 8, 1953.

144. Every man, woman and child lives under a nuclear sword of Damocles, hanging by the slenderest of threads, capable of being cut at any moment by accident or miscalculation or by madness.

• President John F. Kennedy, speech to United Nations General Assembly, September 25, 1961.

145. There is no evil in the atom; only in men's souls.

• Adlai E. Stevenson, Presidential campaign speech in Hartford, September 18, 1952.

146. We have spent two billion dollars on the greatest scientific gamble in history—and won.

• President Harry S Truman, statement after bombing of Hiroshima, August 6, 1945.

147. Never in history has society been confronted with a power so full of promise for the future of man and for the peace of the world.

• President Harry S Truman, message to Congress, October 3, 1945.

ATTITUDES

(See also Courage, Determination, Symbols, War)

---

151. Good nature is worth more than knowledge, more than money, more than honor, to the persons who possess it.

• Reverend Henry Ward Beecher, *Proverbs from Plymouth Pulpit,* 1887.

152. This is the age of the expert, while just those few years ago, it was the age of the man who didn't mind trying.

• Gertrude Berg, *Molly and Me,* 1961.

153. The price of hating other human beings is loving oneself less.

• Eldridge Cleaver, *Soul on Ice,* 1968.*

154. He will hew to the line of right, let the chips fall where they may.

• Senator Roscoe Conkling of New York, presenting the name of former President Ulysses S. Grant for the Republican Presidential nomination at the party's convention in Chicago, June 5, 1880.

155. The first and great commandment is, Don't let them scare you.

• Elmer Davis, *But We Were Born Free,* copyright 1952, 1953, 1954 by Elmer Davis, reprinted by permission of the publisher, The Bobbs-Merrill Company, Inc.

156. By uniting we stand, by dividing we fall.

• John Dickinson, "The Liberty Song," 1768. Whether this was original with Dickinson or not, it made a lasting impression. For similar language, see the state motto of Kentucky, below.

157. Men may believe what they cannot prove.

• Associate Justice William O. Douglas of Supreme Court, opinion in U.S. v. Ballard, 1944.

158. Whatever America hopes to bring to pass in the world must first come to pass in the heart of America.

• President Dwight D. Eisenhower, Inaugural Address, January 20, 1953.

159. We are afraid of truth, afraid of fortune, afraid of death, and afraid of each other.

• Ralph Waldo Emerson, *Essays, First Series:* Self-Reliance, 1841.

160. . . . reconciliation calls for an act of mercy to bind the nation's wounds and heal the scars of divisiveness.

• President Gerald R. Ford, announcing amnesty program for draft evaders and deserters in Washington, September 16, 1974.

161. We must indeed all hang together, or, most assuredly, we shall all hang separately.

• Benjamin Franklin, at the signing of the Declaration of Independence in Philadelphia, July 4, 1776.

162. America stop pushing. I know what I'm doing.

• Allen Ginsberg, *Howl,* "America," 1956. When these lines were written, it was widely felt that this pioneer "beat" poet did not have as clear an outlook as the lines seemed to suggest.

163. Young Americans are old hands at modern life and too sophisticated to be disappointed in their fathers or their country.

• Paul Goodman, *Growing Up Absurd,* 1960.

164. Millions for defense, but not a cent for tribute.

• Commonly misattributed to U.S. diplomat Charles Cotesworth Pinckney, but actually said by Robert Goodloe Harper, who later invented the name Liberia for a new free black republic in Africa, at a dinner in Philadelphia on June 18, 1798, in honor of John Marshall, the U.S. envoy to France.

165. In every town and every village and every mud hut in the world, there is always a man who loves children, who will fight to make a good world for them.

• Lillian Hellman, "Watch on the Rhine," Act 3, 1941.

166. Men who wish to live have the best chance to live. I wish to live. I wish to live with you.

• Lillian Hellman, "Watch on the Rhine," Act 3, 1941.

167. If this be treason, make the most of it.

• Patrick Henry, speech against the Stamp Act in the Virginia House of Burgesses, 1765.

168. The man who insists he is as good as anybody, believes he is better.

• E. W. Howe, *Country Town Sayings,* 1911.

169. We are against people who push other people around.

• Ralph M. Ingersoll, motto of newspaper *PM,* 1940.

170. We are always equal to what we undertake with resolution.

• Thomas Jefferson, letter to his daughter Martha, March 28, 1787.

171. United we stand, divided we fall.

• Motto of the state of Kentucky, 1792. See John Dickinson quotation above.

172. *It Can't Happen Here.*

• Sinclair Lewis, title of novel about fascism in the United States, 1935.

173. I am for the people of the whole nation doing just what they please in all matters which concern the whole nation; for that of each part doing just as they choose in all matters which concern no other part; and for each individual doing just as he chooses in all matters which concern nobody else.

• Abraham Lincoln, speech in Illinois during Senatorial campaign against Stephen H. Douglas, October 1858.

174. Let us have faith that right makes might; and in that faith let us dare to do our duty as we understand it.

• Abraham Lincoln, speech at Cooper Union in New York City, February 27, 1860.

175. I can die at my post but I cannot desert it.

• Abolitionist editor Elijah P. Lovejoy, speech to a mob attacking his newspaper office in Alton, Ill., November 3, 1837. Four days later Lovejoy was killed by a mob.

176. New times demand new measures and new men . . .

• James Russell Lowell, "A Glance Behind the Curtain," 1843. Lowell was to be one of New England's most outspoken literary and poetic voices in the fight against slavery.

177. These are the times that try men's souls.

• Thomas Paine, "The American Crisis" in *The Pennsylvania Journal,* December 19, 1776.

178. The summer soldier and the sunshine patriot will, in this crisis, shrink from the service of their country.

• Thomas Paine, "The American Crisis" in *The Pennsylvania Journal,* December 19, 1776.

179. Thanks for the Memory.

• Title of song by Leo Robin and Ralph Rainger, 1937, that became the theme of comedian Bob Hope.

180. Far better it is to dare mighty things, to win glorious triumphs, even though checkered by failure, than to take rank with those poor spirits who neither enjoy much nor suffer much, because they live in the gray twilight that knows not victory nor defeat.

• Governor Theodore Roosevelt of New York, speech in Chicago, April 10, 1899. Governor Roosevelt, a leader of the Rough Riders in the Spanish American War the year before, practiced what he preached.

AUTOMOBILES
(See also Travel)

---

181. *The Insolent Chariots.*

• John Keats, title of a book about the automobile, 1958.

182. . . . a car in every garage.

• Part of a Republican campaign slogan in the 1928 Presidential election. ("A chicken in every pot, a car in every garage.")

183. This is the only country that ever went to the poorhouse in an automobile.

• Will Rogers, from about 1930–31 on, in various public appearances.

184. We talk grandly of renovating the society of Brazil or Tanganyika while no American city has been able to solve its own traffic problem.

• Eric Sevareid, *This Is Eric Sevareid,* 1964.

185. Drive carefully; the life you save may be your own.

• Common highway sign and saying in the 1930's and 1940's.

186. Fill 'er up.

• Used widely in the 1920's not only on the occasion of ordering gasoline at a filling station but also as a synonym for "here we go" or "we're on our way."

187. The modern American car is a living room on wheels.

• Anonymous, said particularly in the 1950's of the luxurious cars found in some depressed residential areas of New York City.

188. The most dangerous animal in the U.S.A. is the road hog.

• One of a vast number of jokes about road hogs that began in the 1920's.

189. Too many used car buyers drive a hard bargain.

• One variation of a whole genre of remarks about used cars that came into popularity in the late 1940's and 1950's, when the number of cars on the road began its explosive growth.

190. Would you buy a used car from this man?

• Anonymous, 1960's, widely used as a television gag line and also as a caption by political candidates for their opponents, as well as by comedians.

BASEBALL

191. A baseball club is part of the chemistry of the city. A game isn't just an athletic contest. It's a picnic, a kind of town meeting.

• Michael Burke, President of the New York Yankees, testifying at a New York City Council committee hearing, March 25, 1971.

192. Good field, no hit.

• Mike Gonzalez, Cuban player, scout and coach, is generally credited with having filed this report about a major league prospect, probably in the early 1930's. It is sometimes credited to another Cuban player-scout-coach in the National League, Adolfo Luque.

193. Hit 'em where they ain't.

• Willie Keeler, regarded at the turn of the century as the greatest place hitter in baseball, summarized his batting tactics this way.

194. Casey at the Bat.

• Ernest L. Thayer, title of a poem, 1888. It became synonymous with spectacular failure—see notes on quotations from the poem below.

195. But there is no joy in Mudville—mighty Casey has struck out.

• Ernest L. Thayer, "Casey at the Bat," 1888. This is the climactic last line of the classic poem of baseball, now a part of American folklore.

196. Kill the umpire!

• Anonymous, but old enough to have been included in quotation marks by Ernest L. Thayer in "Casey at the Bat" in 1888.

197. Slide, Kelly, slide.

• A turn-of-the-century song refrain based on the cheers of fans in the 1890's over the feats of a baseball player named Kelly who excelled in running the bases; it became a catchword generally meaning, "try a little harder."

198. Three strikes you're out.

• Umpire's words, applied often over the past century to fields other than baseball to mean you only get so many chances at something.

BEHAVIOR

201. Because you're mine / I walk the line.

• John R. (Johnny) Cash, "I Walk the Line," 1956. The song is Copyright © 1956 by Hi Lo Music, Inc. All rights administered by Hill and Range Songs, Inc. Used by permission.

202. Nothing is often a good thing to do, and always a clever thing to say.

• Will Durant in a newspaper interview in New York, June, 1958.

203. . . . a beautiful behavior is better than a beautiful form.

• Ralph Waldo Emerson, *Essays, Second Series:* Manners, 1844.

204. Be civil to all; sociable to many; familiar with few; friend to one; enemy to none.

• Benjamin Franklin, *Poor Richard's Almanac,* 1756.

205. What is moral is what you feel good after and what is immoral is what you feel bad after.

• Ernest Hemingway, *Death in the Afternoon,* 1932.

206. Give up money, give up fame, give up science, give up the earth itself and all it contains, rather than do an immoral act.

• Thomas Jefferson, letter to his nephew Peter Carr, August 19, 1785. This may well be the most sweeping statement Jefferson ever made.

207. To get along, go along.

• Speaker of the House Sam Rayburn's basic advice to new members of Congress, 1950's.

208. The way you behave is the way you'll be judged.

• Anonymous, probably originating as schoolbook maxim of early 19th century.

BIRTH

211. Birth: The first and direst of all disasters.

• Ambrose Bierce, *The Devil's Dictionary,* 1906.

212. The gracious boy who did adorn / The world whereinto he was born . . .

• Ralph Waldo Emerson, "Threnody," 1847.

213. Born for the future, to the future lost!

• Ralph Waldo Emerson, "Threnody," 1847.

214. Why is it that we rejoice at a birth and grieve at a funeral? It is because we are not the person involved.

• Mark Twain, *The Tragedy of Pudd'nhead Wilson,* Pudd'nhead Wilson's Calendar, 1894.

215. Not a day passes, not a minute or second without an accouchement . . .

• Walt Whitman, "To Think of Time," 1853.

216. Infanticipating.

• Walter Winchell, who did not invent the term "blessed event," which he used widely to announce forthcoming births in his Broadway gossip column in the 1930's, did invent his own word to describe the state of expectant couples.

BLACKS

(See also Races)

221. It is a great shock at the age of five or six to find that in a world of Gary Coopers you are the Indian.

• James Baldwin, speech at Cambridge University in England, February 17, 1965.

222. . . . the practical aspects of the needs of the ghetto people are so much clearer to the people there than they are to anyone else.

• Mayor Alfonso J. Cervantes of St. Louis, testimony before the National Advisory Commission on Civil Disorders, 1967.

223. Yet do I marvel at this curious thing: / To make a poet black, and bid him sing!

• Countee Cullen, "Yet Do I Marvel," 1925.

224. I know the Negro race has a long road to go. I believe the life of the Negro race has been a life of tragedy, of injustice, of oppression. The law has made him equal, but man has not.

• Clarence Darrow, plea to the jury in trial of Henry Sweet and other Blacks on murder charges in Detroit, 1926. The defendants in the case, which grew out of a bitter dispute over Black settlement in a white residential area, were all acquitted.

225. Though the colored man is no longer subject to be bought and sold, he is still surrounded by an adverse sentiment which fetters all his movements. In his downward course he meets with no resistance, but his course upward is resisted at every step of his progress.

• Frederick Douglass, speech in Louisville, Ky., September 24, 1883.

226. Nobody wishes more than I do to see such proofs as you exhibit, that nature has given to our black brethren, talents equal to those of the other colors of men, and that the appearance of a want of them is owing merely to the degraded condition of their existence, both in Africa and America.

• Secretary of State Thomas Jefferson, letter to Benjamin Banneker, the first great Black American scientist, August 30, 1791. Banneker was one of the principal figures in the laying out of the city of Washington. He had sent Jefferson a copy of his scientific Almanac, which Jefferson forwarded to the Academy of Sciences in Paris.

227. The real hero of this struggle is the American Negro. His actions and protests, his courage to risk safety and even to risk his life, have awakened the conscience of this nation.

• President Lyndon B. Johnson, speech to a joint session of Congress presenting a voting rights bill, March 15, 1965.

228. . . . the Negro neither wants nor needs condescension . . .

• President John F. Kennedy, message to Congress, June 19, 1963.

229. There are no "white" or "colored" signs on the foxholes or graveyards of battle.

• President John F. Kennedy, message to Congress, June 19, 1963.

230. Whatever else the Negro is, he is American. Whatever he is to become—integrated, unintegrated, or disintegrated—he will become it in America . . . whatever future awaits America awaits the Negro; whatever future awaits the Negro, awaits America.

• Louis E. Lomax, *The Negro Revolt,* 1963.

231. . . . eating soul food will not solve a single problem of housing, employment or education.

• Bayard Rustin, commencement address at Cheyney State College in Cheyney, Penna., June 1971.

232. What a happy country this will be, if the whites will listen.

• David Walker, "Walker's Appeal," September 28, 1829. He was one of the first Black abolitionist journalists and leaders.

233. Black is beautiful.

• Adopted by the Black community in the 1960's as a self-rallying cry.

BORROWING

241. The Borrower is a Slave to the Lender.

• Benjamin Franklin, "The Way to Wealth," 1757. Much of this collection of adages from Franklin's *Poor Richard* archives deals with borrowing and the problems of credit.

242. He that goes a-borrowing, goes a-sorrowing.

• Benjamin Franklin, "The Way to Wealth," 1757.

243. Let us all be happy and live within our means, even if we have to borrow the money to do it with.

• Artemus Ward (Charles Farrar Browne), lecture in the 1860's.

244. God bless our mortgaged home.

• Traditional U.S. sampler motto.

245. Trouble is the only thing you can borrow that you don't have to pay back.

• Anonymous, New England saying of early 19th century.

BROADCASTING

(See also Freedom, Newspapers, Rights)

251. The most powerful social force in the world's most powerful nation—this is what broadcasting, and television broadcasting in particular, has been called with increasing frequency during the past two decades.

• DuPont-Columbia Survey and Awards Jurors, 1969.

252. . . . broadcasting has consistently demonstrated a remarkable and ever-expanding capacity to serve the needs of both commerce and society.

• CBS Chairman William S. Paley, address at annual shareholders meeting of CBS, Los Angeles, April 18, 1973.

253. The fact that the government licenses broadcasting does not make radio and television instrumentalities of the government. Rather, government has the positive obligation to maintain and enhance the climate of freedom in which U.S. broadcasting has served the people of this nation.

• Frank Stanton, statement to Democratic Platform Committee, June 15, 1972. Dr. Stanton was then Vice Chairman of CBS.

254. The preceding program was pre-recorded.

• An announcement that became familiar to radio listeners, particularly in the 1940's, and carried over into the age of television; used to identify material that was not being broadcast live.

255. We pause for station identification.

• Because government regulations require regular and periodic identification by broadcasting stations, this phrase was adopted to introduce an identification pause that interrupted programming.

256. We will return following this message.

• Since the pause for station identification was also used for spot advertising announcements, some on-air announcers and entertainers found it smoother to use this phrase, which could introduce any form of interruption to the program, 1940's.

BUSINESS AND TRADE

(See also Accomplishments, Economy, Prosperity)

---

261. Civilization and profits go hand in hand.

• Vice President-Elect Calvin Coolidge, speech in New York, November 27, 1920. Mr. Coolidge was a prime exponent of the New England work ethic.

262. The business of America is business.

• President Calvin Coolidge, addressing a group of newspaper editors in Washington, D.C., January 17, 1925.

263. It is just as important that business keep out of government as that government keep out of business.

• Republican Presidential candidate Herbert Hoover, speech in New York, October 22, 1928.

264. American industry is concerned—just as concerned as the man in Government is—about a better life for our children, a cleaner America, an America in which we can have the clean air, the clean water and the quality of life that we believe is the American heritage.

• President Richard M. Nixon, statement on anti-pollution campaign, February 10, 1971.

265. I hold it to be our duty to see that the wage-worker, the small producer, the ordinary consumer, shall get their fair share of the benefit of business prosperity. But it either is or ought to be evident to everyone that business has to prosper before anybody can get any benefit from it.

• Theodore Roosevelt, address in Ohio, February 1, 1912.

266. This world is a place of business.

• Henry D. Thoreau, "Life Without Principle," published in *The Atlantic Monthly* in 1863, after his death in 1862.

267. . . . I thought what was good for the country was good for General Motors and vice versa.

• Charles E. Wilson, General Motors executive testifying before Senate committee considering his nomination to be Secretary of Defense, Washington, D.C., January 22, 1953. (It is often credited to January 23 because that is when it appeared in print.)

268. Business underlies everything in our national life, including our spiritual life.

• New Jersey Governor Woodrow Wilson, speech in New York, May 23, 1912.

CANDIDATES

(See also Politics, Presidency, Voting)

---

271. Nominate: To designate for the heaviest political assessment. To put forward a suitable person to incur the mudgobbing and deadcatting of the opposition.

• Ambrose Bierce, *The Devil's Dictionary,* 1906.

272. I do not choose to run for President in 1928.

• President Calvin Coolidge, statement issued from his summer stay in South Dakota, August 2, 1927. While there has been some speculation as to whether he really meant it, the country took him at his word, and his word became a standard phrase for declining a nomination.

273. Offices are acceptable here as elsewhere, and whenever a man has cast a longing eye on them, a rottenness begins in his conduct.

• Vice President Thomas Jefferson, letter to Tench Coxe, May 21, 1799. Jefferson had already cast a longing eye on the Presidency and finished second to John Adams. Next time around, he was to be elected.

274. The idea that you can merchandise candidates for high office like breakfast cereal . . . is, I think, the ultimate indignity to the democratic process.

• Illinois Governor Adlai E. Stevenson, accepting the Democratic Presidential nomination in Chicago, August 18, 1956.

275. The people's choice.

• Its origins are lost deep in the 19th century, but it was used for many years to refer favorably to a candidate for office.

CAUSES

281. The humblest citizen of all the land, when clad in the armor of a righteous cause, is stronger than all the hosts of Error.

• William Jennings Bryan in his "Cross of Gold" speech at the Democratic National Convention in Chicago, July 8, 1896.

282. Our cause is just. Our union is perfect. Our internal resources are great . . .

• John Dickinson, "Declaration . . . Setting Forth the Causes and Necessity of Their Taking Up Arms," presented to the Continental Congress, July 6, 1775.

283. Great causes are never tried on their merits.

• Ralph Waldo Emerson, *Essays, Second Series:* Nature, 1844.

284. Then conquer we must, for our cause it is just . . .

• Francis Scott Key, "The Star-Spangled Banner," September 14, 1814. Written as he watched the Battle of Fort McHenry in Baltimore Harbor.

CENSORSHIP

291. Should a mature and sophisticated reading public be kept in blinders because a government official thinks reading certain works of power and literary value are not good for him?

• U.S. Circuit of Appeals Judge Charles E. Clark, in decision that D. H. Lawrence's *Lady Chatterley's Lover* could indeed be sent through the U.S. mails, March 25, 1960.

292. Don't join the book burners. Don't think you are going to conceal thoughts by concealing evidence that they ever existed.

• President Dwight D. Eisenhower, speech at Dartmouth College, June 14, 1953.

293. No man and no force can take from the world the books that embody men's eternal fight against tyranny of every kind.

• President Franklin D. Roosevelt, statement to the American Booksellers Association, April 23, 1941.

294. The moment we begin to fear the opinions of others and hesitate to tell the truth that is in us, and from motives of policy are silent when we should speak, the divine floods of light and life flow no longer into our souls.

• Elizabeth Cady Stanton, address to National American Woman Suffrage Association, 1890.

295. Once a government is committed to the principle of silencing the voice of opposition, it has only one way to go, and that is down the path of increasingly repressive measures, until it becomes a source of terror to all its citizens and creates a country where everyone lives in fear.

• President Harry S Truman, message to Congress, August 8, 1950.

CHANGE

301. The American system is the greatest engine of change and progress the world has ever seen. The American system has produced more goods, more widely distributed than any other system, any time, any place.

• Vice President Spiro T. Agnew, address to the American Legion, Portland, Ore., September 2, 1970.

302. Weep not that the world changes—did it keep / A stable, changeless state, 'twere cause indeed to weep.

• William Cullen Bryant, "Mutation," 1824.

303. We do not fear this world of change.

• President Dwight D. Eisenhower, second inaugural address, Washington, D.C., January 21, 1957.

304. The country needs to be born again; she is polluted with the lust of power, the lust of gain.

• Margaret Fuller in *The New York Tribune,* July 4, 1845. She was the literary critic of the *Tribune* at the time.

305. Change is the law of life.

• President John F. Kennedy, speech in Frankfurt, Germany, June 25, 1963.

306. . . . it is best not to swap horses while crossing the river . . .

• President Abraham Lincoln, remark to a delegation from the National Union League, commenting on possible reasons why the League had endorsed him for reelection, June 9, 1864. He did not say, as often supposed, "Don't swap horses in the middle of the stream."

307. . . . it is possible to achieve fundamental social change in this country. Customs and practices which seemed fixed in concrete have been overturned.

• Senator Edmund S. Muskie of Maine, speech referring to race relations in the South, May 2, 1971.

308. Nations succeed only as they are able to respond to challenge, and to change when circumstances and opportunities require change.

• President Richard M. Nixon, message to Congress, April 18, 1973, offering a program for conservation and development of energy resources.

309. Things do not change; we change.

• Henry D. Thoreau, *Walden,* 1854.

310. Change is avalanching upon our heads and most people are grotesquely unprepared to cope with it.

• Alvin Toffler, *Future Shock,* 1970.

CHARITY
(See also Philanthropy)

---

311. In charity to all mankind, bearing no malice or ill-will to any human being . . .

• Representative John Quincy Adams of Massachusetts (and ex-President), letter to A. Bronson Alcott, July 30, 1838. (See Lincoln quotation below.)

312. . . . one of the serious obstacles to the improvement of our race is indiscriminate charity.

• Andrew Carnegie, *The Gospel of Wealth,* 1889.

313. We do not quite forgive a giver. The hand that feeds us is in some danger of being bitten.

• Ralph Waldo Emerson, *Essays, Second Series:* Gifts, 1844.

314. . . . charity must be built on justice.

• Henry George, *The Condition of Labor,* 1891.

315. It has been said that we feed the hungry, clothe the naked, bind up the wounds of the man beaten by thieves, pour oil and wine into them, set him on our own beast and bring him to the inn, because we receive ourselves pleasure from these acts.

• Thomas Jefferson, letter to Thomas Law, June 13, 1814.

316. With malice toward none; with charity for all; with firmness in the right, as God gives us to see the right . . .

• President Abraham Lincoln, second inaugural address, March 4, 1865. (See Adams quotation above.)

317. Those of us who walk in light / must help the ones in darkness up.

• Rod McKuen, *Lonesome Cities,* 1968.

CITIZENSHIP

321. Political action is the highest responsibility of a citizen.

• Senator John F. Kennedy of Massachusetts, speech in New York City, October 20, 1960.

322. The first requisite of a good citizen in this republic of ours is that he shall be able and willing to pull his weight.

• President Theodore Roosevelt, speech in New York City, November 11, 1902.

323. Citizenship is man's basic right, for it is nothing less than the right to have rights.

• Chief Justice Earl Warren, dissenting opinion in Perez v. Brownell, 1958.

324. When we assumed the soldier, we did not lay aside the citizen.

• George Washington, address to provincial Congress of New York, June 26, 1775.

325. Citizens by birth or choice of a common country, that country has a right to concentrate your affections.

• President George Washington, Farewell Address, 1796. (Published September 19.)

CITY LIFE

331. Burn down your cities and leave our farms, and your cities will spring up again; but destroy our farms and the grass will grow in the streets of every city in the country.

• William Jennings Bryan, "Cross of Gold" speech at Democratic National Convention in Chicago, July 8, 1896.

332. The city is recruited from the country.

• Ralph Waldo Emerson, *Essays, Second Series:* Manners, 1844.

333. Washington is not a place to live in. The rents are high, the food is bad, the dust is disgusting and the morals are deplorable.

• Horace Greeley, *New York Tribune,* July 13, 1865. (While this quotation could have been placed in the Places section, the editors prefer to view it as a comment on city life rather than on the District of Columbia.)

334. We will neglect our cities to our peril, for in neglecting them we neglect the nation.

• President John F. Kennedy, message to Congress, January 30, 1962.

335. . . . a town life makes one more tolerant and liberal in one's judgment of others.

• Henry Wadsworth Longfellow, *Hyperion,* 1839.

336. Trees are monuments to God / cities monuments to man.

• Rod McKuen, *Lonesome Cities,* 1968.

337. No city government can make any suburb do anything.

• Cleveland, O., Mayor Carl B. Stokes, April 30, 1971.

338. We need help, and we need it yesterday.

• Cleveland, O., Mayor Carl B. Stokes at Senate subcommittee hearing in Washington, June 3, 1971.

339. I love to see the other mayors; misery loves company.

• Seattle Mayor Wesley C. Uhlman, at a meeting of big-city mayors in New York, April 21, 1971.

340. A great city is that which has the greatest men and women . . .

• Walt Whitman, "Song of the Broad-Axe," 1856.

CLOTHING
(See also Dress)

341. Clothes and manners do not make the man; but when he is made, they greatly improve his appearance.

• Reverend Henry Ward Beecher, *Proverbs from Plymouth Pulpit,* 1887. Reverend Beecher was probably the most elegant preacher of his day, and Plymouth Church in Brooklyn in his day probably the most popular of congregations.

342. . . . Pat doesn't have a mink coat. But she does have a respectable Republican cloth coat.

• Senator Richard M. Nixon of California, speech in Los Angeles and over television, September 23, 1952, during campaign in which he was running for Vice President. He was defending himself against charges of questionable financing, and alluded to mink coats because they had become somewhat of a symbol for payment for favors in the preceding Truman administration.

343. King James loved his old shoes best. Who does not? Indeed these new clothes are often won and worn after a most painful birth. . . . A man who has at length found out something important to do will not have to get a new suit to do it in.

• Henry D. Thoreau, *Journal,* undated (about 1846).

344. On the whole, I think that it cannot be maintained that dressing has in this or any country risen to the dignity of an art.

• Henry D. Thoreau, *Walden:* Economy, 1854.

345. Beware of all enterprises that require new clothes . . .

• Henry D. Thoreau, *Walden:* Economy, 1854.

CLUBS

351. I don't want to belong to any club that will accept me as a member.

• Groucho Marx, perhaps as early as the 1930's.

352. A country club is part park and part parking lot.

• Radio joke, 1930's.

353. If you want to be a member of the club, you have to pay your dues.

• Its origins are unknown, but this saying became popular first in the early 20th century and again in the 1950's as a summary of civic duty.

COLLEGES
(See also Education)

361. Administering a college today is like playing chess on the open deck of the sinking *Titanic* . . .

• Dr. Edward Bloustein, on accepting the Presidency of Rutgers University, May 14, 1971.

362. The ideal college for me is Mark Hopkins on one end of a log and me on the other.

• James A. Garfield, in a speech in New York on December 28, 1871, paid tribute in words similar to these (exact text was not preserved) to Mark Hopkins, who served for many years as President of Williams College.

363. It might be said that I have the best of both worlds: a Harvard education and a Yale degree.

• President John F. Kennedy, upon receiving an honorary degree at Yale, June 11, 1962.

364. I find that the three major administrative problems on a campus are sex for the students, athletics for the alumni and parking for the faculty.

• President Clark Kerr of the University of California, quoted in *Time* magazine, November 17, 1958.

365. The most conservative persons I ever met are college undergraduates.

• Princeton University President Woodrow Wilson, speech in New York, November 19, 1905.

366. The use of a university is to make young gentlemen as unlike their fathers as possible.

• President Woodrow Wilson, speech in Pittsburgh, October 24, 1914.

367. A college diploma is a license to look for a job.

• Anonymous; originally said during the Depression days of the 1930's, but since used with a different meaning. In the 1930's jobs were very difficult to find, and college graduates were regarded as possibly having an advantage because of superior education. Today the phrase is used to imply that virtually everybody is a college graduate.

COMPETITION

371. . . . while . . . sometimes hard for the individual, it is best for the race, because it insures the survival of the fittest in every department.

• Andrew Carnegie, *The Gospel of Wealth,* 1889. As a self-made multi-millionaire, Carnegie's view of competition was hardly surprising.

372. Of all human powers operating on the affairs of mankind, none is greater than that of competition.

• Senator Henry Clay of Kentucky, speech in the Senate, February 2, 1832.

373. Nice guys finish last.

• Leo Durocher, managing the Brooklyn Dodgers in the 1940's, said this about his team's arch rivals, the New York Giants, and their manager, Mel Ott.

374. So the rat race is run desperately by bright fellows who do not believe in it because they are afraid to stop.

• Paul Goodman, *Growing Up Absurd,* 1960.

375. . . . free competition is worth much more to society than it costs . . .

• Justice Oliver Wendell Holmes, Jr., of Massachusetts Supreme Judicial Court, in a dissenting opinion in 1896.

376. . . . the best test of truth is the power of the thought to get itself accepted in the competition of the market . . .

• Associate Justice Oliver Wendell Holmes, Jr., of Supreme Court, dissenting opinion in Abrams v. United States, November 10, 1919.

377. Don't look back. Someone might be gaining on you.

• Leroy (Satchel) Paige, great Black baseball pitcher, quoted in *Collier's* magazine on June 13, 1953.

378. A money player.

• Term originated probably in the 1920's to describe a sports competitor who played best when the stakes were highest.

CONFEDERACY

381. . . . putting our trust in God, and in our own firm hearts and strong arms, we will vindicate the right as best we may.

• Jefferson Davis, resigning from the U.S. Senate on the secession of Mississippi, January 21, 1861. He became the President of the Confederate States of America.

382. All we ask is to be left alone.

• Jefferson Davis, Inaugural Address as President of the Confederate States of America, February 18, 1861, in Montgomery, Alabama.

383. In Dixie's land we'll take our stand / To live and die in Dixie!

• Dan (Daniel Decatur) Emmett, pioneer minstrel performer, wrote the song "Dixie" in 1859. It became the rallying song of the Confederacy.

384. Wayward sisters, depart in peace.

• Lieutenant General Winfield Scott, commander of the U.S. Army, suggested this message be sent to the Confederate states, in a letter to Senator William H. Seward, who was about to become Lincoln's Secretary of State, on March 3, 1861.

CONGRESS

391. Congress is the great commanding theatre of this nation . . .

• President Thomas Jefferson, letter to William Wirt, 1808, after Jefferson had been serving as Chief Executive and coping with Congress for almost eight years.

392. . . . this home of legislative debate represents human liberty in the purest form yet devised.

• General of the Army Douglas MacArthur, address to joint session of Congress, April 19, 1951, after he had been removed as commander of U.S. forces in Korea.

393. With Congress, every time they make a joke it's a law, and every time they make a law it's a joke.

• Will Rogers, 1930's, on air and in lecture appearances.

394. I have taken an oath to do impartial justice according to the Constitution and laws, and trust that I shall have the courage to vote according to the dictates of my judgment and for the highest good of the country.

• Senator Edmund G. Ross of Kansas, reply to message from D. R. Anthony and 1000 Others regarding his vote in the impeachment trial of President Andrew Johnson, May 16, 1868. It was Ross's key vote that defeated the impeachment proceedings.

395. This is a Senate of equals, of men of individual honor and personal character, and of absolute independence. We know no masters; we acknowledge no dictators.

• Senator Daniel Webster of Massachusetts, speech in the Senate in debate with Senator Hayne of South Carolina, January 26, 1830.

CONSCIENCE
(See also Ethics)

401. Government cannot coerce individual conscience. A way of law does not automatically become a way of life.

• Vice President Spiro T. Agnew, speech in Cincinnati, February 11, 1969.

402. . . . you will always find those who think they know what is your duty better than you know it.

• Ralph Waldo Emerson, *Essays, First Series:* Self-Reliance, 1841.

403. So nigh is grandeur to our dust, / So near is God to man, / When Duty whispers low, "Thou must," / The youth replies, "I can."

• Ralph Waldo Emerson, "Voluntaries," 1863.

404. In a democratic society like ours, relief must come through an aroused popular conscience that sears the conscience of the people's representatives.

• Associate Justice Felix Frankfurter, Supreme Court opinion in Baker v. Carr, March 26, 1962.

405. A good conscience is a continual Christmas.

• Benjamin Franklin, *Poor Richard's Almanac,* 1749.

406. The moral sense, or conscience, is as much a part of man as his leg or arm.

• Thomas Jefferson, letter to his nephew Peter Carr, August 10, 1787.

407. Nothing strengthens the judgment and quickens the conscience like individual responsibility.

• Elizabeth Cady Stanton, speech to National American Woman Suffrage Association, 1892.

408. The courage of New England is the courage of conscience.

• Senator Daniel Webster of Massachusetts, speech in Senate January 26, 1830.

CONSERVATIVES
(See also Colleges)

---

411. We expect old men to be conservatives, but when a nation's young men are so, its funeral bells are already rung.

• Reverend Henry Ward Beecher, *Proverbs from Plymouth Pulpit,* 1887. Little if anything in this collection of quotations from the great clergyman's sermons, published in the year of his death, suggested that as an old man he had become conservative. He was the pastor of Plymouth Church in Brooklyn for 40 years, as well as a major editor and journalist of his time.

412. Men are conservatives when they are least vigorous, or when they are most luxurious. They are conservatives after dinner.

• Ralph Waldo Emerson, *Essays, Second Series:* New England Reformers, 1844.

413. . . . the conservative is an old democrat.

• Ralph Waldo Emerson, *Representative Men:* Napoleon, 1850.

414. What is conservatism? Is it not adherence to the old and tried, against the new and untried?

• Abraham Lincoln, speech at Cooper Union, New York City, February 27, 1860.

415. The true conservative seeks to protect the system of private property and free enterprise by correcting such injustices and inequalities as arise from it.

• President Franklin D. Roosevelt, speech to Democratic State Convention in Syracuse, N.Y., September 30, 1936.

416. A conservative is a man with two perfectly good legs who, however, has never learned to walk.

• President Franklin D. Roosevelt, radio address, October 26, 1939.

417. A conservative believes in lasting values; a liberal believes in changing values.

• Used in several variations by supporters of Republican candidate Barry M. Goldwater during the 1964 Presidential campaign.

CONSTITUTION

421. The Constitution of the United States was made not merely for the generation that then existed, but for posterity—unlimited, undefined, endless, perpetual posterity.

• Senator Henry Clay of Kentucky, speech in the Senate on the Compromise Bill of 1850, February 6, 1850.

422. The Constitution of the United States is a law for rulers and people, equally in war and in peace, and covers with the shield of its protection all classes of men, at all times, and under all circumstances.

• Associate Justice David Davis, Supreme Court decision in *Ex Parte Milligan,* December 1866, declaring martial law unconstitutional in an area away from the scene of war and where civil courts were functioning. The case had arisen during Civil War in Indiana.

423. Our Constitution works. Our great republic is a government of laws and not of men. Here, the people rule.

• President Gerald R. Ford, inaugural address in Washington, D.C., August 9, 1974.

424. We are under a Constitution, but the Constitution is what the judges say it is.

• Governor Charles Evans Hughes of New York, speech at Elmira, N.Y., May 3, 1907. Three and a half years later Governor Hughes himself was appointed to the U.S. Supreme Court.

425. Our peculiar security is in the possession of a written Constitution. Let us not make it a blank paper by construction.

• President Thomas Jefferson to Wilson C. Nicholas, letter written September 7, 1803.

426. The government of the United States, then, though limited in its powers, is supreme; and its laws, when made in pursuance of the Constitution, form the supreme law of the land, "anything in the constitution or laws of any State to the contrary notwithstanding."

• Chief Justice John Marshall, Supreme Court decision in McCulloch v. Maryland, March 6, 1819. This historic decision established the Constitution as the fundamental law of the U.S., overriding state law and confirming the sovereignty of the federal government.

427. The United States Constitution has proven itself the most marvelously elastic compilation of rules of government ever written.

• Franklin D. Roosevelt, radio address, March 2, 1930. Some years later, when instead of being Governor of New York he was President Roosevelt, he sought to enlarge the Supreme Court because he was dissatisfied with the judgments of "nine old men" applied to the Constitution. Congress rejected the idea.

428. Keep your eye on the Constitution. This is the guarantee, that is the safeguard, that is the night watchman of democratic representative government . . .

• Alfred E. Smith, remarks at Harvard University, June 22, 1933.

429. Constitutions are checks upon the hasty action of a majority. They are the self-imposed restraints of a whole people upon a majority of them to secure sober action and a respect for the rights of the minority, and of the individual . . .

• President William Howard Taft, veto of Arizona Enabling Act, August 22, 1911. The veto was based on the provision in the Arizona constitution for the recall of judges. Resubmitted without that provision, the Act passed and Arizona was admitted to the union; then, as a state, Arizona put the recall provision back in its constitution.

430. The basis of our political systems is the right of the people to make and to alter their constitutions of government. But the constitution which at any time exists, until changed by an explicit and authentic act of the whole people, is sacredly obligatory upon all.

• President George Washington, Farewell Address, published September 19, 1796.

431. Let us then stand by the Constitution, as it is, and by our country as it is, one, united, and entire; let it be a truth engraven on our hearts . . . that we have one country, one constitution, one destiny.

• Senator Daniel Webster of Massachusetts, speech in New York, March 15, 1837.

432. We may be tossed upon an ocean where we can see no land—nor, perhaps, the sun or stars. But there is a chart and a compass for us to study, to consult, and to obey. That chart is the Constitution.

• Senator Daniel Webster of Massachusetts, address at Springfield, Mass., September 29, 1847.

COURAGE
(See also Symbols, War)

441. *The Red Badge of Courage.*

• Stephen Crane, title of novel of the Civil War, 1895.

442. At any age it is better to be a dead lion than a living dog —though better still, of course, to be a living and victorious lion . . .

• Elmer Davis, *But We Were Born Free,* 1954.*

443. Damn the torpedoes, full steam ahead!

• Rear Admiral David G. Farragut, August 5, 1864, as he led his U.S. Navy fleet through a narrow channel, heavily mined, to capture Mobile Bay in the Civil War.

444. To have *faith* requires courage, the ability to take a risk, the readiness even to accept pain and disappointment. Whoever insists on safety and security as primary conditions of life cannot have faith . . .

• Erich Fromm, *The Art of Loving,* 1956.

445. I have not yet begun to fight. (Sometimes quoted as I have just begun to fight.)

• Captain John Paul Jones aboard the American warship *Bonhomme Richard,* in battle with British *H.M.S. Serapis,* September 23, 1779, when asked by the British whether he was prepared to surrender. The *Bonhomme Richard* burned and sank, but not before Jones and his men boarded and captured the *Serapis.*

446. Don't give up the ship!

• Captain James Lawrence, commander of the U.S. frigate *Chesapeake,* mortally wounded in the War of 1812 battle with the British frigate *Shannon,* is supposed to have said this as his last command to his men on June 1, 1813. It has also been attributed to other U.S. Navy heroes.

447. Nuts!

• Reply of Major General Anthony C. McAuliffe to German demand for surrender of his forces at Bastogne, Belgium, December 22, 1944, in World War II.

448. I shall never surrender nor retreat . . . I am determined to sustain myself as long as possible and die like a soldier who never forgets what is due to his own honor and that of his country.

• Colonel William B. Travis, commander at the Alamo, San Antonio, Texas, February 24, 1836. Less than two weeks later, he and his entire garrison were wiped out by Mexican forces.

449. When the going gets tough, the tough get going.

• Anonymous, used in the late 1960's.

COURTESY
(See also Attitudes, Manners)

---

451. . . . the first point of courtesy must always be truth . . .

• Ralph Waldo Emerson, *Essays, Second Series:* Manners, 1844.

452. How sweet and gracious, even in common speech, / Is that fine sense which men call Courtesy!

• James T. Fields, "Courtesy," about the 1850's.

453. To be humble to superiors is duty, to equals courtesy, to inferiors nobleness.

• Benjamin Franklin, *Poor Richard's Almanac,* 1735.

454. How cheap a price for the good will of another!

• President Thomas Jefferson, letter to his grandson, Thomas Jefferson Randolph, November 24, 1808.

455. Common courtesy is increasingly uncommon.

• Anonymous, believed to have originated after the Civil War.

COURTS
(See also Constitution, Justice, Law)

461. No matter whether th' constitution follows th' flag or not, th' supreme coort follows th' iliction returns.

• Finley Peter Dunne, *Mr. Dooley: "The Supreme Court's Decisions,"* 1900. The comment was inspired by the Democratic platform in that election year, which noted that "The Constitution follows the flag . . ." (See fuller quotation under Foreign Relations.)

462. Judges are apt to be naive, simple-minded men.

• Associate Justice Oliver Wendell Holmes, Jr. of the Supreme Court, speech in New York, February 15, 1913.

463. The Supreme Court of the United States is different from all other courts, past and present. It decides fundamental social and political questions that would never be put to judges in other countries . . .

• Anthony Lewis, *Gideon's Trumpet,* 1964.

464. It is emphatically the province and duty of the judicial department to say what the law is.

• Chief Justice John Marshall, Supreme Court decision in Marbury v. Madison, February 24, 1803, which helped establish the power of the Court.

465. I have always thought, from my earliest youth till now, that the greatest scourge an angry Heaven ever inflicted upon an ungrateful and sinning people was an ignorant, a corrupt, or a dependent judiciary.

• Chief Justice John Marshall, a resident of Virginia, as recorded in the Debates of the Virginia (Constitutional) Convention of 1829–31.

466. The decisions of the courts on economic and social questions depend on their economic and social philosophy.

• President Theodore Roosevelt, message to Congress, December 8, 1908.

467. Court—where a suit is pressed and a man can be taken to the cleaners.

• Anonymous, post-World War II.

CRIME

471. Crime is contagious. If the government becomes a lawbreaker, it breeds contempt for law.

• Associate Justice Louis D. Brandeis of the Supreme Court, dissenting opinion in Olmstead v. United States, June 4, 1928. The reference to government law-breaking was prompted by the fact that the case involved government wire-tapping.

472. . . . each act, criminal or otherwise, follows a cause; . . . given the same conditions, the same result will follow forever and ever . . .

• Clarence Darrow, *Crime: Its Cause and Treatment,* 1922.

473. The chief problem in any community cursed with crime is not the punishment of the criminals, but the preventing of the young from being trained to crime.

• W. E. B. DuBois, *The Souls of Black Folk,* 1903.

474. Commit a crime and the earth is made of glass. There is no such thing as concealment.

• Ralph Waldo Emerson, *Essays, First Series:* Compensation, 1841. Emerson wrote these lines in a less complicated and clearly bygone world.

475. What have we better than a blind guess to show that the criminal law in its present form does more good than harm? I do not stop to refer to the effect which it has had in degrading prisoners and in plunging them further into crime, or to the question whether fine and imprisonment do not fall more heavily on a criminal's wife and children than on himself. I have in mind more far-reaching questions. Does punishment deter? Do we deal with criminals on proper principles?

• Judge Oliver Wendell Holmes, Jr. of the Supreme Judicial Court of Massachusetts, "The Path of Law," speech in Boston, January 8, 1897.

476. The thousands of criminals I have seen in 40 years of law enforcement have had one thing in common: every single one was a liar.

• Federal Bureau of Investigation Director J. Edgar Hoover, article in *Family Weekly*, July 14, 1963.

477. Crime doesn't pay.

• Anonymous maxim probably originating in the 19th century.

478. Public enemy.

• The term arose in the late 1920's or early 1930's and gained great attention when first Chicago crime-fighters and then the Federal Bureau of Investigation used it to designate most-wanted criminals.

CULTURE
(See also Art, Literature)

---

481. *Modern Man Is Obsolete.*

• Title of book by Norman Cousins, 1945.

482. No country ever saw learning so broadly diffused through every class of people, or could boast of so sensible, so discerning a Commonality.

• Timothy Dwight, address at Yale University, July 25, 1776. Reverend Dwight later became President of Yale.

483. Culture opens the sense of beauty.

• Ralph Waldo Emerson, *The Conduct of Life:* Culture, 1860.

484. I cannot live without books.

• Thomas Jefferson, letter to John Adams, 1815.

485. The engineers and the scientists can take us to the moon, but we need the poet or the painter to take us to the heights of understanding and perception. Doctors are enabling us to live longer and healthier lives, but we need the musician and the dancer and the filmmaker to bring beauty and meaning to our lives.

• President Richard M. Nixon, seeking broader support of the arts, May 26, 1971.

486. A civilization without culture and art is no civilization.

• New York Governor Nelson A. Rockefeller, message to New York State Commission on Cultural Resources, August 1970.

487. A cult of culture has risen from the general increase in wealth, leisure and education.

• Eric Sevareid, *This Is Eric Sevareid,* 1964.

488. The too exquisitely cultured I avoid as I do the theatre. Their life lacks reality. They offer me wine instead of water. They are surrounded by things that can be bought.

• Henry D. Thoreau, *Journal,* June 26, 1852.

489. The first four letters of culture have no special significance. There is no true culture cult.

• This statement is unattributable, being a synthesis of various passing observations of the 1960's, when the word culture and the word cult were sometimes used interchangeably. Literary and art cultism has almost always claimed to be the true and real culture of its time.

CUSTOM

491. Customs represent the experience of mankind.

• Reverend Henry Ward Beecher, *Proverbs from Plymouth Pulpit,* 1887. One of many aphorisms from the most prominent orator of his time, published in the year of his death but spoken in the pulpit of Plymouth Church in Brooklyn at an earlier time.

492. . . . if we are a materialistic people, no people on earth so relentlessly denounces materialism or strives so hard to share its materials with other people who do not have them; if we are a conformist society, there is no other society that worries out loud so much about the evils of conformity; if we are the richest country on the globe, in no other country do riches alone attract less awe and public merit than in the United States.

• Eric Sevareid, *This Is Eric Sevareid,* 1964.

493. All men are partially buried in the grave of custom, and of some we see only the crown of the head above ground.

• Henry D. Thoreau, *A Week on the Concord and Merrimack Rivers,* 1849.

494. It's an old country custom.

• Used in variations by Mark Twain, who seems to have adapted an old country saying.

495. One man's cuss is another man's custom.

• Saying of late 19th century in defense of the language of Western frontiersmen.

DEATH

501. . . . in this world nothing is certain but death and taxes.

• Benjamin Franklin, letter to Jean-Baptiste Leroy, November 13, 1789.

502. Why fear death? It is the most beautiful adventure in life.

• Charles Frohman, May 7, 1915. These are reputed to have been the last words of the great American theatrical producer, who died in the torpedoing of the British liner *Lusitania* by a German submarine in World War I.

503. A man over ninety is a great comfort to all his elderly neighbors: he is a picket-guard at the extreme outpost; and the young folks of sixty and seventy feel that the enemy must get by him before he can come near their camp.

• Oliver Wendell Holmes, *The Guardian Angel,* 1867.

504. I have a rendezvous with Death / At some disputed barricade.

• Alan Seeger, "I Have a Rendezvous with Death," 1916, the year he was killed in World War I.

505. . . . Adam, the first great benefactor of our race. He brought death into the world.

• Mark Twain (Samuel L. Clemens), *The Tragedy of Pudd'nhead Wilson,* Pudd'nhead Wilson's Calendar, 1894.

506. The report of my death was an exaggeration.

• Mark Twain (Samuel L. Clemens), cablegram to New York news service, June 2, 1897. While in Europe, he had been reported dead.

507. Nothing can happen more beautiful than death.

• Walt Whitman, "Starting from Paumanok," 1860.

DEBT
(See also Borrowing)

---

511. Remember, a patch on your coat, and money in your pocket, is better and more creditable than a writ on your back, and no money to take it off.

• Benjamin Franklin, *Poor Richard's Almanac,* 1756.

512. A national debt, if not excessive, will be to us a national blessing.

• Alexander Hamilton, letter to Robert Morris, April 30, 1781.

513. It is incumbent on every generation to pay its own debts as it goes—a principle which, if acted on, would save one-half the wars of the world.

• Thomas Jefferson, letter to Comte Destutt de Tracy, French philosopher, 1820.

514. No nation ought to be without a debt. A national debt is a national bond; and when it bears no interest, is in no case a grievance.

• Thomas Paine, *Common Sense,* 1776.

515. It's not the principle of the thing, it's the interest.

• Radio joke in the 1930's, part of the wry humor of the bitter Depression.

516. Oh debt, where is thy sting?

• Anonymous, commentary on post-World War II inflation.

DECLARATION OF INDEPENDENCE

521. We hold these truths to be self-evident: That all men are created equal; that they are endowed by their Creator with certain unalienable rights; that among these are life, liberty and the pursuit of happiness. That, to secure these rights, governments are instituted among men, deriving their just powers from the consent of the governed; that, whenever any form of government becomes destructive of these ends, it is the right of the people to alter or abolish it, and to institute new government . . .

• Declaration of Independence, adopted by Continental Congress in Philadelphia, July 4, 1776.

522. We, therefore, the representatives of the United States of America . . . solemnly publish and declare, that these united colonies are, and of right ought to be, free and independent states . . .

• Declaration of Independence, adopted by Continental Congress in Philadelphia, July 4, 1776.

523. And, for the support of this declaration, with a firm reliance on the protection of Divine Providence, we mutually pledge to each other our lives, our fortunes, and our sacred honor.

• Declaration of Independence, adopted by Continental Congress in Philadelphia, July 4, 1776.

524. . . . we must, indeed all hang together, or most assuredly we shall all hang separately.

• Benjamin Franklin, upon the signing of the Declaration of Independence in Philadelphia, July 4, 1776.

525. . . . the flames kindled on the 4th of July, 1776, have spread over too much of the globe to be extinguished by the feeble engines of despotism; on the contrary, they will consume these engines and all who work them . . .

• Thomas Jefferson, letter to John Adams, September 12, 1821. Jefferson was the principal drafter of the Declaration of Independence, Adams a principal editor on the same committee. They were both signers of the Declaration, both Presidents of the United States—and they both died on the very same day, the fiftieth anniversary of the day they affixed their names to this historic document, July 4, 1826.

526. The assertion that "all men are created equal" was of no practical use in effecting our separation from Great Britain; and it was placed in the Declaration not for that, but for future use. Its authors meant it to be—as, thank God, it is now proving itself—a stumbling-block to all those who in after times might seek to turn a free people back into the hateful paths of despotism.

• Abraham Lincoln, speech at Springfield, Ill., 1857.

DEMOCRACY
(See also Freedom, People)

531. . . . not all people in this world are ready for democratic processes.

• Senator Barry M. Goldwater of Arizona, in television interview, April 7, 1963.

532. Not only will we fight for democracy, we will make it more worth fighting for.

• Secretary of the Interior Harold L. Ickes, speech in New York City, May 18, 1941. The United States was not yet engaged in World War II, but the Roosevelt Administration was making clear its antipathy to the Fascist powers and its friendship for England.

533. I am persuaded myself that the good sense of the people will always be found to be the best army.

• Thomas Jefferson, letter to Colonel Edward Carrington, January 16, 1787.

534. If there be any among us who wish to dissolve this Union or to change its Republican form, let them stand undisturbed, as monuments of the safety with which error of opinion may be tolerated where reason is left free to combat it.

• President Thomas Jefferson, first inaugural address, Washington, D.C., March 4, 1801.

535. A democracy, that is, a government of all the people, by all the people, for all the people . . .

• Reverend Theodore Parker, speech at New England Anti-Slavery Convention in Boston, May 29, 1850. The language pre-dated Abraham Lincoln's Gettysburg Address (see Government) by 13 years, and others before Reverend Parker had used somewhat similar phrases; but Parker was known to Lincoln, and the Parker phrase is believed also to have been well-known to the President.

536. All the ills of democracy can be cured by more democracy.

• Alfred E. Smith, speech in Albany, N.Y., June 27, 1933.

537. Self-criticism is the secret weapon of democracy . . .

• Governor Adlai E. Stevenson of Illinois, speech at opening of Democratic National Convention in Chicago, July 21, 1952. He became the party's nominee for the Presidency five days later.

538. Democracy works only when the people are informed.

• U.S. Circuit Court of Appeals Judge J. Skelly Wright, dissenting opinion in case involving order to *Washington Post* not to publish Pentagon Papers, June 19, 1971.

DEMOCRATS
(See also Politics, Republicans)

541. The Democratic party is like a mule. It has neither pride of ancestry nor hope of posterity.

• Ignatius Donnelly, speech in the Minnesota legislature, September 13, 1860. Donnelly, a Republican when this remark was made, later founded the Populist party. The same quotation has also been attributed to at least three other people.

542. . . . some of the best friends that Democrats have are not in the Democratic Party.

• Senator John F. Kennedy of Massachusetts, Democratic candidate for the Presidency, accepting the nomination of the Liberal Party of New York State, September 1960.

543. . . . if the Democratic Party cannot be helped by the many who are poor, it cannot be saved by the few who are rich.

• President John F. Kennedy, on several occasions in 1961–1962.

544. I am not a member of any organized political party. I am a Democrat.

• Attributed to Will Rogers in the 1920's, when the Democratic Party was losing three Presidential elections in a row.

545. A Democratic convention is always a political party.

• Anonymous observation of various political reporters. Democratic conventions traditionally have been regarded by the press as much livelier than Republican ones.

546. The Democrats always disagree, until Election Day.

• Political axiom, particularly since 1930's.

DESTINY

551. Destiny is not a matter of chance; it is a matter of choice.

• William Jennings Bryan, speech in Washington, D.C., February 22, 1899.

552. Whatever limits us, we call Fate.

• Ralph Waldo Emerson, *The Conduct of Life:* Fate, 1860.

553. All are architects of Fate, / Working in these walls of Time;

• Henry Wadsworth Longfellow, "The Builders," written in 1846, published in 1849.

554. Duty determines destiny.

• President William McKinley, speech in Chicago, October 19, 1898. In 1901 President McKinley's duty took him to the Pan American Exposition in Buffalo, N.Y., where he was assassinated—a sardonic postscript to his earlier remark.

555. Our manifest destiny to overspread the continent allotted by Providence . . .

• John L. O'Sullivan created the phrase in *United States Magazine* and *Democratic Review* in the summer of 1845. It was adopted by politicians as the explanation of U.S. territorial expansion for the rest of the 19th century.

556. This generation of Americans has a rendezvous with destiny.

• President Franklin D. Roosevelt, accepting renomination of Democratic Party for Presidency, June 27, 1936.

557. America's noblest destiny is not empire. It is to demonstrate the possibility of conquering poverty and keeping freedom in a land at peace.

• Norman Thomas, radio speech, June 29, 1941. Norman Thomas was the leader and many times Presidential candidate of the Socialist Party. At the time of this speech, the U.S. government was siding more and more openly with Britain against the Fascist nations in World War II.

DETERMINATION
(See also Attitudes)

---

561. Sink or swim, live or die, survive or perish with my country was my unalterable determination.

• John Adams, conversation with Jonathan Sewall, 1774.

562. I am in earnest—I will not equivocate—I will not excuse—I will not retreat a single inch—AND I WILL BE HEARD.

• William Lloyd Garrison, *The Liberator,* January 1, 1831.

563. I propose to fight it out on this line if it takes all summer.

• General Ulysses S. Grant, dispatch to Secretary of War Edwin M. Stanton, May 11, 1864, as he began his bloody and inexorable campaign against the army of Confederate General Robert E. Lee in the Civil War.

564. Resolve, and thou art free.

• Henry Wadsworth Longfellow, *The Masque of Pandora,* 1875.

565. I can die at my post but I cannot desert it.

• Elijah P. Lovejoy, speech in Alton, Ill., November 3, 1837. Four days later this courageous abolitionist editor was murdered when a mob attacked his press.

DIPLOMACY

(See also Foreign Relations)

571. . . . never trust a man who speaks the language of the country where he's stationed.

• Art Buchwald, "Sheep on the Runway," 1970.

572. American diplomacy is easy on the brain but hell on the feet.

• Ambassador (to Great Britain) Charles G. Dawes, speech in Washington, June 2, 1931. The American view of diplomacy was more simplistic at that time.

573. There are three species of creatures who when they seem coming are going, / When they seem going they come: diplomats, women, and crabs.

• John Hay, "Distichs," probably early 1870's. Hay, who became U.S. Secretary of State, was one of our better diplomats himself.

574. Let us never negotiate out of fear. But let us never fear to negotiate.

• President John F. Kennedy, inaugural address, Washington, D.C., January 20, 1961.

575. We live in a time in world history when the old organizations and the old approaches many times do not speak to the problems that we face today.

• President Richard M. Nixon, remarks at reception for Organization of American States, Washington, D.C., April 13, 1973.

576. The United States never lost a war or won a conference.

• Will Rogers, early 1930's.

577. Protocol, Geritol and alcohol.

• U.S. Ambassador to the United Nations Adlai E. Stevenson's description of the ingredients of a diplomat's life, first quoted in 1964.

DISSENT

(See also Attitudes)

---

581. Here in America we are descended in blood and in spirit from revolutionists and rebels—men and women who dared to dissent from accepted doctrine. As their heirs, we may never confuse honest dissent with disloyal subversion.

• President Dwight D. Eisenhower, speech at Columbia University Bi-centennial in New York City, May 31, 1954. He spoke against the backdrop of loose charges of subversion in the midst of the Senate's "Army-McCarthy" hearings.

582. Whoso would be a man, must be a nonconformist.

• Ralph Waldo Emerson, *Essays, First Series:* Self-Reliance, 1841.

583. The heresy of one age becomes the orthodoxy of the next.

• Helen Keller, *Optimism,* 1903.

584. Let us not be afraid of debate or dissent—let us encourage it.

• Senator John F. Kennedy of Massachusetts, address in Washington, D.C. to National Civil Liberties Conference, April 16, 1959.

585. A house divided against itself cannot stand.

• Abraham Lincoln, speech in Springfield, Ill., June 16, 1858. The phrase was a paraphrase of the Bible (Mark III, 25), but it has become associated more with Lincoln of late than with scripture.

586. It is difference of opinion that makes horse-races.

• Mark Twain (Samuel L. Clemens), *The Tragedy of Pudd'nhead Wilson,* Pudd'nhead Wilson's Calendar, 1894.

DREAMS

591. I walked beside the evening sea / And dreamed a dream that could not be; / The waves that plunged along the shore / Said only: "Dreamer, dream no more!"

• George William Curtis, "Ebb and Flow," late 19th century.

592. Judge of your natural character by what you do in your dreams.

• Ralph Waldo Emerson, *Journals,* 1833.

593. I dream of Jeanie with the light brown hair . . .

• Stephen Foster, "Jeanie with the Light Brown Hair," 1854. Believed to have been written about his wife.

594. Beautiful dreamer, wake unto me, / Starlight and dewdrops are waiting for thee . . .

• Stephen Foster, "Beautiful Dreamer," 1862. The publisher who issued it in 1864 capitalized on the composer's death by describing this song as the last one Foster ever wrote, but the claim was false.

595. We need men who can dream of things that never were.

• President John F. Kennedy, speech in Dublin, Ireland, June 28, 1963.

596. There's a long, long trail awinding / Into the land of my dreams . . .

• Stoddard King, "There's A Long, Long Trail Awinding," prior to 1913; it was later put to music and became a popular song of World War I.

597. Men are dreaming animals, and the incapacity to dream makes a man less than human.

• Irving Kristol, speech at Hillsdale College, Hillsdale, Mich., April 1973.

598. All that we see or seem / Is but a dream within a dream.

• Edgar Allan Poe, "A Dream Within a Dream," 1827.

DRESS AND FASHION
(See also Clothing)

601. Eat to please thyself, but dress to please others.

• Benjamin Franklin, *Poor Richard's Almanac,* 1738.

602. Fond pride of dress is sure a very curse; / Ere fancy you consult, consult your purse.

• Benjamin Franklin, *The Way to Wealth,* 1757.

603. On the whole, I think that it cannot be maintained that dressing has in this or any country risen to the dignity of an art.

• Henry D. Thoreau, *Walden:* Economy, 1854.

604. Every generation laughs at the old fashions, but follows religiously the new.

• Henry D. Thoreau, *Walden:* Economy, 1854.

605. It is the luxurious and dissipated who set the fashions which the herd so diligently follow.

• Henry D. Thoreau, *Walden:* Economy, 1854.

606. When seen in the perspective of half-a-dozen years or more, the best of our fashions strike us as grotesque, if not unsightly.

• Thorstein Veblen, *The Theory of the Leisure Class,* 1899.

DRINK
(See also Prohibition)

611. A man will be eloquent if you give him good wine.

• Ralph Waldo Emerson, *Representative Men:* Montaigne, 1850.

612. He that drinks fast, pays slow.

• Benjamin Franklin, *Poor Richard's Almanac,* 1733.

613. For it's always fair weather / When good fellows get together / With a stein on the table and a good song ringing clear.

• Richard Hovey, "A Stein Song," late 19th century.

614. The Elixir of Perpetual Youth, / Called Alcohol . . .

• Henry Wadsworth Longfellow, "The Golden Legend," 1851. The words are spoken in the poetic narrative by Lucifer.

615. The drinks are on the house.

• Traditional invitation to a saloon crowd, used in the 19th century to get the customers started drinking. The theory was that very few would stop at the one free drink.

616. I'll drink to that.

• Response to a toast; though not American in origin, it has become a familiar U.S. conversational phrase.

617. I would rather forget to drink than drink to forget.

• Temperance slogan of early 20th century.

DRUGS

621. Opiate: An unlocked door in the prison of Identity. It leads into the jail yard.

• Ambrose Bierce, *The Devil's Dictionary,* 1906.

622. The spirit of the world, the great calm presence of the Creator, comes not forth to the sorceries of opium or of wine.

• Ralph Waldo Emerson, *Essays, Second Series:* The Poet, 1844.

623. A shot in the arm can be fatal.

• Anti-narcotics grafitti, 1960's.

624. Better a party-pooper than a pill-popper.

• Radio public service announcement, 1960's.

625. People who will try anything once may not get a second chance.

• Anonymous, cited in 1960's as a saying of the 1920's.

ECOLOGY

631. We must realize that we can no longer throw our wastes away because there is no "away."

• New Jersey Governor William T. Cahill, statement when signing law against coastal dumping, Trenton, New Jersey, 1971.

632. Nature works on a method of all for each and each for all.

• Ralph Waldo Emerson, *Society and Solitude:* Farming, 1870.

633. We have met the enemy and he is us.

• Walt Kelly, "Pogo" comic strip, 1970.

634. It were happy if we studied nature more in natural things, and acted according to nature, whose rules are few, plain and most reasonable.

• William Penn, *Fruits of Solitude,* 1693.

635. Men and Nature must work hand in hand. The throwing out of balance of the resources of Nature throws out of balance also the lives of men.

• President Franklin D. Roosevelt, message to Congress, January 24, 1933. FDR established the Civilian Conservation Corps as a Depression measure to provide work and improve the land at the same time.

636. The nation that destroys its soil destroys itself.

• President Franklin D. Roosevelt, letter to states seeking standard conservation laws, February 26, 1937. The problem of the Dust Bowl was fresh in everybody's minds.

637. I see an America whose rivers and valleys and lakes, hills and streams and plains, the mountains over our land and nature's wealth deep under the earth, are protected as the rightful heritage of all the people.

• President Franklin D. Roosevelt, speech in the final phase of the 1940 election, November 2, 1940.

638. The conservation of our natural resources and their proper use constitute the fundamental problem which underlies almost every other problem of our national life.

• President Theodore Roosevelt, message to Congress, December 3, 1907.

639. . . . the laws of nature are the same everywhere. Whoever violates them anywhere must always pay the penalty.

• Carl Schurz, speech in Philadelphia, 1889. Statesman, reformer and editor, he also qualified as somewhat of a prophet with this comment.

ECONOMY

(See Business, Labor, Prosperity)

---

641. After order and liberty, economy is one of the highest essentials of a free government. . . . Economy is always a guarantee of peace . . .

• Vice President Calvin Coolidge, speech in Northampton, Mass., May 30, 1923. When he became President a few months later, on the death of President Harding, Calvin Coolidge had an administration in which economy, peace and prosperity all flourished—but none of them lasted very long after.

642. . . . banking establishments are more dangerous than standing armies.

• Thomas Jefferson, letter to John Taylor, 1816. Jefferson pinned his faith in tilling the soil; banking, he felt, soiled the till.

643. Any government, like any family, can for a year spend a little more than it earns. But you and I know that a continuance of that habit means the poorhouse.

• President Franklin D. Roosevelt, radio fireside chat, July 30, 1932. Not long thereafter, President Roosevelt was accused of adopting the very policy he criticized and unbalancing the budget.

644. The State cannot get a cent for any man without taking it from some other man. . . . The latter is the Forgotten Man.

• William Graham Sumner, *What Social Classes Owe to Each Other,* 1883. President Franklin D. Roosevelt 50 years later popularized the phrase, the Forgotten Man, along with his opposite number, the "economic royalist."

645. That man is the richest whose pleasures are the cheapest.

• Henry D. Thoreau, *Journal,* March 11, 1856.

EDUCATION

(See also Ancestry, Colleges, Poverty, Races, Science, Taxes, Welfare, Youth)

---

651. Next in importance to freedom and justice is popular education, without which neither freedom nor justice can be permanently maintained.

• Representative James A. Garfield of Ohio, letter accepting Republican nomination for the Presidency, July 12, 1880.

652. . . . the consequences of foreign education are alarming to me, as an American.

• Thomas Jefferson, letter to J. Banister, Jr., October 15, 1785. Jefferson later struck a major blow for native American education by founding the University of Virginia.

653. Preach, my dear Sir, a crusade against ignorance; establish and improve the law for educating the common people.

• Thomas Jefferson, letter to noted lawyer George Wythe, August 13, 1786.

654. A child miseducated is a child lost.

• President John F. Kennedy, message to Congress, January 11, 1962.

655. Our educational system teaches us not to think, but to know the answer.

• Norman Mailer, *The Presidential Papers,* 1963.

656. Learn to live, and live to learn.

• Bayard Taylor, "To My Daughter," mid-19th century.

657. Today, education is perhaps the most important function of state and local government.

• Chief Justice Earl Warren, Supreme Court decision in Brown v. Board of Education of Topeka, May 17, 1954. This was the case which made school segregation illegal, reversing the 19th century doctrine of "separate but equal."

EFFICIENCY

661. There is always a best way of doing everything, if it be to boil an egg.

• Ralph Waldo Emerson, *The Conduct of Life:* Behavior, 1860.

662. Get there fustest with the mostest.

• Attributed to Confederate General Nathan Bedford Forrest as a description of successful military tactics.

663. Get it first and get it right.

• Journalistic maxim.

664. There are three ways of doing something—the right way, the wrong way and the Army way.

• Maxim of U.S. Army men since at least World War I.

EQUALITY
(See Declaration of Independence)

671. Conceiving the defense of freedom, like freedom itself, to be one and indivisible, we hold all continents and peoples in equal regard and honor. We reject any insinuation that one race or another, one people or another, is in any sense inferior or expendable.

• President Dwight D. Eisenhower, inaugural address, January 20, 1953.

672. The man who insists he is as good as anybody, believes he is better.

• E. W. Howe, *Country Town Sayings,* 1911.

673. All of us do not have equal talent, but all of us should have an equal opportunity to develop our talents.

• President John F. Kennedy, speech in San Diego, Calif., June 6, 1963. The American concept of equality has expanded over the years—first with the 1776 Declaration that "all men are created equal," then with the ending of slavery almost a century later, which gave Black people recognition that they were finally covered by the Declaration, and, in our own time, with the recognition that equality also should include equal opportunity.

674. Four score and seven years ago our fathers brought forth on this continent a new nation, conceived in liberty and dedicated to the proposition that all men are created equal.

• President Abraham Lincoln, address at Gettysburg, Penna., November 19, 1863, dedicating the national cemetery at the site of an epic battle of a few months earlier in the Civil War. Today it is being suggested that the phrase should be rewritten as "all men and women are created equal."

675. . . . perfect equality affords no temptation.

• Thomas Paine, *Common Sense,* 1776.

676. You cannot be friends upon any other terms than upon the terms of equality.

• President Woodrow Wilson, address on Latin American policy in Mobile, Alabama, October 27, 1913.

ETHICS
(See also Conscience)

681. Expedients are for the hour, but principles are for the ages.

• Reverend Henry Ward Beecher, *Proverbs from Plymouth Pulpit,* 1887, a collection of his memorable remarks published the year of his death.

682. A people that values its privileges above its principles soon loses both.

• President Dwight D. Eisenhower, inaugural address, January 20, 1953.

683. The shield against the stingings of conscience is the universal practice of our contemporaries.

• Ralph Waldo Emerson, *Representative Men:* On the Uses of Great Men, 1850. Or, as we say it today, "Everybody's doing it."

684. We want individuals to whom all eyes may turn as examples of the practicability of virtue. We want shining examples.

• Margaret Fuller, *New York Tribune,* July 4, 1845. Pioneer woman journalist Margaret Fuller, friend of Emerson, was in some ways a shining example herself, proving that her sex was fully capable of competing with men.

685. Everybody has a little bit of Watergate in him.

• Reverend Billy Graham, remark at dedication of church in Fort Lauderdale, Fla., February 3, 1974. The Watergate affair and the question of impeaching the President over it were much in the news.

686. Whenever you are to do a thing, though it can never be known but to yourself, ask yourself how you would act were all the world looking at you, and act accordingly.

• Thomas Jefferson, letter to his nephew, Peter Carr, August 19, 1785.

687. Goodness is the only investment that never fails.

• Henry D. Thoreau, *Walden:* Higher Laws, 1854.

EXECUTIVES

691. A man is known by the company that he organizes.

• Ambrose Bierce, *The Devil's Dictionary,* 1906.

692. What is worth doing is worth the trouble of asking someone to do it.

• Ambrose Bierce, *The Devil's Dictionary,* 1906. *The Devil's Dictionary* was a periodical published at weekly or often longer intervals on a very irregular basis until 1906, when much of it was published in a single collection under another title. For the purpose of simplicity, we have used the 1906 date for virtually all quotations from the *Dictionary.*

693. All decisions should be made as low as possible in the organization. The Charge of the Light Brigade was ordered by an officer who wasn't there looking at the territory.

• Robert Townsend, *Up the Organization,* 1970.

694. The buck stops here.

• Sign on President Harry S Truman's desk, circa 1950.

695. Blessed are they who go around in circles, for they shall be known as wheels.

• Anonymous, popular saying of 1950's.

696. Some people get ulcers and some people give them.

• Gag novelty sign of the 1960's.

EXPLORATION

701. That's one small step for a man, one giant leap for mankind.

• Astronaut Neil Armstrong, first words spoken on the moon by the first human being to set foot on the moon, July 20, 1969. Part of the miracle was that the words were broadcast from the moon back to earth.

702. In the next twenty centuries, the age of Aquarius of the great year, the age for which our young people have such high hopes, humanity may begin to understand its most baffling mystery—where are we going? The earth is, in fact, traveling many thousands of miles per hour in the direction of the constellation Hercules—to some unknown destination in the cosmos. Man must understand his universe in order to understand his destiny.

• *Apollo 11* astronaut Neil Armstrong, first man on the moon, address to joint session of Congress, September 16, 1969. This was the climax of the official national welcome for Armstrong, Edwin Aldrin, Jr. and Michael Collins, the crew of *Apollo 11.*

703. Our efforts today and what we have done so far are but small building blocks in a huge pyramid to come . . .

• Lt. Col. John H. Glenn, Jr., Marine who became first U.S. astronaut to orbit the earth (on February 20, 1962), speech to joint session of Congress, February 26, 1962.

704. Knowledge begets knowledge. The more I see, the more impressed I am—not with what we know—but with how tremendous the areas are that are as yet unexplored.

• Lt. Col. John H. Glenn, Jr., first American to orbit the earth, speech to joint session of Congress, February 26, 1962.

705. Certainly the most thrilling and romantic happening of these years is the adventure in space, surpassing in promise the voyages of the fifteenth and sixteenth centuries. This adventure makes life worth the trouble again.

• Paul Goodman, *Growing Up Absurd,* 1960.

706. The sky is no longer the limit.

• President Richard M. Nixon, speech in both New York and Los Angeles in tribute to *Apollo 11* astronauts, August 13, 1969. President Nixon and the astronauts attended ceremonies in New York, Chicago and Los Angeles on the same day.

FAME

711. My advice to a young man seeking deathless fame would be to espouse an unpopular cause and devote his life to it.

• George William Curtis, "Wendell Phillips," later 19th century. Phillips was an abolitionist leader, then a crusader for women's rights, prison reform and other causes in which he was both fiery and ahead of his time.

712. Fame is a bee. / It has a song— / It has a sting— / Ah, too, it has a wing.

• Emily Dickinson, poems, circa 1870.

713. I trust a good deal to common fame . . . If a man can write a better book, preach a better sermon, or build a better mousetrap than his neighbor, though he builds his house in the woods, the world will make a beaten path to his door.

• Generally credited to Ralph Waldo Emerson, in a lecture, but also claimed, in much the same form, by Elbert Hubbard many years later. Probably first said in 1860's or 1870's.

714. Fame usually comes to those who are thinking about something else.

• Oliver Wendell Holmes, *The Autocrat of the Breakfast-Table,* 1858. Dr. Holmes was one to whom fame came early and very likely when he was thinking about something else, since he was a physician before he gained fame as a writer.

715. Lives of great men all remind us / We can make our lives sublime. / And departing, leave behind us / Footprints on the sands of time.

• Henry Wadsworth Longfellow, "A Psalm of Life," 1839.

716. No true and permanent fame can be found except in labors which promote the happiness of mankind.

• Charles Sumner, address at Amherst, Mass., August 11, 1847.

FAMILY

(See also Ancestry)

721. Sometimes I get the feeling that Dr. Freud invented mothers and fathers for their children to hate.

• Gertrude Berg, *Molly and Me,* 1961.

722. It is not observed in history that families improve with time.

• George William Curtis, *Prue and I,* 1856.

723. Men are what their mothers made them.

• Ralph Waldo Emerson, *The Conduct of Life:* Fate, 1860. Emerson himself was only eight when his father died.

724. Late children, early orphans.

• Benjamin Franklin, *Poor Richard's Almanac,* 1742.

725. Back of every achievement is a proud wife and a surprised mother-in-law.

• Brooks Hays, former Congressman, on being sworn in as an aide to President Kennedy, December 1, 1961.

726. . . . how convenient it would be to many of our great men and great families of doubtful origin, could they have the privilege of the heroes of yore, who, whenever their origin was involved in obscurity, modestly announced themselves descended from a god . . .

• Washington Irving, *A History of New York by Diedrich Knickerbocker,* 1809.

727. The family is one of nature's masterpieces.

• George Santayana, *The Life of Reason, Vol. 2, Reason in Society,* 1905.

728. . . . I do not condemn nepotism, provided the relatives really work.

• Senator Margaret Chase Smith of Maine, speech to National Women's Republican Conference, April 16, 1962.

729. Do wise Christian legislators need any arguments to convince them that the sacredness of the family relation should be protected at all hazards? The family—that great conservator of national virtue and strength—how can you hope to build it up in the midst of violence, debauchery and excess?

• Mrs. Elizabeth Cady Stanton, testimony to New York State Senate Judiciary Committee on proposed divorce bill, 1861.

730. The time not to become a father is eighteen years before a world war.

• E. B. White, *The Second Tree from the Corner,* 1945.

FEAR

731. Fear is an instructor of great sagacity and the herald of all revolutions.

• Ralph Waldo Emerson, *Essays, First Series:* Compensation, 1841.

732. He has not learned the lesson of life who does not every day surmount a fear.

• Ralph Waldo Emerson, *Society and Solitude:* Courage, 1870.

733. We should not let our fears hold us back from pursuing our hopes.

• Senator John F. Kennedy of Massachusetts, speech in Washington, D.C., December 11, 1959.

734. Let us never negotiate out of fear. But let us never fear to negotiate.

• President John F. Kennedy, inaugural address, Washington, D.C., January 20, 1961.

735. Our hearts, our hopes, our prayers, our tears, / Our faith triumphant o'er our fears, / Are all with thee—are all with thee.

• Henry Wadsworth Longfellow, "The Building of the Ship," 1850.

736. . . . the only thing we have to fear is fear itself . . .

• President Franklin D. Roosevelt, first inaugural address, Washington, D.C., March 4, 1933. These words became the rallying catch-phrase that helped lift the spirits of the American people in the midst of a great depression.

FLAG

741. I pledge allegiance to the flag of the United States of America and to the Republic for which it stands, one Nation under God, indivisible, with liberty and justice for all.

• The original pledge, written by the Reverend Francis Bellamy, was first said at the dedication of the World's Fair Grounds in Chicago, October 21, 1892. It was altered several times before the words "under God" were added by Joint Resolution of Congress, signed by President Eisenhower on June 14, 1954. The original authorship has been claimed by both Reverend Bellamy and James B. Upham, but Bellamy is credited in the official U.S. government history of the Pledge.

742. The Republic never retreats. Its flag is the only flag that has never known defeat. Where that flag leads we follow, for we know that the hand that bears it onward is the unseen hand of God.

• Albert J. Beveridge, speech in Philadelphia, February 15, 1899. Beveridge, about to start the first of his two terms as a U.S. Senator from Indiana, was one of the early Progressive Republicans supporting Theodore Roosevelt.

743. *You're a Grand Old Flag!*

• George M. Cohan, song from his musical comedy, "George Washington, Jr.," 1906.

744. Oh, say, does that star-spangled banner yet wave / O'er the land of the free, and the home of the brave?

• Francis Scott Key, "The Star-Spangled Banner," September 14, 1814, written as he kept an anxious eye on the flag at Fort McHenry in Baltimore Harbor as its guns dueled with those of British ships in the War of 1812.

745. "Shoot, if you must, this old, gray head, / But spare your country's flag," she said.

• John Greenleaf Whittier, "Barbara Frietchie," 1863. The incident which provided the basis for this stirring Civil War poem became part of American folklore, but in fact it was not the elderly Barbara Frietchie but a younger woman who showed the U.S. flag while Frederick, Md., was occupied by Confederate troops.

746. The flag is the embodiment, not of sentiment but of history. It represents the experiences made by men and women, the experiences of those who do and live under that flag.

• President Woodrow Wilson, Flag Day address in New York City, June 14, 1915.

FLOWERS

751. Where are the flowers, the fair young flowers that lately sprang and stood / In brighter light and softer airs, a beauteous sisterhood?

• William Cullen Bryant, "The Death of the Flowers," 1825. His sister's death prompted this poem about the cycle of nature.

752. Earth laughs in flowers . . .

• Ralph Waldo Emerson, "Hamatreya," 1847.

753. . . . these stars of earth, these golden flowers.

• Henry Wadsworth Longfellow, "Flowers," 1839.

754. In all places, then, and in all seasons, / Flowers expand their light and soul-like wings, / Teaching us, by most persuasive reasons, / How akin they are to human things.

• Henry Wadsworth Longfellow, "Flowers," 1839.

755. A weed is no more than a flower in disguise.

• James Russell Lowell, *A Fable for Critics,* 1848.

756. Say it with flowers.

• Patrick F. O'Keefe, advertising slogan for the Society of American Florists, 1917.

FOOD

761. Man cannot live by bread, it is true, but the man who cannot live on bread and water is not fit to live.

• Reverend Henry Ward Beecher, sermon at Plymouth Church in Brooklyn, July 22, 1877.

762. Man does not live by bread alone, but by faith, by admiration, by sympathy.

• Ralph Waldo Emerson, *Lectures and Biographical Sketches,* edited and published in 1884, posthumously; Emerson died in 1882.

763. Eat to live and not live to eat.

• Apparently a slightly revised version of an old proverb, published by Benjamin Franklin in *Poor Richard's Almanac,* 1733.

764. Kill no more pigeons than you can eat.

• Benjamin Franklin, letter to his friend Catherine Ray, October 16, 1755.

765. Life, within doors, has few pleasanter prospects than a neatly arranged and well-provisioned breakfast table.

• Nathaniel Hawthorne, *The House of the Seven Gables,* 1851.

766. . . . like the hidalgo's dinner, very little meat and a great deal of tablecloth.

• Henry Wadsworth Longfellow, *The Spanish Student,* 1843.

767. Avoid fried meats, which angry the blood.

• Leroy (Satchel) Paige, quoted in *Collier's* magazine, June 13, 1953.

768. The way to a man's heart is through his stomach.

• There is some question as to whether this was an anonymous proverb or was created by Sara Payson Willis Parton (Fanny Fern), author of *Fern Leaves from Fanny's Portfolio,* 1853.

769. It's ironic that in this age when anybody who's cut his second molars considers himself a gourmet, the quality of our staple foods is so dreary.

• Harriet Van Horne, *Never Go Anywhere Without a Pencil,* 1972.

770. A chicken in every pot, a car in every garage.

• Republican slogan in 1928 Presidential campaign. Today it is doubtful that the vision of plentiful fowl would be considered to have as much appeal as a cheaper price for red meat.

FOOTBALL

771. Football today is far too much a sport for the few who can play it well; the rest of us, and too many of our children, get our exercise from climbing up the seats in stadiums, or from walking across the room to turn on our television sets.

• President John F. Kennedy, who described himself as having been "an obscure member of the junior varsity at Harvard," speech at National Football Foundation Dinner in New York City, December 4, 1961.

772. Football compels us primarily with its explosive choreography, its terse blend of skill pirouetting a field mined with danger. It is a game of action that must be seen to be enjoyed.

• Larry Merchant, *The National Football Lottery,* 1973.

773. In short, in life, as in a football game, the principle to follow is: Hit the line hard; don't foul and don't shirk, but hit the line hard.

• Theodore Roosevelt, *The Strenuous Life,* 1910. In similar words, he had advocated this doctrine all his life.

774. Monday morning quarterback . . .

• First used when football became a mass audience sport in the 1920's; sometimes attributed to Grantland Rice. An alternative phraseology was and is "grandstand quarterback," used to describe spectators who question the play calls by the quarterback on the field.

775. Triple-threat man . . .

• A football player who could run with the ball, kick or pass with equal skill. The term arose in the 1920's and faded after World War II, when football became a sport of individual specialists rather than all-around players.

FOREIGN RELATIONS
(See also Business, Diplomacy, Hunger, Patriotism)

---

781. . . . we are today in the midst of a cold war.

• Bernard M. Baruch, speech in Columbia, S.C., April 16, 1947. This is often credited with having been the first use of the phrase, but it came so quickly into common usage that its original authorship may be moot.

782. . . . sovereign nations cannot allow their policies to be dictated, or their fate decided, by artificial rigging and distortion of world commodity markets.

• President Gerald R. Ford, address to World Energy Conference, Detroit, September 23, 1974.

783. Millions for defense but not a cent for tribute.

• Robert Goodloe Harper (though commonly misattributed to U.S. diplomat Charles Cotesworth Pinckney), at a dinner in Philadelphia for John Marshall, U.S. envoy to France, June 18, 1798. A member of the U.S. House of Representatives from Maryland at the time, Harper made another contribution later to the American lexicon when he suggested the name Liberia for the new free Black republic in Africa.

784. . . . peace, commerce, and honest friendship, with all nations—entangling alliances with none.

• President Thomas Jefferson, first inaugural address, Washington, D.C., March 4, 1801.

785. The less we have to do with the amities or enmities of Europe, the better.

• Thomas Jefferson, letter to Thomas Leiper, 1815.

786. The country is as strong abroad only as it's strong at home.

• President John F. Kennedy, speech in St. Paul, Minn., October 6, 1962.

787. Our policy is directed not against any country or doctrine but against hunger, poverty, desperation, and chaos.

• Secretary of State George C. Marshall, commencement address at Harvard University, Cambridge, Mass., June 5, 1947, introducing what became known as the Marshall Plan for helping nations devastated by World War II.

788. . . . the American continents, by the free and independent condition which they have assumed and maintain, are henceforth not to be considered as subjects for future colonization by any European powers.

• President James Monroe, message to Congress, December 2, 1823. This was the message which laid down what became known as the Monroe Doctrine.

789. We seek friendly relations with all nations. Any nation can be our friend without being any other nation's enemy.

• President Richard M. Nixon, broadcast to nation announcing his plan to visit the People's Republic of China, July 15, 1971.

790. I am confident that our free and vigorous American economy can more than hold its own in open world competition. But we must always insist that such competition take place under equitable rules.

• President Richard M. Nixon, message to Congress, April 10, 1973.

791. We live in a time in world history when the old organizations and the old approaches many times do not speak to the problems that we face today.

• President Richard M. Nixon, remarks at reception for Organization of American States in Washington, D.C., April 13, 1973.

792. We must be the great arsenal of democracy.

• President Franklin D. Roosevelt, radio fireside chat, December 29, 1940, referring to the need for supporting democratic nations in World War II.

793. There is a homely adage which runs, "Speak softly and carry a big stick; you will go far." If the American nation will speak softly and yet build and keep at a pitch of the highest training a thoroughly efficient navy, the Monroe Doctrine will go far.

• Vice President Theodore Roosevelt, speech at Minnesota State Fair, September 2, 1901.

794. I believe that it must be the policy of the United States to support free peoples who are resisting attempted subjugation by armed minorities or by outside pressures.

• President Harry S Truman, speech to joint session of Congress, March 12, 1947, presenting what became known as the Truman Doctrine.

795. It is our true policy to steer clear of permanent alliances with any portion of the foreign world . . .

• President George Washington, farewell address, published September 19, 1796 in *Philadelphia Daily American Advertiser.* (It was never delivered as a speech, and was published on the 19th with the date of September 17 on the text.)

796. America cannot be an ostrich with its head in the sand.

• President Woodrow Wilson, speech in Des Moines, February 1, 1916.

797. . . . the Constitution follows the flag. . . . We warn the American people that imperialism abroad will lead quickly and inevitably to despotism at home . . .

• Democratic Party platform in election of 1900; adopted in Kansas City in July. (For another quotation inspired by this one, see quote number 461.)

FREEDOM

(See also Attitudes, Constitution, Government, History, Justice, Rights)

---

801. My individual freedom stops where your nose begins, so far as the swinging of my fist is concerned. My right to demonstrate my disagreement with a law does not give me the privilege of interfering with the rights of other people.

• Vice President Spiro T. Agnew, speech in Atlanta, February 21, 1970.

802. Republics are not in and of themselves better than other forms of government, except insofar as they carry with them and guarantee to the citizens that liberty of thought and action for which they were established.

• Senator William E. Borah of Idaho, speech in Senate opposing proposal for new espionage law, April 19, 1917, just after our entry in World War I.

803. Experience should teach us to be most on our guard to protect liberty when the government's purposes are beneficent. . . . The greatest dangers to liberty lurk in insidious encroachment by men of zeal, well-meaning but without understanding.

• Associate Justice Louis D. Brandeis of the Supreme Court, dissenting opinion in Olmstead v. U.S., a wiretapping case, June 4, 1928.

804. The Union—next to our liberty, the most dear!

• Vice President John C. Calhoun, toast at a dinner in Washington, D.C., April 13, 1840. Calhoun, the apostle of states' rights, used the toast to contradict President Andrew Jackson's view that the Federal government was paramount. (For Jackson's words see quote number 911.)

805. Our consciousness of and concern about the potential dangers to our cherished liberties is the best, and in the last analysis, perhaps the only protection for our liberties.

• Senator Sam J. Ervin, Jr., of North Carolina, speech at Miami University, Hamilton, Ohio, June 28, 1973.

806. The history of liberty has largely been the history of the observance of procedural safeguards.

• Associate Justice Felix Frankfurter of the Supreme Court, opinion in McNabb v. U.S., 1943.

807. Now, we Americans understand freedom. We have earned it; we have lived for it, and we have died for it. This nation and its people are freedom's models in a searching world. We can be freedom's missionaries in a doubting world.

• Senator Barry M. Goldwater of Arizona, accepting Republican Presidential nomination in San Francisco, July 16, 1964.

808. I would remind you that extremism in the defense of liberty is no vice.

• Senator Barry M. Goldwater of Arizona, accepting Republican Presidential nomination in San Francisco, July 16, 1964. (See also quotation number 1163.)

809. . . . armed in the holy cause of liberty . . .

• Patrick Henry, speech to the Virginia Assembly, March 23, 1775.

810. Give me liberty or give me death!

• Patrick Henry, speech to the Virginia Assembly, March 23, 1775. The full sentence is: "I know not what course others may take; but as for me, give me liberty or give me death!"

811. The very aim and end of our institutions is just this: that we may think what we like and say what we think.

• Oliver Wendell Holmes, *The Professor at the Breakfast-Table,* 1860. Dr. Holmes' son, Associate Justice Oliver Wendell Holmes, Jr., of the Supreme Court, echoed these sentiments in his years on the Court; but not always. See below.

812. The most stringent protection of free speech would not protect a man in falsely shouting fire in a theatre and causing a panic.

• Associate Justice Oliver Wendell Holmes, Jr., of the Supreme Court, decision in Schenck v. U.S., March 3, 1919.

813. If there is any principle of the Constitution that more imperatively calls for attachment than any other it is the principle of free thought—not free thought for those who agree with us but freedom for the thought we hate . . .

• Associate Justice Oliver Wendell Holmes, Jr., of the Supreme Court, dissenting opinion in U.S. v. Schwimmer, May 27, 1929.

814. We Americans know that freedom, like peace, is indivisible.

• Secretary of the Interior Harold L. Ickes, speech in New York City, May 18, 1941.

815. The arms we have been compelled by our enemies to assume we will, in defiance of every hazard, with unabating firmness and perseverance, employ for the preservation of our liberties; being with one mind resolves to die free men rather than live slaves.

• Thomas Jefferson and John Dickinson, "Declaration . . . Setting Forth the Causes and Necessity of . . . Taking Up Arms," adopted by Continental Congress July 6, 1775.

816. The tree of liberty must be refreshed from time to time with the blood of patriots and tyrants. It is its natural manure.

• Thomas Jefferson, letter to Colonel W. S. Smith, November 13, 1787.

817. . . . we are likely to preserve the liberty we have obtained only by unremitting labors and perils.

• Thomas Jefferson, letter to his friend Phillip Mazzei, April 24, 1796.

818. It behooves every man who values liberty of conscience for himself, to resist invasions of it in the case of others . . .

• President Thomas Jefferson, letter to Dr. Benjamin Rush, April 21, 1803.

819. Where the press is free and every man able to read, all is safe.

• Thomas Jefferson, letter to Charles Yancey, 1816.

820. Only the strength and progress and peaceful change that come from independent judgment and individual ideas—and even from the unorthodox and the eccentric—can enable us to surpass that foreign ideology that fears free thought more than it fears hydrogen bombs.

• Senator John F. Kennedy of Massachusetts, *Profiles in Courage,* 1956.

821. In the long history of the world, only a few generations have been granted the role of defending freedom in its hour of maximum danger. I do not shrink from this responsibility.

• President John F. Kennedy, inaugural address, Washington, D.C., January 20, 1961.

822. We stand for freedom.

• President John F. Kennedy, message to Congress, May 25, 1961.

823. Our reliance is in the love of liberty which God has planted in us. Our defense is in the spirit which prized liberty as the heritage of all men, in all lands everywhere. Destroy this spirit and you have planted the seeds of despotism at your own doors.

• Abraham Lincoln, speech in Edwardsville, Ill., September 11, 1858, during campaign against Stephen H. Douglas.

824. Four score and seven years ago our fathers brought forth on this continent a new nation, conceived in liberty and dedicated to the proposition that all men are created equal.

• President Abraham Lincoln, address at Gettysburg, Penna., November 19, 1863.

825. . . . that this nation, under God, shall have a new birth of freedom . . .

• President Abraham Lincoln, address at Gettysburg, Penna., November 19, 1863.

826. Since the general civilization of mankind, I believe that there are more instances of the abridgment of the freedom of the people by gradual and silent encroachments of those in power than by violent and sudden usurpations.

• James Madison, speech to the Virginia Convention, June 16, 1788.

827. We gave our freedom away a long time ago. We gave it away in all the revolutions we did not make, all the acts of courage we found a way to avoid, all the roots we destroyed in fury at that past which still would haunt our deeds.

• Norman Mailer, *Presidential Papers,* 1963.

828. . . . the freedom of the press is one of the great bulwarks of liberty, and can never be restrained but by despotic governments.

• George Mason, Virginia Bill of Rights, adopted June 12, 1776.

829. We look forward to a world founded upon four essential human freedoms. The first is freedom of speech and expression—everywhere in the world. The second is freedom of every person to worship God in his own way—everywhere in the world. The third is freedom from want . . . everywhere in the world. The fourth is freedom from fear . . . everywhere in the world.

• President Franklin D. Roosevelt, message to Congress, January 6, 1941. The "four freedoms" became a rallying point in the gathering fight against dictatorship overseas, in the shadow of World War II.

830. My country, 'tis of thee, / Sweet land of liberty, / Of thee I sing: / Land where my fathers died, / Land of the pilgrims' pride, / From every mountain-side / Let freedom ring.

• Reverend Dr. Samuel F. Smith, "America," sung for the first time in public at Park Street Church in Boston on July 4, 1831.

831. You don't negotiate free speech.

• Dr. Frank Stanton, then Vice Chairman of CBS, speech in Memphis, Tenn., October 4, 1972.

832. A free press stands as one of the great interpreters between the government and the people. To allow it to be fettered is to fetter ourselves.

• Associate Justice George Sutherland of the Supreme Court, decision in Grosjean v. American Press Co., February 10, 1936. The case involved Louisiana's attempt to levy a tax on the gross advertising of newspapers, at a time when the state's major newspapers and the Huey Long political machine were at loggerheads.

833. God grants liberty only to those who love it, and are always ready to guard and defend it.

• Senator Daniel Webster of Massachusetts, speech in the Senate, June 3, 1834.

834. Liberty exists in proportion to wholesome restraint; the more restraint on others to keep off from us, the more liberty we have.

• Senator Daniel Webster of Massachusetts, speech in Charleston, S.C., May 10, 1847.

835. This nation will survive, this state will prosper, the orderly business of life will go forward if only men can speak in whatever way given them to utter what their hearts hold—by voice, by posted card, by letter, or by press. Reason has never failed men. Only force and repression have made the wrecks in the world.

• William Allen White, *The Emporia Gazette,* July 27, 1922.

FRIENDSHIP

841. Friendship: A ship big enough to carry two in fair weather, but only one in foul.

• Ambrose Bierce, *The Devil's Dictionary,* 1906.

842. The only way to have a friend is to be one.

• Ralph Waldo Emerson, *Essays, First Series:* Friendship, 1841.

843. There are three faithful friends—an old wife, an old dog, and ready money.

• Benjamin Franklin, *Poor Richard's Almanac,* 1738.

844. It only takes an outstretched hand.

• Rod McKuen, *Lonesome Cities:* Los Angeles, "An Outstretched Hand," 1968.

845. I never met a man I didn't like.

• Will Rogers, 1920's. One of the late comedian's most enduring and repeated remarks.

846. A man cannot be said to succeed in this life who does not satisfy one friend.

• Henry D. Thoreau, *Journal,* February 19, 1857.

847. You cannot be friends upon any other terms than upon the terms of equality.

• President Woodrow Wilson, speech in Mobile, Ala., October 27, 1913.

FRONTIER
(See also Pioneering)

(See also Pioneering)

851. We stand today on the edge of a new frontier—the frontier of the 1960's—a frontier of unknown opportunities and perils—a frontier of unfulfilled hopes and threats.

• Senator John F. Kennedy of Massachusetts, speech accepting Democratic Presidential nomination in Los Angeles, July 15, 1960.

852. . . . that restless, nervous energy; that dominant individualism, working for good and for evil, and withal that buoyancy and exuberance which comes with freedom—these are traits of the frontier, or traits called out elsewhere because of the existence of the frontier.

• Frederick Jackson Turner, "The Significance of the Frontier in American History," 1893.

853. . . . the most important effect of the frontier has been in the promotion of democracy . . .

• Frederick Jackson Turner, "The Significance of the Frontier in American History," 1893.

FUTURE

861. . . . the intimation of the future comes only with the sense of the past.

• S. N. Behrman, "Biography," Act II, 1932.

862. I know of no way of judging the future but by the past.

• Patrick Henry, speech at the Virginia Assembly, March 23, 1775.

863. I like the dreams of the future better than the history of the past . . .

• Thomas Jefferson, letter to John Adams, August 1, 1816. The two former Presidents had seen their dreams of the past become a reality with U.S. independence.

864. Yesterday is not ours to recover, but tomorrow is ours to win or lose.

• President Lyndon B. Johnson, nationally televised address, November 23, 1963, the day after he had succeeded the assassinated John F. Kennedy as President.

865. Thou, too, sail on, O Ship of State! / Sail on, O Union, strong and great! / Humanity with all its fears, / With all the hopes of future years, / Is hanging breathless on thy fate!

• Henry Wadsworth Longfellow, "The Building of the Ship," 1850.

866. We cannot always build the future for our youth, but we can build our youth for the future.

• President Franklin D. Roosevelt, speech in Philadelphia, September 20, 1940.

867. Attempts to forecast the future inevitably alter it.

• Alvin Toffler, *Future Shock,* 1970.

868. I say that the century on which we are entering—the century which will come of this war—can be and must be the century of the common man.

• Vice President Henry A. Wallace, speech in New York City, May 8, 1942.

GAMBLING

871. There are two things that are no fun for me in gambling then. One is gambling so recklessly that you must lose. The other is gambling so carefully that you aren't gambling.

• Larry Merchant, *The National Football Lottery,* 1973.

872. Somebody loses whenever somebody wins.

• Carl Sandburg, *Smoke and Steel,* "Crapshooters," 1920.

873. Don't bet on fights.

• Slogan on the sports pages of *The New York Sun,* popularized in the 1920's and continued thereafter until the paper's demise.

874. . . . the child of avarice, the brother of iniquity, and the father of mischief.

• General George Washington, definition of gambling in a letter to his nephew, Bushrod Washington, January 15, 1783.

875. Now you see it, now you don't.

• Spiel of the operators of shell games and three-card monte stands in the traveling shows of the latter half of the 19th century.

876. Put up or shut up.

• Anonymous, believed to have originated in the late 18th century in the early stock markets, and soon thereafter transferred to the gaming tables.

877. Put your money where your mouth is.

• Anonymous, same derivation as quotation immediately above.

878. Winner take all.

• Believed to have originated in either the stake races or individual contests of strength at the fairs of the early 19th century.

GEOGRAPHY
(See also Places)

---

881. In the world today, with air the means of communication, with time and space almost annihilated, geography still remains a fact.

• Secretary of State John Foster Dulles, speech in Washington, D.C., April 11, 1955.

882. The difference between landscape and landscape is small, but there is a great difference in the beholders.

• Ralph Waldo Emerson, *Essays, Second Series:* Nature, 1844.

883. In America, the geography is sublime, but the men are not . . .

• Ralph Waldo Emerson, *The Conduct of Life:* Considerations by the Way, 1860.

884. *There Are No Islands Any More.*

• Edna St. Vincent Millay, *There Are No Islands Any More,* 1940. The book's title reflected the impact of World War II on England and on insular thinking.

885. Geography can be defined as "What on earth!"

• Anonymous schoolboy wit of the turn of the century.

GOLF

891. Cow pasture pool.

• Attributed to O. K. Bovard of the *St. Louis Post-Dispatch,* used by sports writers beginning in the late 20's or early 30's.

892. The dirty little pill . . . rolling down the hill . . .

• From a novelty song broadcast by Frank Crumit in the early '30's.

893. If you want them to play your course—don't put rocks on the green!

• Terry Southern, *The Magic Christian,* "Grand Guy Grand," 1960.

894. A game in which the balls lie on the ground and the players lie in the clubhouse.

• Vaudeville gag of the 1930's.

895. The only activity in which finishing under par is considered a big success.

• Anonymous saying since 1930's.

896. The 19th hole.

• Beginning in the 1920's, this became a popular euphemism for the bar section of the country club.

GOVERNMENT

(See also City Life, Constitution, Freedom, Law, People)

---

901. As the happiness of the people is the sole end of government, so the consent of the people is the only foundation of it.

• John Adams, *Thoughts on Government,* 1776.

902. The worst thing in this world, next to anarchy, is government.

• Reverend Henry Ward Beecher, *Proverbs from Plymouth Pulpit,* 1887.

903. . . . government is not an exact science . . .

• Associate Justice Louis D. Brandeis of the Supreme Court, dissenting opinion in Truax v. Corrigan, 1921.

904. Government is a trust, and the officers of the government are trustees; and both are created for the benefit of the people.

• Henry Clay, speech in Kentucky, 1829.

905. While the people should patriotically and cheerfully support their Government, its functions do not include the support of the people.

• President Grover Cleveland, veto message, February 16, 1887. This was a period when President Cleveland was vetoing benefit bills that provided public funds for expanded pension lists, or other special classes of subsidy.

906. The government of the United States is a device for maintaining in perpetuity the rights of the people, with the ultimate extinction of all privileged classes.

• President Calvin Coolidge, speech in Philadelphia, September 25, 1924.

907. The prospect of domination of the nation's scholars by Federal employment, project allocations, and the power of money is ever present—and is gravely to be regarded. Yet, we should, we must also be alert to the equal and opposite danger that public policy could itself become the captive of a scientific-technological elite.

• President Dwight D. Eisenhower, farewell address in nationwide broadcast, January 17, 1961. This was the speech in which President Eisenhower warned also of "the military-industrial complex" (see Armed Forces).

908. Our best protection against bigger government in Washington is better government in the states.

• Dwight D. Eisenhower, speech to National Governors Conference in Cleveland, June 8, 1964. The former President was definitely not in favor of big government, either during his administration or thereafter.

909. God reigns and the Government at Washington still lives!

• Representative James A. Garfield of Ohio, remarks to a crowd in Wall Street, New York, after the news of the death of President Lincoln, April 15, 1865. Sixteen years later, when he, himself, was President of the United States, James A. Garfield, like Lincoln, was assassinated.

910. A government that is big enough to give you all you want is big enough to take it all away.

• Senator Barry M. Goldwater of Arizona, Republican Presidential candidate, speech in West Chester, Penna., October 21, 1964.

911. Our federal union! It must and shall be preserved.

• President Andrew Jackson, toast at a Jefferson's Birthday dinner in Washington, April 13, 1830. (In some accounts the words "it shall" are not included in the quotation.) President Jackson took the occasion to throw down the gauntlet to the advocates of states' rights—and Vice President John C. Calhoun promptly replied. (See Calhoun quotation under Freedom.)

912. The natural progress of things is for liberty to yield and government to gain ground.

• Thomas Jefferson, letter to Colonel Edward Carrington, May 27, 1788.

913. . . . the republican is the only form of government which is not eternally at open or secret war with the rights of mankind.

• Thomas Jefferson, letter to Mayor William Hunter of Alexandria, Va., March 11, 1790.

914. The basis of effective government is public confidence.

• President John F. Kennedy, message to Congress about governmental conduct and ethics, April 27, 1961.

915. No man is good enough to govern another man without that other's consent.

• Abraham Lincoln, speech in Peoria, Ill., October 16, 1854.

916. . . . and that government of the people, by the people, for the people, shall not perish from the earth.

• President Abraham Lincoln, address dedicating national cemetery at Gettysburg, Penna., November 19, 1863. Although the Gettysburg Address popularized the "of the people, by the people, for the people" phrase, it had been used in similar form by many others. (See Parker and Webster quotations below.)

917. . . . a government of all the people, by all the people, for all the people.

• Reverend Theodore Parker, speech to anti-slavery convention in Boston, May 29, 1850. (See also Lincoln and Webster quotations in this section.)

918. If men be good, government cannot be bad.

• William Penn, "Fruits of Solitude," 1693. Technically this should not be included in a book of American sayings, since it was written by Penn in England, but he was the founder of Pennsylvania and an American pioneer.

919. . . . government should do only those things the people cannot do for themselves.

• California Governor Ronald Reagan, statement in Los Angeles, June 23, 1971.

920. The government is us; we are the government, you and I.

• President Theodore Roosevelt, speech at Asheville, N.C., September 9, 1902.

921. The basis of our political systems is the right of the people to make and to alter the constitutions of government. But the constitution, which at any time exists, until changed by an explicit and authentic act of the whole people, is sacredly obligatory upon all.

• President George Washington, Farewell Address, dated September 17 and published September 19, 1796. The President never delivered the address. It was published in the *Philadelphia Daily American Advertiser.*

922. It is, Sir, the people's Constitution, the people's government, made for the people, made by the people, and answerable to the people.

• Senator Daniel Webster of Massachusetts, speech in the Senate, January 26, 1830. This phrase, in Webster's historic reply to Senator Hayne on the issue of states' rights, was an adaptation of many earlier phrases of many other people; it preceded both Theodore Parker's and Abraham Lincoln's use of similar phrases, quoted in 916 and 917.

GRATITUDE

931. Next to ingratitude, the most painful thing to bear is gratitude.

• Reverend Henry Ward Beecher, *Proverbs from Plymouth Pulpit,* 1887.

932. I sincerely wish ingratitude was not so natural to the human heart as it is.

• Alexander Hamilton, letter to George Washington, March 25, 1783.

933. Thanks: A really neglected form of compensation.

• Robert Townsend, *Up the Organization,* 1970.

934. Gratitude can only be given. It cannot be taken.

• One version of schoolday riddle of the 19th century.

935. Thanksgiving is the only kind of giving some people know.

• Anonymous, used as the theme of many Thanksgiving Day services.

GULLIBILITY

941. There's a sucker born every minute.

• Attributed to Phineas T. Barnum, the great 19th century showman.

942. Hello, sucker!

• Texas Guinan, nightclub hostess during the speakeasy era of the 1920's, used this greeting for her customers.

943. Never buy what you do not want because it is cheap; it will be dear to you.

• Thomas Jefferson, letter to Thomas Jefferson Smith, son of an old friend, February 21, 1825. The elder Smith had asked Jefferson to give some advice to his son.

944. You can fool some of the people all of the time, and all of the people some of the time, but you can't fool all of the people all of the time.

• Abraham Lincoln is credited with this statement, but historians cannot agree as to when he said it, or where. The date was sometime between 1856 and 1863.

HABITS

951. . . . order breeds habit.

• Henry B. Adams, *The Education of Henry Adams,* 1907.

952. The best way to stop a habit is never to start it.

• Attributed to J. C. Penney, 20th century merchant and moralist.

953. For the ordinary business of life, an ounce of habit is worth a pound of intellect.

• Thomas B. Reed, former Speaker of the House of Representatives, speech at Bowdoin College, Brunswick, Me., 1902.

954. It's easy to give up smoking; I've done it a thousand times.

• Mark Twain (Samuel L. Clemens), remark used in his lecture appearances in late 19th century and early 20th.

955. Nothing so needs reforming as other people's habits.

• Mark Twain (Samuel L. Clemens), *The Tragedy of Pudd'nhead Wilson,* Pudd'nhead Wilson's Calendar, 1894.

HAPPINESS

961. . . . the happiness of man, as well as his dignity, consists in virtue.

• John Adams, *Thoughts on Government,* 1776.

962. Happiness is speechless.

• George William Curtis, *Prue and I,* 1856.

963. To fill the hour—that is happiness . . .

• Ralph Waldo Emerson, *Essays, Second Series:* Experience, 1844.

964. . . . men's happiness depends upon their expectations —and the expectations of modern men have grown tremendously.

• Charles Frankel, *The Case for Modern Man,* 1956.

965. Happiness is the only good. / The time to be happy is now. / The place to be happy is here. / The way to be happy is to make others so.

• Robert G. Ingersoll, "Creed," late 19th century. Ingersoll, regarded as the most eloquent orator of his time, was an aggressive agnostic in an age of worship.

966. . . . the pursuit of happiness . . .

• Thomas Jefferson, phrase in the Declaration of Independence, July 4, 1776.

967. . . . the tranquil, permanent felicity with which domestic society in America blesses most of its inhabitants . . .

• Thomas Jefferson, letter to Charles Bellini, September 30, 1785.

968. It is the inalienable right of all to be happy.

• Elizabeth Cady Stanton, address to New York State Judiciary Committee on proposal to reform state divorce law, February 1861. The proposal failed.

969. Man is the artificer of his own happiness.

• Henry D. Thoreau, *Journal,* January 21, 1838.

970. Happy days are here again.

• Democratic Party motto in 1932, drawn from title of song by Jack Yellen of 1929.

HEALTH
(See also Medicine)

---

971. Health is not a condition of matter, but of Mind . . .

• Mary Baker Eddy, *Science and Health,* 1908. The founder of Christian Science wrote these words at the same time that the infant science of psychiatry was also exploring the question of mind over matter.

972. The first wealth is health.

• Ralph Waldo Emerson, *The Conduct of Life,* Power, 1860.

973. Early to bed, and early to rise, makes a man healthy, wealthy and wise.

• Benjamin Franklin, *The Way to Wealth,* 1757.

974. . . . health is worth more than learning . . .

• Thomas Jefferson, letter to his young cousin John Garland Jefferson, June 11, 1790.

975. The first medical right of all Americans is care within their means.

• Senator Edmund S. Muskie of Maine, commencement address at Albert Einstein College of Medicine in New York City, May 27, 1971.

976. Health that mocks the doctor's rules. / Knowledge never learned of schools.

• John Greenleaf Whittier, "The Barefoot Boy," 1855.

HEROES

981. Every hero becomes a bore at last.

• Ralph Waldo Emerson, *Representative Men,* Uses of Great Men, 1850.

982. Hail, Columbia! Happy land! / Hail, ye heroes! Heaven-born band!

• Joseph Hopkinson, "Hail Columbia," 1798. (He wrote words to an earlier piece of music.)

983. The idol of today pushes the hero of yesterday out of our recollection; and will, in turn, be supplanted by his successor of tomorrow.

• Washington Irving, *The Sketch Book,* Westminster Abbey, 1820.

984. In the world's broad field of battle, / In the bivouac of life, / Be not like dumb, driven cattle! / Be a hero in the strife!

• Henry Wadsworth Longfellow, "A Psalm of Life," 1838.

HISTORY
(See also Past)

---

991. History fades into fable . . .

• Washington Irving, *The Sketch Book,* Westminster Abbey, 1820.

992. Four score and seven years ago our fathers brought forth on this continent a new nation, conceived in liberty and dedicated to the proposition that all men are created equal.

• President Abraham Lincoln, speech dedicating national cemetery at Gettysburg, Penna. four and a half months after the great Civil War battle there, November 19, 1863. Recalling our nation's history, the Gettysburg Address itself became one of the most eloquent pages in that history.

993. Vos you dere, Sharlie?

• Familiar gag line used by radio dialect comedian Jack Pearl in the 1930's became a colloquial expression meaning, approximately, "Did you see it happen?"

994. Thrice happy is the nation that has a glorious history.

• Governor Theodore Roosevelt of New York, speech in Chicago, April 10, 1899.

995. Those who cannot remember the past are condemned to repeat it.

• George Santayana, *The Life of Reason, Volume 1,* 1905. Spanish-born, Santayana wrote and taught at Harvard before returning to Europe. These much-quoted words were written during his Harvard tenure.

996. The greatness of this country was not won by people who were afraid of risks.

• Senator Margaret Chase Smith of Maine, speech in the Senate about the Communist presence in Laos and its impact on U.S. policy, March 23, 1961.

997. Lafayette, we are here.

• Colonel Charles E. Stanton (not General John J. Pershing, to whom it is sometimes attributed), at Lafayette's grave in Paris, July 4, 1917, paralleling the arrival of the American Expeditionary Forces in France during World War I with Lafayette's help to the U.S. in the American Revolutionary War.

998. . . . the frontier has gone, and with its going has closed the first period of American history.

• Frederick Jackson Turner, "The Significance of the Frontier in American History," 1893. When Turner read this paper at a meeting of the American Historical Association he started a whole new school of American history. (See also Frontier.)

999. It has been said that the only thing we learn from history is that we do not learn.

• Chief Justice Earl Warren, memorial eulogy of assassinated President John F. Kennedy, Washington, D.C., November 24, 1963.

HOLIDAYS

1001. *Memorial Day:* Let no ravages of time testify to coming generations that we have forgotten as a people the cost of a free and undivided Republic.

• General John A. Logan, Commander of the Grand Army of the Republic, the organization of Civil War veterans, in a message to his members instructing them to observe the first Memorial Day, May 5, 1868.

1002. *Independence Day:* I am apt to believe that it will be celebrated by succeeding generations as the great anniversary festival. . . . with pomp and parade, with shows, games, sports, guns, bells, bonfires, and illuminations, from one end of this continent to the other, from this time forward forevermore.

• John Adams made what must be regarded as one of the most prescient predictions in American history with a letter he wrote to his wife Abigail predicting how America would celebrate Independence Day. The only trouble is that Adams wrote the letter on July 3, 1776, and the day he predicted would be celebrated by succeeding generations was July 2, not July 4. It was on July 2 that the Continental Congress adopted a resolution that "these United Colonies are, and of right ought to be, Free and Independent States." Two days later the Congress adopted and signed the more detailed and eloquent Declaration of Independence.

1003. *Thanksgiving:* Wise lawgivers and great patriots have acknowledged the salutary effect of appointed times for national reunions which combine religious sentiment with domestic and social enjoyment . . .

• Mrs. Sarah J. Hale, editorial in *Godey's Lady Book* magazine, September 1863. The editorial helped mightily in persuading Abraham Lincoln to proclaim the first modern Thanksgiving Day (although in both colonial and Revolutionary War times there had been special occasion days).

HOME

1011. As the homes, so the state.

• A. Bronson Alcott, *Tablets,* 1868.

1012. All up and down the whole creation, / Sadly I roam, / Still longing for the old plantation, / And for the old folks at home.

• Stephen Foster, "The Old Folks at Home," about 1851. Also known as "Way Down Upon the Swanee River."

1013. Home, home on the range . . .

• Attributed to a number of authors, but generally credited to Dr. Brewster Higley, under the original title of "The Western Home," about 1873.

1014. The happiness of the domestic fireside is the first boon of heaven . . .

• Thomas Jefferson, letter to John Armstrong, February 1813.

1015. 'Mid pleasures and palaces though we may roam, / Be it ever so humble, there's no place like home.

• John Howard Payne, "Home, Sweet Home," song from the opera "Clari, the Maid of Milan," 1823, music by Sir Henry R. Bishop.

1016. Home, Sweet Home.

• Title of song from the opera "Clari, the Maid of Milan," by John Howard Payne, 1823, music by Sir Henry R. Bishop.

HONESTY

1021. The louder he talked of his honor, the faster we counted our spoons.

• Ralph Waldo Emerson, *The Conduct of Life:* Worship, 1860.

1022. When knaves fall out, honest men get their goods . . .

• Benjamin Franklin, *Poor Richard's Almanac,* 1742.

1023. You cannot adopt politics as a profession and remain honest.

• Louis McHenry Howe, speech at Columbia University, January 17, 1933. The remark came back in a small way to haunt Howe, who was President Franklin D. Roosevelt's most trusted aide when the New Deal began two months later.

1024. . . . nobody thinks of drawin' the distinction between honest graft and dishonest graft. There's all the difference in the world between the two.

• William L. Riordon, *Plunkitt of Tammany Hall,* 1905. Riordon was quoting George Washington Plunkitt, a Tammany politician in New York who defined honest graft with this example: You hear the city is going to create a new park, so you go out and buy up land at the site, and when the park plan is made public you sell the land at a big profit. He defined dishonest graft as blackmailing people for protection money and that sort of thing.

1025. I cannot tell a lie.

• Attributed to George Washington by Mason Locke Weems (who quoted it as "I can't tell a lie," although it is most cited without the contraction) in *The Life and Memorable Actions of George Washington,* 1806. Whether or not George Washington ever said it in confessing that he chopped down a cherry tree is highly moot, but Parson Weems apparently was not equally careful of his truths.

HONOR
(See also Courage)

1031. A nation reveals itself not only by the men it produces but also by the men it honors, the men it remembers.

• President John F. Kennedy, speech at Amherst College, Amherst, Mass., October 26, 1963, at dedication of Robert Frost Library.

1032. A really great people, proud and high-spirited, would face all the disasters of war rather than purchase that base prosperity which is bought at the price of national honor.

• President Theodore Roosevelt, speech at Harvard University, Cambridge, Mass., February 23, 1907.

1033. When faith is lost, when honor dies, / The man is dead!

• John Greenleaf Whittier, "Ichabod," 1850.

HOSPITALITY

1041. Hospitality consists of a little fire, a little food, and an immense quiet.

• Ralph Waldo Emerson, *Journal,* 1856.

1042. The ornament of a house is the friends who frequent it.

• Ralph Waldo Emerson, *Society and Solitude:* Domestic Life, 1870.

1043. Fish and visitors smell in three days.

• Benjamin Franklin, *Poor Richard's Almanac,* 1736. Franklin was a man of moderation in most things, which meant that even good things had their limits.

1044. The red carpet treatment . . .

• Anonymous, but popularized by the much-publicized rolling out of the red carpet in the first half of the current century for the arrival of the *Twentieth Century Limited* when it was the great luxury train connection between Chicago and New York.

1045. The thoughtful host puts the first stain on the dinner tablecloth himself.

• Anonymous, possibly of European origin.

HOTELS

1051. It used to be a good hotel, but that proves nothing—I used to be a good boy.

• Mark Twain (Samuel L. Clemens), dispatch to *San Francisco Daily, Alta California,* 1867.

1052. The borscht circuit . . .

• Term originated by *Variety* in the 1930's, referring to the Jewish resort hotels in the Catskill Mountains of New York State. Entertainers were booked on a circuit of such hotels during the summer, and a term was devised as a sort of shorthand to describe this booking within show business.

1053. Where you exchange dollars for quarters.

• Comedy definition of the 1950's.

1054. Your home away from home.

• Advertising sub-title used by various hotels, particularly in the 1920's.

HOUSING
(See also Home)

1061. A man builds a fine house; and now he has a master, and a task for life; he is to furnish, watch, show it, and keep it in repair the rest of his days.

• Ralph Waldo Emerson, *Society and Solitude:* Works and Days, 1870.

1062. Let me live in my house by the side of the road / And be a friend of man.

• Sam Walter Foss, "The House by the Side of the Road," 1897.

1063. Little Boxes on the hillside, / Little Boxes made of ticky tacky; / Little Boxes on the hillside, / Little Boxes all the same.

• Malvina Reynolds, "Little Boxes," 1962. A popular song about popular developments.

1064. I see one-third of a nation ill-housed, ill-clad, and ill-nourished.

• President Franklin D. Roosevelt, second inaugural address, Washington, D.C., January 20, 1937.

1065. Our houses are such unwieldy property that we are often imprisoned rather than housed in them.

• Henry D. Thoreau, *Walden:* Economy, 1854. Thoreau preferred to live in a cabin at Walden Pond.

HUMOR

1071. Men will let you abuse them if only you will make them laugh.

• Reverend Henry Ward Beecher, *Proverbs from Plymouth Pulpit,* 1887.

1072. Wit makes its own welcome, and levels all distinctions. No dignity, no learning, no force of character, can make any stand against good wit.

• Ralph Waldo Emerson, *Letters and Social Aims:* The Comic, 1876.

1073. Thou canst not joke an enemy into a friend, but thou may'st a friend into an enemy.

• Benjamin Franklin, *Poor Richard's Almanac,* 1739. Franklin's own career suggested that while the adage applied to most people, he, himself, was an exception. Few people either had the sense of humor or the number of friends that Franklin could claim in his long lifetime.

1074. Laugh and the world laughs with you; / Weep and you weep alone . . .

• Ella Wheeler Wilcox, "Solitude" 1883. Mr. Wilcox was still Miss Ella Wheeler when these lines were first published, in a New York newspaper.

1075. He who laughs, lasts.

• Early 20th century adaptation of the ancient maxim that he who laughs last laughs longest.

1076. I'm too big to cry and it hurts too much to laugh.

• Paraphrased by Adlai E. Stevenson in 1952, after he was defeated in the Presidential election, and credited by him to Abraham Lincoln; but Lincoln himself attributed it to "a boy in Kentucky."

HUNGER
(See also Food)

1081. I've never known a country to be starved into democracy.

• Senator George D. Aiken of Vermont, March 27, 1964. Senator Aiken made the comment to reporters covering the Senate in connection with a discussion of economic boycotts of non-democratic nations.

1082. I see one-third of a nation ill-housed, ill-clad, ill-nourished.

• President Franklin D. Roosevelt, second inaugural address, Washington, D.C., January 20, 1937. In his first term, President Roosevelt had rallied the nation against economic panic; now he called for a new wave of social reform.

1083. People who are hungry and out of a job are the stuff of which dictatorships are made.

• President Franklin D. Roosevelt, message to Congress, January 11, 1944.

1084. A hungry man is not a free man.

• Adlai E. Stevenson, Presidential campaign speech in Kasson, Minn., September 6, 1952.

1085. No one can worship God or love his neighbor on an empty stomach.

• President Woodrow Wilson, speech in New York City, May 23, 1912.

1086. Hunger does not breed reform; it breeds madness and all the ugly distempers that make an ordered life impossible.

• President Woodrow Wilson, address to Congress on the day World War I ended, November 11, 1918. A week later he announced he would go to the Peace Conference in Europe, triggering the domestic dispute that ended with U.S. rejection of the idea of a League of Nations.

IDEALS

(See also Attitudes, Causes, Peace)

1091. In charity to all mankind, bearing no malice or ill-will to any human being, and even compassionating those who hold in bondage their fellow-men, not knowing what they do.

• Representative John Quincy Adams of Massachusetts, letter to A. Bronson Alcott, July 30, 1838. See the Lincoln quotation for March 4, 1865, below, for a similar phrasing a generation later.

1092. What is a great man who has made his mark upon history? Every time, if we think far enough, he is a man who has looked through the confusion of the moment and has seen the moral issue involved . . .

• Jane Addams, Washington's Birthday Address at the Union League Club in Chicago, February 23, 1903.

1093. . . . I had rather be right than President.

• Senator Henry Clay of Kentucky, probably first said to fellow Senators in February 1839 in response to warnings that his attempt to reach a compromise on the issue of slavery might cost him the Presidency in the next election. Many reference books give the date of the quotation as 1850, which would vitiate much of the idealism with which it is associated; for in 1850 Henry Clay was 73, not in the best of health and highly unlikely to be a candidate again for the Presidency.

1094. We shall overcome.

• Great rallying cry of the civil rights movement of the 1960's, made into a song by Zilphia Horton, Frank Hamilton, Guy Carawan and Pete Seeger, 1960.

1095. Some men see things as they are and say why. I dream things that never were and say, why not?

• Attributed to Senator Robert F. Kennedy of New York by his brother, Senator Edward M. Kennedy of Massachusetts, at memorial service in New York following the assassination of Robert, June 9, 1968.

1096. I think that the ideals of youth are fine, clear and unencumbered; and that the real art of living consists in keeping alive the conscience and sense of values we had when we were young.

• Rockwell Kent, quoted in obituary in *New York Times,* March 14, 1971, as having been said "a few years ago."

1097. Let us have faith that right makes might, and in that faith let us to the end dare to do our duty as we understand it.

• Abraham Lincoln, address at Cooper Union, New York City, February 27, 1860. This address captured great public attention and was instrumental in winning the Republican Presidential nomination for Lincoln later that year.

1098. With malice toward none, with charity for all, with firmness in the right, as God gives us to see the right, let us strive on to finish the work we are in . . .

• President Abraham Lincoln, second inaugural address, Washington, D.C., March 4, 1865. See quotation of John Quincy Adams above.

1099. For we, too, have our ideals, even if we differ from those who have tried to establish a monopoly of idealism.

• Senator Henry Cabot Lodge of Massachusetts, speech in the Senate opposing U.S. membership in the League of Nations, August 12, 1919.

1100. For when the One Great Scorer comes to write against your name, / He marks—not that you won or lost—but how you played the game.

• Grantland Rice, *Sportlights of 1923:* "Alumnus Football," 1924.

1101. Ideal society is a drama enacted exclusively in the imagination.

• George Santayana, *The Life of Reason: Reason in Society,* 1905.

1102. There is such a thing as a man being too proud to fight.

• President Woodrow Wilson, speech in Philadelphia, May 10, 1915. The President was opposed to entering the Great War in Europe. He campaigned for re-election the following year on the basis of having kept the nation out of war. But in 1917, after the Germans' unrestricted submarine warfare, Wilson reversed his "too proud to fight" dictum and led the U.S. into the conflict.

1103. America is the only idealist nation in the world.

• President Woodrow Wilson, speech in Sioux Falls, S.D., September 8, 1919. President Wilson toured the nation to try to win support for his idealistic concept of the League of Nations, but he failed to get it accepted.

IMMIGRANTS

1111. We are the Romans of the modern world—the great assimilating people.

• Oliver Wendell Holmes, *The Autocrat of the Breakfast-Table,* 1858. The great wave of immigration was really just beginning when Dr. Holmes wrote these lines.

1112. I think it fortunate for the United States to have become the asylum for so many virtuous patriots of different denominations.

• Thomas Jefferson, letter to M. de Meusnier, a French scholar, April 29, 1795. Jefferson wrote this about a young nation where slavery still existed and freedom of religion was not quite complete in all the states, but he more than most other men opened the doors for the whole world.

1113. "Keep, ancient lands, your storied pomp!" cries she / With silent lips. "Give me your tired, your poor, / Your huddled masses yearning to breathe free, / The wretched refuse of your teeming shore. / Send these, the homeless, tempest-tossed to me, / I lift my lamp beside the golden door!"

• Emma Lazarus, "The New Colossus," 1883. In 1903 the poem was affixed to the base of the Statue of Liberty in a memorial tablet. It had been written about the Statue of Liberty when that great monument was being installed in New York Harbor.

1114. My folks didn't come over on the *Mayflower,* but they were there to meet the boat.

• Will Rogers, probably first said in the 1920's. The cowboy monologist, wit and actor was part Indian by birth.

1115. Remember, remember always that all of us, and you and I especially, are descended from immigrants and revolutionists.

• President Franklin D. Roosevelt, speech to the Daughters of the American Revolution in Washington, D.C., April 21, 1938.

1116. Some Americans need hyphens in their names because only part of them has come over.

• President Woodrow Wilson, speech in Washington, D.C., May 16, 1914.

1117. We may have come over on different ships, but we're all in the same boat now.

• Whitney M. Young, Jr., speech in New York City, May 7, 1970. Mr. Young was the Executive Director of the National Urban League.

INDEPENDENCE
(See also Declaration of Independence, Freedom)

1121. Independence forever!

• John Adams, last words. The second President of the United States died, like his successor, Thomas Jefferson, on July 4, 1826. (See Daniel Webster quotation, number 1125, below.)

1122. We have no other alternative than independence, or the most ignominious and galling servitude. . . . You are now the guardians of your own liberties.

• Samuel Adams, speech in Philadelphia, August 1, 1776, saluting the first month of American independence.

1123. Peace upon any other basis than national independence, peace purchased at the cost of any part of our national integrity, is fit only for slaves, and even when purchased at such a price it is a delusion, for it cannot last.

• Senator William E. Borah of Idaho, speech in the Senate opposing U.S. approval of the League of Nations, November 19, 1919. For President Woodrow Wilson's proposal of such a League, see Wilson quotation below.

1124. Let independence be our boast, / Ever mindful what it cost; / Ever grateful for the prize, / Let its altar reach the skies!

• Joseph Hopkinson, "Hail Columbia," 1798. He wrote lyrics to a musical composition originally prepared for the first Presidential inauguration in 1789. The music was originally entitled "The President's March," composed by a composer variously identified as Philip Roth and Philip Phile.

1125. It is my living sentiment, and by the blessing of God it shall be my dying sentiment—Independence now and Independence forever!

• Representative Daniel Webster of Massachusetts, eulogy of John Adams and Thomas Jefferson, both of whom had died on July 4, 1826, delivered at Faneuil Hall in Boston, August 2, 1826. The reported last words of John Adams, Massachusetts' first citizen to become President (see quotation 1121 above), inspired the Webster speech.

1126. A general association of nations must be formed under specific covenants for the purpose of affording mutual guarantees of political independence and territorial integrity to great and small states alike.

• President Woodrow Wilson, address to joint session of Congress, January 8, 1918. Announcing a program of Fourteen Points for peace, the President made this proposal for a League of Nations his fourteenth point. When the League was set up as part of the peace settlement of World War I, in accordance with Wilson's Fourteen Points, the Senate rejected it. Senator Borah's comment, quoted above, expressed the principal reason for the rejection—the fear that our own national sovereignty and independence would be compromised by membership in the world association of nations Wilson had proposed. The battle for the League of Nations was instrumental in destroying Wilson's health and effectiveness in his last years in office.

INDIANS
(See also Immigrants)

1131. The aboriginal inhabitants of these countries I have regarded with the commiseration their history inspires. Endowed with the faculties and the rights of men, breathing an ardent love of liberty and independence, and occupying a country which left them no desire but to be undisturbed, the stream of overflowing population from other regions directed itself on these shores; without power to divert, or habits to contend against, they have been overwhelmed by the current, or driven before it; now reduced within limits too narrow for the hunter's state, humanity enjoins us to teach them agriculture and the domestic arts; to encourage them to that industry which alone can enable them to maintain their place in existence; and to prepare them in time for that state of society, which to bodily comforts adds the improvement of the mind and morals.

• President Thomas Jefferson, second inaugural address, Washington, D.C., March 4, 1805. For its time, this was one of the white man's most sympathetic commentaries on the American Indian.

1132. The Indian of falcon glance and lion bearing, the theme of the touching ballad, the hero of the pathetic tale, is gone.

• Charles Sprague, "The American Indian," around the 1830's. Far from being a frontier authority, Sprague was a Boston banker and writer.

1133. Give it back to the Indians.

• Anonymous, believed to have originated with disgusted homesteaders of the 1870's and thereafter, who found their new land not quite the blessing they had anticipated.

1134. Paleface (or white man) speak with forked tongue.

• Popular translation of a repeated accusation by the Indians, particularly in the middle part of the 19th century, about the broken promises of the U.S. government. Later used by Stephen Vincent Benet in "The Devil and Daniel Webster."

1135. Too many chiefs, not enough Indians.

• Believed to have originated among the Indians themselves as a commentary on their problems of survival in the Indian wars.

INDIVIDUALISM

1141. Nature never rhymes her children, nor makes two men alike.

• Ralph Waldo Emerson, *Essays, Second Series:* Character, 1844.

1142. When the war closed . . . we were challenged with a peacetime choice between the American system of rugged individualism and a European philosophy of diametrically opposed doctrines—doctrines of paternalism and state socialism.

• Herbert Hoover, Presidential campaign speech in New York City, October 22, 1928. The phrase "rugged individualism" moved into the American vocabulary, but from that point on it seemed to mean different things to different people. It was, one might say, interpreted individually.

1143. Let me emphasize that serious as have been the errors of unrestrained individualism, I do not believe in abandoning the system of individual enterprise.

• President Franklin D. Roosevelt, radio address, August 24, 1935.

1144. What a man does, compared with what he is, is but a small part.

• Henry D. Thoreau, *Journal,* March 28, 1842.

1145. If a man does not keep pace with his companions, perhaps it is because he hears a different drummer. Let him step to the music which he hears, however measured or far away.

• Henry D. Thoreau, *Walden,* Conclusion, 1854.

1146. . . . the frontier is productive of individualism.

• Frederick Jackson Turner, "The Significance of the Frontier in American History," 1893.

INGENUITY AND INVENTION

1151. Genius is one percent inspiration and 99 percent perspiration.

• Thomas A. Edison is believed to have said this first in the 1890's; he repeated it in subsequent interviews.

1152. Invention breeds invention.

• Ralph Waldo Emerson, *Society and Solitude:* Works and Days, 1870.

1153. What good is a new-born baby?

• Reported as having been said by Benjamin Franklin on August 27, 1783, when somebody asked what purpose was served by the first balloon ascension, in Paris.

1154. What hath God wrought!

• Samuel F. B. Morse, first message on the opening of the first telegraph line between Washington, D.C. and Baltimore, May 24, 1844. Morse, the inventor of the telegraph, sent the message from the Supreme Court chamber in the Capitol, which may have been prophetic; ten years later the Supreme Court finally upheld the validity of his patent claims against various other claimants.

1155. Good old American know-how.

• Phrase used in the 20th century, particularly after World War II, to describe American efficiency.

1156. It's not what you do, it's how you do it.

• Anonymous, gained popularity in 1920's.

1157. Yankee ingenuity.

• Phrase which arose in early 19th century, possibly of British origin.

JUSTICE

1161. I am pleading that all life is worth saving and that mercy is the highest attribute of man.

• Clarence Darrow, plea to the judge on the sentencing of Nathan Leopold and Richard Loeb in a sensational "thrill murder" case of the 1920's, July 1924.

1162. Peace and justice are two sides of the same coin.

• President Dwight D. Eisenhower, news reports, February 6, 1957.

1163. . . . moderation in the pursuit of justice is no virtue.

• Senator Barry M. Goldwater, speech accepting Republican Presidential nomination in San Francisco, July 16, 1964. This was the speech in which Senator Goldwater also said that "extremism in the defense of liberty is no vice."

1164. Police officers should be judged by the quality, not the quantity of arrests.

• Manhattan District Attorney Frank S. Hogan, report to the Mayor of New York, February 21, 1971.

1165. Equal and exact justice to all men, of whatever state or persuasion, religious or political . . .

• President Thomas Jefferson, First Inaugural Address, Washington, D.C., March 4, 1801.

1166. Justice delayed is democracy denied.

• Robert F. Kennedy, *To Secure These Rights,* 1964.

1167. Justice delayed is not only justice denied—it is also justice circumvented, justice mocked, and the system of justice undermined.

• President Richard M. Nixon, address to National Conference on the Judiciary, Williamsburg, Va., March 11, 1971. (See Robert F. Kennedy quotation immediately above.)

1168. Expedience and justice frequently are not even on speaking terms.

• Senator Arthur H. Vandenberg of Michigan, speech in the Senate, March 8, 1945. (See Wilson quotation below.)

1169. Judging from the main portions of the history of the world, so far, justice is always in jeopardy.

• Walt Whitman, *Democratic Vistas,* 1870.

1170. Justice has nothing to do with expediency.

• President Woodrow Wilson, speech in Washington, D.C., February 26, 1916. (See Vandenberg quotation above.)

KNOWLEDGE
(See also Education)

1171. Defeat is a fact and victory can be a fact. If the idea is good, it will survive defeat, it may even survive the victory.

• Stephen Vincent Benet, *John Brown's Body,* 1928.

1172. We are wiser than we know.

• Ralph Waldo Emerson, *Essays, First Series:* The Over-Soul, 1841.

1173. Knowledge is the antidote to fear . . .

• Ralph Waldo Emerson, *Society and Solitude:* Courage, 1870.

1174. To be proud of knowledge is to be blind with light.

• Benjamin Franklin, *Poor Richard's Almanac,* 1756.

1175. The enemy of the conventional wisdom is not ideas but the march of events.

• John K. Galbraith, *The Affluent Society,* 1958.

1176. Knowledge and timber shouldn't be much used till they are seasoned.

• Oliver Wendell Holmes, *The Autocrat of the Breakfast-Table,* 1858. Dr. Holmes may have been more prophetic than he realized, for his son was past 60 when he was appointed to the Supreme Court of the United States and thereafter became a giant of American jurisprudence.

1177. It is the province of knowledge to speak and it is the privilege of wisdom to listen.

• Oliver Wendell Holmes, *The Poet at the Breakfast-Table,* 1872.

1178. I think by far the most important bill in our whole code, is that for the diffusion of knowledge among the people. No other sure foundation can be devised, for the preservation of freedom and happiness.

• Thomas Jefferson, letter to his teacher and friend, George Wythe, August 13, 1786.

1179. I think this is the most extraordinary collection of talent, of human knowledge, that has ever been gathered together at the White House—with the possible exception of when Thomas Jefferson dined alone.

• President John F. Kennedy, remarks at a dinner for U.S. winners of the Nobel prizes at the White House, Washington, D.C., April 29, 1962.

1180. Promote then as an object of primary importance, institutions for the general diffusion of knowledge. In proportion as the structure of a government gives force to public opinion, it is essential that public opinion be enlightened.

• President George Washington, Farewell Address, dated September 17 and published September 19, 1796, in *Philadelphia Daily American Advertiser.* (It was never delivered as an oration.)

LABOR

(See also Business, Prosperity, Work)

1181. Wages is a cunning device of the devil, for the benefit of tender consciences, who would retain all the advantages of the slave system, without the expense, trouble, and odium of being slave-holders.

• Orestes A. Brownson, in his publication, *The Boston Quarterly Review,* July, 1840.

1182. . . . you shall not press down upon the brow of labor this crown of thorns; you shall not crucify mankind upon a cross of gold.

• William Jennings Bryan, speech at Democratic National Convention in Chicago, July 8, 1896. This great speech, which made Bryan a national figure, is remembered as the "cross of gold" speech attacking the gold standard.

1183. There can be no distress, there can be no hard times, when labor is well paid. The man who raises his hand against the progress of the workingman raises his hand against prosperity.

• W. Bourke Cockran, speech in New York City, August 18, 1896. Cockran, one of the Democratic Party's great orators, was opposed to William Jennings Bryan's economic idea. (See quotation directly above.)

1184. There is no right to strike against the public safety by anybody, anywhere, any time.

• Governor Calvin Coolidge of Massachusetts, telegram to Samuel Gompers, President of the American Federation of Labor, concerning a strike by members of the Boston police, September 14, 1919.

1185. Take not from the mouth of labor the bread it has earned.

• President Thomas Jefferson, inaugural address, Washington, D.C., March 4, 1801.

1186. American labor, whenever it gathers, does so with love for its flag and country and loyalty to its government.

• Mayor Fiorello H. LaGuardia of New York, speech at Chicago World's Fair on Labor Day, September 3, 1934.

1187. We have learned that unless there is employment for all there will be profits for none.

• Mayor Fiorello H. LaGuardia of New York, speech at Chicago World's Fair on Labor Day, September 3, 1934. Depression unemployment was then the problem.

LAND

1191. It is a noble land that God has given us; a land that can feed and clothe the world; a land whose coastlines would inclose half the countries of Europe; a land set like a sentinel between the two imperial oceans of the globe, a greater England with a nobler destiny.

• Albert J. Beveridge, "The March of the Flag," speech in Indianapolis, September 16, 1898.

1192. If a man owns land, the land owns him.

• Ralph Waldo Emerson, *The Conduct of Life:* Wealth, 1860. And this was written before the era of high taxes.

1193. What we call real estate—the solid ground to build a house on—is the broad foundation on which nearly all the guilt of this world rests.

• Nathaniel Hawthorne, *The House of the Seven Gables,* 1851.

1194. The earth is given as a common stock for men to labor and live on.

• Thomas Jefferson, letter to Reverend James Madison, Virginia churchman and educator (and cousin of the James Madison who became President), October 28, 1785.

1195. My country, 'tis of thee, / Sweet land of Liberty, / Of thee I sing; / Land where my fathers died, / Land of the pilgrims' pride, / From every mountain-side / Let freedom ring.

• Reverend Samuel F. Smith, "America," written to the tune of "God Save the King" and first performed on July 4, 1832.

1196. We in America have from the beginning been cleaving and baring the earth, attacking, reforming the enormity of nature we were given which we took to be hostile.

• John Updike, "Packed Dirt, Churchgoing, A Dying Cat, A Traded Car," from *Pigeon Feathers and Other Stories,* 1962.

LANGUAGE

1201. Language is the archives of history. . . . each word was at first a stroke of genius.

• Ralph Waldo Emerson, *Essays, Second Series:* The Poet, 1844.

1202. Language gradually varies, and with it fade away the writings of authors who have flourished their allotted time . . .

• Washington Irving, *The Sketch Book:* The Mutability of Literature, 1820.

1203. It is the man who determines what is said, not the words.

• Henry D. Thoreau, *Journal,* July 11, 1840.

1204. Language, as well as the faculty of speech, was the immediate gift of God.

• Noah Webster, *American Dictionary of the English Language,* preface, 1828. Webster demonstrated his love of language by creating the definitive American dictionary.

1205. Wondrous the English language, language of live men . . .

• Walt Whitman, "As I Sat Alone," 1856.

1206. Watch your language!

• Familiar caution which originated as warning to men that with ladies present they should not use rough or obscene modes of speech. It was later adopted by some English teachers as a reminder to their students to use the language properly.

LAW
(See also Courts)

1211. Law is not self-executing. Unfortunately, at times its execution rests in the hands of those who are faithless to it. And even when its enforcement is committed to those who revere it, law merely deters some human beings from offending, and punishes other human beings for offending. This does not make men good. This task can be performed only by ethics or religion or morality.

• Senator Sam J. Ervin, Jr., of North Carolina, statement as Chairman of Senate Watergate Committee with its final report, July 12, 1974.

1212. Laws too gentle are seldom obeyed; too severe, seldom executed.

• Benjamin Franklin, *Poor Richard's Almanac,* prior to 1757.

1213. There are not enough jails, not enough policemen, not enough courts to enforce a law not supported by the people.

• Vice President Hubert H. Humphrey, speech in Williamsburg, Va., May 1, 1965.

1214. . . . a strict observance of the written laws is doubtless *one* of the high duties of a good citizen, but it is not the *highest.* The laws of necessity, of self-preservation, of saving our country when in danger, are of higher obligation.

• Thomas Jefferson, letter to Maryland editor John B. Colvin, September 20, 1810.

1215. Our nation is founded on the principle that observance of the law is the eternal safeguard of liberty and defiance of the law is the surest road to tyranny.

• President John F. Kennedy, television speech, September 20, 1962.

1216. Lawyers are the great public servants of America . . .

• Martin Mayer, *The Lawyers,* 1966.

1217. The legal structure still changes only in response to crisis: lawyers and judges, like laymen, are forever crying that there ought to be a law.

• Martin Mayer, *The Lawyers,* 1966.

1218. We will no longer be permitted to sacrifice each generation in turn while the law catches up with life.

• President Franklin D. Roosevelt, speech in Washington, D.C., September 17, 1937. President Roosevelt chose Citizenship Day of the year in which he proposed his "court packing plan" to level this oratorical sideswipe, however disguised, at the Supreme Court he had earlier labeled "nine old men."

1219. Law and order enforced with justice and by strength lie at the foundations of civilization. Law must be based on justice, else it cannot stand, and it must be enforced with resolute firmness, because weakness in enforcing it means in the end that there is no justice and no law, nothing but the rule of disorderly and unscrupulous strength.

• President Theodore Roosevelt, speech in Spokane, Wash., May 26, 1903.

1220. To make laws that man cannot, and will not obey, serves to bring all law into contempt.

• Elizabeth Cady Stanton, testimony before New York State Senate Judiciary Committee on proposed divorce reform bill, 1861. Despite the efforts of the women's rights movement led by Mrs. Stanton, this particular bill failed of passage.

LEISURE
(See also Sports)

1221. Employ thy time well if thou meanest to gain leisure.

• Benjamin Franklin, *Poor Richard's Almanac,* 1758.

1222. No man is so methodical as a complete idler, and none so scrupulous in measuring out his time as he whose time is worth nothing.

• Washington Irving, *Wolfert's Roost,* "My French Neighbor," 1855.

1223. He enjoys true leisure who has time to improve his soul's estate.

• Henry D. Thoreau, *Journal,* February 11, 1840.

1224. The number of acceptable pastimes, hobbies, games, sports and entertainments is climbing rapidly, and the growth of a distinct subcult built around surfing, for example, demonstrates that, at least for some, a leisure-time commitment can also serve as the basis for an entire life style.

• Alvin Toffler, *Future Shock,* 1970.

1225. In itself and in its consequences the life of leisure is beautiful and ennobling in all civilized men's eyes.

• Thorstein Veblen, *The Theory of the Leisure Class,* 1899.

LIBERALS

1231. A liberal is a man who is willing to spend somebody else's money.

• Attributed to Senator Carter Glass of Virginia, 1938.

1232. Liberalism should be found not striving to spread bureaucracy but striving to set bounds to it.

• Herbert Hoover, Presidential campaign speech in New York City, October 22, 1928.

1233. I believe a man can be a liberal without being a spendthrift.

• Governor Alfred M. Landon of Kansas, the Republican Presidential nominee, used this statement prominently in his election campaign in 1936. President Franklin D. Roosevelt won re-election that year in one of the biggest landslides in U.S. election history.

1234. The liberal party is a party which believes that, as new conditions and problems arise beyond the power of men and women as individuals, it becomes the duty of the government itself to find new remedies with which to meet them.

• President Franklin D. Roosevelt, Introduction to 1938 volume of *Public Papers and Addresses.*

1235. Self-styled liberals change as the styles change.

• Popular saying of 1950's and 1960's.

1236. You can always tell a liberal, but you can't tell him much.

• Maxim of the 1960's, applied to various situations but notably the school busing dispute.

LINCOLN

1241. In him was vindicated the greatness of real goodness and the goodness of real greatness.

• Reverend Phillips Brooks, sermon at Independence Hall, Philadelphia, April 1865.

1242. His heart was as great as the world, but there was no room in it to hold the memory of a wrong.

• Ralph Waldo Emerson, *Letters and Social Aims:* Greatness, 1876.

1243. That nation has not lived in vain which has given the world Washington and Lincoln, the best great men and the greatest good men whom history can show.

• Senator Henry Cabot Lodge of Massachusetts, speech in Boston, February 12, 1909. (See Brooks quote above.)

1244. . . . the well assured and most enduring memorial to Lincoln is invisibly there, today, tomorrow and for a long time yet to come in the hearts of lovers of liberty, men and women who understand that wherever there is freedom there have been those who fought, toiled and sacrificed for it.

• Carl Sandburg, speech to joint session of Congress on Lincoln's 150th birthday, February 12, 1909.

1245. Now he belongs to the ages.

• Secretary of War Edwin M. Stanton, the day Lincoln died, April 15, 1865.

1246. Oh Captain! My Captain!

• Walt Whitman, "Oh Captain! My Captain!," poem in memory of Lincoln, 1865.

LITERATURE

1251. All literature is yet to be written.

• Ralph Waldo Emerson, "Literary Ethics," 1838.

1252. An old author is constantly rediscovering himself in the more or less fossilized productions of his earlier years.

• Oliver Wendell Holmes, *Over the Teacups,* 1891. Past 80 when this book was published, the elder Holmes' writings haven't fossilized even now.

1253. The literary world is made up of little confederacies, each looking upon its own members as the lights of the universe; and considering all others as mere transient meteors, doomed soon to fall and be forgotten, while its own luminaries are to shine steadily on to immortality.

• Washington Irving, attributed to "a literary man by the name of 'Buckthorne' " in *Tales of a Traveller:* Literary Life, 1824.

1254. Our American professors like their literature clear and cold and pure and very dead.

• Sinclair Lewis, speech accepting Nobel Prize for Literature, Stockholm, Sweden, December 12, 1930.

1255. It is not all books that are as dull as their readers.

• Henry D. Thoreau, *Walden:* Reading, 1854.

1256. How many a man has dated a new era in his life from the reading of a book.

• Henry D. Thoreau, *Walden:* Reading, 1854.

1257. In the civilization of today, it is undeniable that, over all the arts, literature dominates, serves beyond all.

• Walt Whitman, *Democratic Vistas,* 1871.

LONELINESS

1261. In a universe whose size is beyond human imagining, where our world floats like a dust mote in the void of night, men have grown inconceivably lonely.

• Loren Eiseley, *The Immense Journey,* "Little Men and Flying Saucers," 1957.

1262. Nevertheless, in any city there are true wildernesses where a man can be alone. It can happen in a hotel room, or on the high roofs at dawn.

• Loren Eiseley, *The Immense Journey,* "The Judgment of the Birds," 1957.

1263. Ships that pass in the night, and speak each other in passing . . .

• Henry Wadsworth Longfellow, *Tales of a Wayside Inn,* "The Theologian's Tale," "Elizabeth," 1863.

LONGEVITY
(See also Age)

1271. I have been asked, "How do you grow old so easily?" I reply, "Very easily. I give all my time to it."

• Representative Emanuel Celler of New York, dean of the House, on his 83rd birthday, in Washington, D.C., May 6, 1971.

1272. Few envy the consideration enjoyed by the oldest inhabitant.

• Ralph Waldo Emerson, *Society and Solitude:* Old Age, 1870.

1273. Wish not so much to live long as to live well.

• Benjamin Franklin (who did both), *Poor Richard's Almanac,* 1738.

1274. All would live long, but none would be old.

• Benjamin Franklin, *Poor Richard's Almanac,* 1749.

1275. . . . Age is opportunity no less / Than Youth itself, though in another dress.

• Henry Wadsworth Longfellow, "Morituri Salutamus," written in 1874, read in 1875 by the author at the 50th anniversary of his class at Bowdoin College.

1276. If you don't carouse, you will live a long time; or maybe it will just seem to be a long time.

• One version of a vaudeville gag line of the 1920's and 1930's, also used with varying phrases such as "If you don't smoke, or drink, or play around. . . ."

1277. Life is habit forming.

• Graffiti of 1960's.

LOVE

1281. . . . any love is better than none.

• Paddy Chayefsky, "The Middle of the Night," 1957.

1282. All mankind love a lover.

• Ralph Waldo Emerson, *Essays, First Series:* Love, 1841.

1283. Most people see the problem of love primarily as that of *being loved,* rather than that of *loving,* of one's capacity to love. Hence the problem to them is how to be loved, how to be lovable.

• Erich Fromm, *The Art of Loving,* 1956. If there had ever been any doubt about popular preoccupation with being loved, the tremendous sales of Dr. Fromm's book around the world should have proven the point.

1284. There's nothing in this world so sweet as love, / And next to love the sweetest thing is hate.

• Henry Wadsworth Longfellow, *The Spanish Student,* 1842.

1285. There is no remedy for love but to love more.

• Henry D. Thoreau, *Journal,* July 25, 1839.

1286. . . . love has never known a law / Beyond its own sweet will.

• John Greenleaf Whittier, "Amy Wentworth," 1862.

LOYALTY

1291. Since this country was founded, each generation of Americans has been summoned to give testimony to its national loyalty.

• President John F. Kennedy, inaugural address in Washington, D.C., January 20, 1961.

1292. My kind of loyalty was loyalty to one's country, not to its institutions or its office-holders.

• Mark Twain (Samuel L. Clemens), *A Connecticut Yankee in King Arthur's Court,* 1889.

1293. I do solemnly swear (or affirm) that I will support and defend the Constitution of the United States against all enemies, foreign and domestic; that I will bear true faith and allegiance to the same; that I take this obligation freely, without any mental reservation or purpose of evasion, and that I will well and truthfully discharge the duties of the office on which I am about to enter. So help me God.

• U.S. Oath of Office, adopted July 11, 1868. It replaced one used during the Civil War which demanded that the affirmer or swearer attest to his past loyalty as well as his future intentions. In the Reconstruction period, such an oath would have deprived the government of the services of many honorable men who had fought for a cause they believed in during the life of the Confederate States of America.

LUCK
(See also Gambling)

1301. Shallow men believe in luck.

• Ralph Waldo Emerson, *The Conduct of Life:* Worship, 1860.

1302. Diligence is the mother of good luck.

• Benjamin Franklin, *Poor Richard's Almanac,* 1735.

1303. Luck is a mighty queer thing. All you know about it for certain is that it's bound to change.

• Bret Harte, "The Outcasts of Poker Flat," 1869.

1304. True luck consists not in holding the best of the cards at the table: / Luckiest he who knows just when to rise and go home.

• John Hay, "Distichs," latter 19th century.

1305. What men call luck / Is the prerogative of valiant souls, / The fealty life pays its rightful kings.

• James Russell Lowell, "A Glance Behind the Curtain," 1843.

1306. Every day was Sunday / and every month was May / and every girl who came along / was sure to come your way.

• Rod McKuen, *Lonesome Cities,* "Somerset," 1968.

1307. Luck is the residue of design.

• Attributed to Branch Rickey, baseball executive of mid-20th century.

1308. The luck of the draw.

• Anonymous, derived from the game of draw poker.

MAIL

1311. I never received more than one or two letters in my life—I wrote this some years ago—that were worth the postage.

• Henry D. Thoreau, *Walden:* Where I lived, and What I Lived For, 1854.

1312. A "Dear John Letter"

• World War II slang for a letter from his sweetheart advising him that she had found someone else.

1313. As welcome as a letter from home.

• Possibly of European origin, gained popularity in first half of 19th century.

1314. The mails must go through.

• Postal Service slogan, origin unknown.

1315. Neither snow, nor rain, nor heat, nor gloom of night stays these couriers from the swift completion of their appointed rounds.

• Inscription on Manhattan Post Office, adapted from "The Histories" of Herodotus.

MANNERS
(See also Courtesy)

1321. Your manners are always under examination, and by committees little suspected—a police in citizens' clothes—but are awarding or denying you very high prizes when you least think of it.

• Ralph Waldo Emerson, *The Conduct of Life:* Culture, 1860.

1322. Fine manners need the support of fine manners in others.

• Ralph Waldo Emerson, *The Conduct of Life:* Behavior, 1860.

1323. We cannot learn from one another until we stop shouting at one another—until we speak quietly enough so that our words can be heard as well as our voices.

• President Richard M. Nixon, inaugural address, Washington, D.C., January 20, 1969.

1324. We meet at meals three times a day, and give each other a new taste of that old musty cheese that we are. We have had to agree on a certain set of rules, called etiquette and politeness, to make this frequent meeting tolerable and that we need not come to open war.

• Henry D. Thoreau, *Walden:* Solitude, 1854.

1325. Manners are changing but the essential need for manners of some kind remains the same. Good manners are the traffic rules for society in general—not in the purely "social" sense. Without good manners, living would be chaotic, human beings unbearable to each other.

• Amy Vanderbilt, *Everyday Etiquette,* 1952.

1326. There are few things that so touch us with instinctive revulsion as a breach of decorum.

• Thorstein Veblen, *The Theory of the Leisure Class,* 1899.

MARINE CORPS, U.S.

1331. The marines have landed, and the situation is well in hand.

• Variously attributed to Richard Harding Davis as a 19th century correspondent in Latin America and to what was regarded as the standard terminology used by Navy or Marine commanding officers in reporting back to headquarters.

1332. Retreat, Hell! We're just advancing in another direction.

• Marine General O. P. Smith, widely quoted remark in Korean War when Communist counter-attack in October-November 1950, with massive Chinese help, pushed United Nations forces back. Sometimes quoted as "We're just *fighting* in another direction."

1333. Semper fidelis. (Ever faithful.)

• Motto of the U.S. Marine Corps.

1334. First to fight for right and freedom / And to keep our honor clean; / We are proud to claim the title / Of United States Marines. . . . If the Army and the Navy / Ever look on Heaven's scenes, / They will find the streets are guarded / By United States Marines.

• The Marines' Hymn, author unknown, written about 1875.

1335. Tell it to the marines.

• Anonymous and very likely not of American derivation. It is cited as an "old saying" by Sir Walter Scott in *Redgauntlet,* 1824.

MARRIAGE
(See also Sex)

1341. Marriage: The state or condition of a community consisting of a master, a mistress and two slaves, making in all, two.

• Ambrose Bierce, *The Devil's Dictionary,* 1906.

1342. Is not marriage an open question, when it is alleged, from the beginning of the world, that such as are in the institution wish to get out, and such as are out wish to get in?

• Ralph Waldo Emerson, *Representative Men:* Montaigne, 1850.

1343. Where there's marriage without love, there will be love without marriage.

• Benjamin Franklin, *Poor Richard's Almanac,* 1734.

1344. Washington is full of famous men and the women they married when they were young.

• Mrs. Oliver Wendell Holmes, Jr. (Fanny Dixwell Holmes), remark at White House dinner for her husband, the new Supreme Court justice from Massachusetts, January 8, 1903.

1345. We believe that personal independence and equal human rights can never be forfeited, except for crime; that marriage should be an equal and permanent partnership, and so recognized by law; that until it is so recognized, married partners should provide against the radical injustice of present laws, by every means in their power.

• Lucy Stone and Henry B. Blackwell, statement read at their marriage in Massachusetts, 1855. She used her maiden name throughout her life, as a leader in the women's rights movement.

MEDICINE

1351. I would not think of having a doctor I didn't like. . . . My liking him won't make him a better doctor, but I think it will make me a better patient.

• Shana Alexander, *The Feminine Eye,* "An Ordeal to Choke a Sword-Swallower," 1966.

1352. God heals, and the doctor takes the fees.

• Benjamin Franklin, *Poor Richard's Almanac,* 1736.

1353. Medicine is always a little behind, and as fast as we meet one problem there's a new one appearing ahead.

• Arthur Hailey, *The Final Diagnosis,* 1959. British-born Arthur Hailey became an expert in descriptions of American institutions.

1354. . . . if the whole materia medica, as now used, could be sunk to the bottom of the sea, it would be all the better for mankind—and all the worse for the fishes.

• Oliver Wendell Holmes, address to the Massachusetts Medical Society in Boston, May 30, 1860. Dr. Holmes, a physician, excluded from his criticism "opium, which the Creator himself seems to prescribe, for we often see the scarlet poppy growing in the cornfields, as if it were foreseen that wherever there is hunger to be fed there must also be pain to be soothed . . ." and "the vapors which produce the miracle of anesthesia . . ."

1355. The patient, treated on the fashionable theory, sometimes gets well in spite of the medicine.

• President Thomas Jefferson, letter to Dr. Casper Wistar, June 21, 1807. Jefferson was not bashful about expressing his own medical convictions even when he was writing to a distinguished professor of medicine.

1356. Just what the doctor ordered.

• Anonymous, probably early 19th century.

1357. The doctors cure all kinds of ills / Except the shock of doctors' bills.

• Graffiti on New York hospital wall, 1972.

MEN

1361. Remember, all men would be tyrants if they could.

• Abigail Adams, letter to her husband, John Adams, March 31, 1776. Mrs. Adams was one of the first feminists in this infant nation.

1362. Men are what their mothers made them.

• Ralph Waldo Emerson, *The Conduct of Life:* Fate, 1860.

1363. Our self-made men are the glory of our institutions.

• Wendell Phillips, speech in Boston, December 21, 1860.

1364. I never met a man I didn't like.

• Will Rogers may not have originated this remark—although he is credited with it—but he most assuredly said it more often than anyone else, over the course of the 1920's and early 1930's.

1365. We do not ask man to represent us; it is hard enough in times like these for man to carry backbone enough to represent himself.

• Elizabeth Cady Stanton, address in Albany, N.Y., March 19, 1860, to an audience of members of the New York State Legislature. Mrs. Stanton, a longtime leader of American feminists, worked for more than half a century in the cause of women's rights.

1366. There is no escape—man drags man down, or man lifts man up.

• Booker T. Washington, "The American Standard," speech to Harvard University alumni after receiving honorary degree, 1896.

MINORITIES
(See also Blacks, Racism)

1371. It is time for America's silent majority to stand up for its rights, and let us remember the American majority includes every minority.

• Vice President Spiro T. Agnew, speech in Tulsa, Oklahoma, May 9, 1969. The term "silent majority" was first used by Richard Nixon.

1372. One, on God's side, is a majority.

• Wendell Phillips, speech at Harper's Ferry, November 1, 1859. Phillips came to the site of John Brown's capture two weeks earlier to use this forum for another eloquent plea for the abolition of slavery. Brown believed his violence was doing the work of God. But violence breeds violence, and the following month Brown was executed. (See Reed quotation below.)

1373. Governments exist to protect the rights of minorities. The loved and the rich need no protection—they have many friends and few enemies.

• Wendell Phillips, speech in Boston, December 21, 1860.

1374. One, with God, is always a majority, but many a martyr has been burned at the stake while the votes were being counted.

• Representative Thomas B. Reed of Maine, speech in the House of Representatives, 1885.

1375. No democracy can long survive which does not accept as fundamental to its very existence the recognition of the rights of minorities.

• President Franklin D. Roosevelt, letter to National Association for Advancement of Colored People, June 25, 1938.

MONEY

(See also Economy, Wealth)

1381. . . . you shall not press down upon the brow of labor this crown of thorns; you shall not crucify mankind upon a cross of gold.

• William Jennings Bryan, speech at Democratic National Convention in Chicago, July 8, 1896. His eloquent championship of "free silver" and abolition of the gold standard won the Nebraskan the Democratic Presidential nomination, but not the unanimous support of his party. (See Cockran quotation below.)

1382. Money can never circulate freely and actively unless there be absolute confidence in its value. If a man doubt whether the money in his pocket will be as valuable tomorrow as it is today, hc will decline to exchange his commodity against it . . .

• W. Bourke Cockran, speech in Madison Square Garden, New York, August 18, 1896. Cockran, a New York Democratic leader and orator, opposed William Jennings Bryan's attacks on the gold standard. (See Bryan quotation above.)

1383. He that is of opinion money will do everything may well be suspected of doing everything for money.

• Benjamin Franklin, *Poor Richard's Almanac,* 1753.

1384. You can't take it with you.

• Phrase popularized in title of play of same name by Moss Hart and George S. Kaufman, 1936.

1385. No people in a great emergency ever found a faithful ally in gold. It is the most cowardly and treacherous of all metals. It makes no treaty that it does not break. It has no friend whom it does not sooner or later betray.

• Senator John J. Ingalls of Kansas, speech in the Senate. February 15, 1878.

1386. The almighty dollar, that great object of devotion throughout our land . . .

• Washington Irving, "The Creole Village," 1836.

MUSIC

1391. Music is invaluable where a person has an ear. Where they have not, it should not be attempted.

• Thomas Jefferson, letter to Nathaniel Burwell, March 14, 1818, on the subject of "female education."

1392. Music is the universal language of mankind . . .

• Henry Wadsworth Longfellow, *Outre-Mer,* 1834.

1393. And the night shall be filled with music, / And the cares that infest the day, / Shall fold their tents, like the Arabs, / And as silently steal away.

• Henry Wadsworth Longfellow, "The Day Is Done," 1845.

1394. Let music swell the breeze, / And ring from all the trees / Sweet Freedom's song; / Let mortal tongues awake, / Let all that breathe partake, / Let rocks their silence break— / The sound prolong.

• Reverend Samuel F. Smith, "America," 1832; written to the tune of "God Save the King" and first performed on July 4th.

1395. . . . music is perpetual, and only hearing is intermittent.

• Henry D. Thoreau, *Journal,* February 8, 1857.

1396. I hear America singing, the varied carols I hear . . .

• Walt Whitman, "I Hear America Singing," 1855.

1397. Mind the music and the step . . .

• Refrain of "Yankee Doodle Dandy," believed to have been written in the late 1760's or 1770's by an Englishman, but popularized as an American fighting song in the American Revolutionary War.

NAVY, U.S.

(See also Armed Forces, Courage)

1401. You may fire when you are ready, Gridley.

• Commodore George Dewey, battle order to Captain Charles Gridley as U.S. fleet entered Manila Bay to fight the Spanish in the Spanish American War, in an engagement which became an epic American victory, May 1, 1898.

1402. Praise the Lord and pass the ammunition.

• Chaplain Howell M. Forgy of the *U.S.S. New Orleans* was reported to have made the remark at Pearl Harbor, Hawaii as sailors fought back against a surprise Japanese air attack on December 7, 1941. It was later picked up as the title and running theme of a World War II song by Frank Loesser.

1403. Sighted sub, sank same.

• U.S. Navy flier Lt. Donald F. Mason, reporting his bombing of a Japanese submarine in the South Pacific in World War II, January 8, 1942. (Credited in some sources to David Mason on February 26, 1942, but listed by the Navy in recent compilations as noted above.)

1404. We have met the enemy and they are ours.

• Commodore Oliver Hazard Perry, reporting to General William Henry Harrison on his naval victory over the British on Lake Erie, September 10, 1813, in the War of 1812.

1405. The Navy has reached a point where we can no longer drift with the tides and winds of change totally oblivious to the demands of our youth, the needs of our civilian society and the dignity of our personnel.

• Admiral Elmo R. Zumwalt, Jr., Chief of Naval Operations, commencement address at U.S. Naval Academy, Annapolis, Md., June 9, 1971.

1406. Join the Navy and see the world.

• U.S. Navy recruiting motto, used extensively in 1920's and 1930's.

NEEDS

1411. What this country needs is a good five-cent nickel.

• Generally attributed to newspaper columnist Franklin P. Adams, 1932; whether he coined it or was the first to pick it up, it became a rueful commentary on the Great Depression. It was a take-off on the remark of Vice President Marshall quoted below.

1412. What the world needs now is love, sweet love, / It's the only thing that there's just too little of.

• Burt Bacharach and Hal David, "What the World Needs Now Is Love," 1965.

1413. What this country really needs is a good five-cent cigar.

• Vice President Thomas R. Marshall, tiring of some pontificating in the Senate as various Senators orated about what the country needed, is supposed to have made this remark to the Chief Clerk of the upper House in 1915.

1414. New technology is needed to balance the costs and injustices of old technology.

• Ralph Nader, speech in Washington, D.C., June 19, 1971.

1415. The country needs, and, unless I mistake its temper, the country demands, bold, persistent experimentation.

• Governor Franklin D. Roosevelt of New York, speech in Atlanta, Ga., May 22, 1932.

1416. Understanding human needs is half the job of meeting them.

• Democratic Presidential candidate Adlai E. Stevenson, speech in Columbus, O., October 3, 1952.

1417. The supreme need of our time is for men to learn to live together in peace and harmony.

• President Harry S Truman, inaugural address, Washington, D.C., January 20, 1949.

1418. We in America need ceremonies . . .

• John Updike, "Packed Dirt, Churchgoing, A Dying Cat, A Traded Car," from *Pigeon Feathers and Other Stories,* 1962.

NEIGHBORS

1421. Nor knowest thou what argument / Thy life to thy neighbor's creed has lent. / All are needed by each one / Nothing is fair or good alone.

• Ralph Waldo Emerson, "Each and All," 1839.

1422. Good fences make good neighbors.

• Robert Frost, "Mending Wall," 1914.

1423. The impersonal hand of government can never replace the helping hand of a neighbor.

• Vice President Hubert H. Humphrey, speech in Washington, D.C., February 10, 1965.

1424. In the field of world policy, I would dedicate this nation to the policy of the good neighbor.

• President Franklin D. Roosevelt, first inaugural address, Washington, D.C., March 4, 1933.

1425. As we have recaptured and rekindled our pioneering spirit, we have insisted that it shall always be a spirit of justice, a spirit of teamwork, a spirit of sacrifice, and, above all, a spirit of neighborliness.

• President Franklin D. Roosevelt, speech to National Conference of Catholic Charities, October 4, 1933.

1426. . . . I am as desirous of being a good neighbor as I am of being a bad subject . . .

• Henry D. Thoreau, *Civil Disobedience,* 1849.

NEUTRALITY
(See also Foreign Relations)

1431. Even to observe neutrality you must have a strong government.

• Alexander Hamilton, discussion at Constitutional Convention in Philadelphia, June 29, 1787. Verbatim minutes of the Convention were not kept, so this may be a summary of Hamilton's remarks, rather than a totally accurate quotation.

1432. He who treats his friends and enemies alike, has neither love nor justice.

• Robert G. Ingersoll, *Prose Poems,* 1884.

1433. I do sincerely wish . . . that we could take our stand on a ground perfectly neutral and independent towards all nations.

• Thomas Jefferson, letter to Elbridge Gerry, May 13, 1797. The infant United States saw very clearly that its best course was to try to avoid entanglement in the wars of Europe.

1434. This nation will remain a neutral nation, but I cannot ask that every American remain neutral in thought as well. Even a neutral has a right to take account of facts. Even a neutral cannot be asked to close his mind or his conscience . . .

• President Franklin D. Roosevelt, radio "fireside chat," September 3, 1939. America was to become increasingly torn between desire to stay out of war and concern over the rise of Adolph Hitler; but the final moment of decision was bypassed when the Japanese attack on Pearl Harbor two years later brought the U.S. fully into World War II. Before then, neutrality had been becoming less and less neutral as the President proclaimed this nation an "arsenal of democracy."

1435. The United States must be neutral in fact as well as in name during these days . . .

• President Woodrow Wilson, proclamation of neutrality at outset of World War I, August 19, 1914.

1436. The basis of neutrality is not indifference; it is not self interest. The basis of neutrality is sympathy for humanity. . . . It is impartiality of spirit and of judgment.

• President Woodrow Wilson, speech in New York City, April 20, 1915.

1437. It depends whom you're neutral for.

• Anonymous, probably as old as the republic. U.S. neutrality in reality has always been seen as benefiting one side or the other in foreign wars.

NEW ENGLAND
(See also Places, Weather)

1441. The courage of New England was the "courage of Conscience." It did not rise to that insane and awful passion, the love of war for itself.

• Rufus Choate, speech at bi-centennial of Ipswich, Mass., his hometown, in 1834. Choate later succeeded Daniel Webster as Senator from Massachusetts but did not remain in public office.

1442. . . . a sup of New England's air is better than a whole draft of old England's ale.

• Reverend Francis Higginson, *New England's Plantation,* 1630. The Reverend Higginson was a new settler recently arrived from England when he wrote this tribute to his new land.

1443. New England has a harsh climate, a barren soil, a rough and stormy coast, and yet we love it, even with a love passing that of dwellers in more favored regions.

• Henry Cabot Lodge, speech in New York City, December 22, 1884. Observing Forefathers' Day, this rising young New Englander saluted his native region some years before his native region began saluting him as one of its great Senators.

1444. The New Englanders are a people of God, settled in those which were once the Devil's territories.

• Reverend Cotton Mather, *Wonders of the Invisible World,* 1693. The description of "the Devil's territories" fitted in with his defense of many of the Salem witch trials.

1445. . . . New England, where the clergy long held a monopoly of what passed for learning.

• Francis Parkman, article in *The Nation,* 1869. Written toward the end of the period in which Ralph Waldo

Emerson, an ordained Unitarian minister, was the undisputed king of American intellectuals. Emerson, however, had abandoned the ministry in the 1830's.

1446. There is a sumptuous variety about the New England weather that compels the stranger's admiration—and regret. . . . In the spring I have counted one hundred and thirty-six different kinds of weather inside four-and-twenty hours.

• Mark Twain (Samuel L. Clemens), speech in New York City, December 22, 1876.

NEWSPAPERS AND PRESS
(See also Broadcasting, Freedom)

1451. . . . were it left to me to decide whether we should have a government without newspapers or newspapers without a government, I should not hesitate a moment to prefer the latter.

• Thomas Jefferson, letter to Colonel Edward Carrington, January 16, 1787.

1452. . . . the man who never looks into a newspaper is better informed than he who reads them; inasmuch as he who knows nothing is nearer to truth than he whose mind is filled with falsehoods and errors.

• President Thomas Jefferson, letter to John Norvell, June 11, 1807. Norvell was thinking of starting a newspaper; this was Jefferson's comment. Some of the most ringing defenses of freedom of the press, and some of the most bitter attacks on the way the press used its freedom, were penned by Jefferson, whose attitude was most liberal when he was a young man, before his later political career made him the target of editorial criticism.

1453. The newspaper does not report history any longer. It must make it.

• Norman Mailer, *Presidential Papers,* 1963.

1454. All I know is what I read in the papers.

• Will Rogers, trademark remark in many of his lectures and radio appearances, particularly in the 1930's.

1455. The men with the muckrakes are often indispensable to the well-being of society; but only if they know when to stop raking the muck . . .

• President Theodore Roosevelt, speech in Washington, D.C., April 14, 1906. President Roosevelt, a reformer and crusader speaking at the height of the great journalistic crusade against corruption in industry, monopoly and shabby practices, feared that overpublicizing of the discovered excesses would disenchant the public with the whole subject.

1456. It is a newspaper's duty to print the news, and raise hell.

• Wilbur F. Storey, editor of the *Chicago Times,* statement of editorial purpose, 1861.

1457. Whenever the press quits abusing me, I know I'm in the wrong pew.

• President Harry S Truman, remark in Washington, April 17, 1948.

OCCUPATIONS
(See also Law, Medicine, Work)

1461. He that hath a trade hath an estate; he that hath a calling hath an office of profit and honor.

• Benjamin Franklin, *The Way to Wealth,* 1757.

1462. Experience teaches, that men are often so much governed by what they are accustomed to see and practise, that the simplest and most obvious improvements, in the most ordinary occupations, are adopted with hesitation, reluctance, and by slow gradations.

• Secretary of the Treasury Alexander Hamilton, Report on Manufactures, December 5, 1791.

1463. . . . there is as much dignity in tilling a field as in writing a poem.

• Booker T. Washington, *Up from Slavery,* 1901.

1464. The difference between a trade and a profession used to be the color of the shirt; now it's mainly a matter of degrees.

• In many forms, this was the point of many comments promoting higher education among returning veterans after World War II under the GI Bill of Rights in the 1940's.

1465. How do you do is a lot more friendly than what do you do.

• Anonymous, 1930's.

OPPORTUNITY

1471. God helps them that help themselves.

• Benjamin Franklin, *The Way to Wealth,* 1757.

1472. Our country has become the land of opportunity to those born without inheritance . . .

• Republican Presidential candidate Herbert Hoover, speech in New York City, October 22, 1928.

1473. All of us do not have equal talent, but all of us should have an equal opportunity to develop our talents.

• President John F. Kennedy, speech in San Diego, June 6, 1963.

1474. I seen my opportunity and I took it.

• George Washington Plunkitt, quoted by William L. Riordon in *Plunkitt of Tammany Hall,* 1905. Plunkitt was describing how he profited in a real estate deal on the basis of inside knowledge of the plans of the city government.

1475. Since the days when the great fleet of Columbus sailed into the waters of the New World, America has been another name for opportunity . . .

• Frederick Jackson Turner, "The Significance of the Frontier in American History," 1893.

OPTIMISM
(See also Attitudes, Hope)

1481. You Can't Keep a Good Man Down.

• M. F. Carey, title of a popular song of 1900.

1482. The one ultimate unforgivable crime is to despair of the republic . . .

• Governor Thomas E. Dewey of New York, speech in Minneapolis, December 6, 1939.

1483. My theory has always been, that if we are to dream, the flatteries of hope are as cheap, and pleasanter than the gloom of despair.

• Thomas Jefferson, letter to Barbe de Marbois, former Secretary of the French Legation in Philadelphia, June 14, 1817.

1484. The American, by nature, is optimistic. He is experimental, an inventor and a builder who builds best when called upon to build greatly.

• Senator John F. Kennedy of Massachusetts, speech in Washington, D.C., January 1, 1960.

1485. An optimist says the bottle is half full when it is half empty. *Sometimes rendered as:* An optimist says the bottle is half full; a pessimist says it is half empty.

• Anonymous, probably early 19th century.

ORATORY

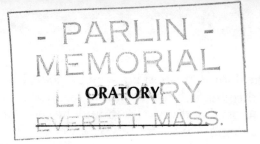

1491. All the great speakers were bad speakers at first.

• Ralph Waldo Emerson, *The Conduct of Life:* Power, 1860.

1492. Every man is eloquent once in his life.

• Ralph Waldo Emerson, *Society and Solitude:* Eloquence, 1870.

1493. A soft tongue may strike hard.

• Benjamin Franklin, *Poor Richard's Almanac,* 1744.

1494. Amplification is the vice of modern oratory. . . . Speeches measured by the hour die by the hour.

• Thomas Jefferson, letter to David Harding, April 20, 1824. Today when we refer to amplification, we refer to volume rather than length, but in either meaning, Jefferson's comment still seems to apply.

1495. True eloquence does not consist in speech. Words and phrases may be marshalled in every way, but they cannot compass it. It must consist in the man, in the subject, and in the occasion.

• Representative Daniel Webster of Massachusetts, speech memorializing John Adams and Thomas Jefferson at services in Boston, August 2, 1826. (Both former Presidents had died on July 4.)

PAST

(See also History)

1501. In every age "the good old days" were a myth. No one ever thought they were good at the time.

• Brooks Atkinson, *Once Around the Sun,* February 8, 1951.

1502. The door to the past is a strange door. It swings open and things pass through it, but they pass in one direction only. No man can return across that threshold, though he can look down still and see the green light waver in the water weeds.

• Loren Eiseley, *The Immense Journey,* The Snout, 1957.

1503. Those who cannot remember the past are condemned to repeat it.

• George Santayana, *The Life of Reason,* Volume 1, 1905. Perhaps the most quoted of all aphorisms about studying the past.

1504. History can contribute nothing in the way of panaceas. But it can assist vitally in the formation of that sense of what is democratic, of what is in line with our republican traditions, which alone can save us.

• Arthur M. Schlesinger, Foreword dated May 7, 1944 to *The Age of Jackson,* 1945.

PATRIOTISM

1511. Oh beautiful for patriot dream / That sees beyond the years / Thine alabaster cities gleam / Undimmed by human tears! / America! America! / God shed his grace on thee, / And crown thy good with brotherhood / From sea to shining sea!

• Katherine Lee Bates, "America the Beautiful," 1895.

1512. Patriotism is easy to understand in America. It means looking out for yourself by looking out for your country.

• Vice President Calvin Coolidge, speech in Northampton, Mass., May 30, 1923.

1513. Our country! In her intercourse with foreign nations, may she always be in the right; but our country, right or wrong!

• Commodore Stephen Decatur, at dinner in his honor in Norfolk, Va., April 1816, after he returned from a triumph over the Barbary pirates. The wording of his statement is sometimes quoted slightly differently, but this is the generally accepted version.

1514. I only regret that I have but one life to lose for my country.

• Nathan Hale, last words as he was about to be hanged by the British as a spy in New York during the American Revolutionary War, September 22, 1776. Some versions of the Connecticut schoolteacher's last words quote him as saying he had but one life to *give*.

1515. He serves his party best who serves the country best.

• President Rutherford B. Hayes, inaugural address in Washington, D.C., March 5, 1877. President Hayes gained his office after an Electoral Commission concluded that although Democrat Samuel J. Tilden had a larger popular vote, the various disputed elections in some states should be decided in favor of the Republicans. It was probably the single election that disserved the nation most.

1516. And so, my fellow Americans, ask not what your country can do for you; ask what you can do for your country.

• President John F. Kennedy, inaugural address in Washington, D.C., January 20, 1961.

1517. Now is the time for all of us to be patriots in the best sense of the word, not content simply to enjoy the blessings of the system we have inherited but to try to make our nation better, to hand on to the next generation a better America, truer to its promise, its potential and its own ideals.

• John D. Rockefeller, III, speech at University of Arkansas, Fayetteville, Ark., May 2, 1973.

1518. A man who is good enough to shed his blood for his country is good enough to be given a square deal afterward. More than that no man is entitled to, and less than that no man shall have.

• President Theodore Roosevelt, speech in Springfield, Ill., July 5, 1903.

1519. There can be no divided allegiance here. We have room for but one flag. . . . We have room for but one language. . . . We have room for but one sole loyalty, and that is loyalty to the American people . . .

• Theodore Roosevelt, letter read to a mass meeting in New York City, January 5, 1919. The former President died the following day.

1520. If we really love this country, if we truly love justice and mercy, if we fervently want to make this nation better for those who are to follow us, we can at least abjure the hatred that consumes people, the false accusations that divide us and the bitterness that begets violence.

• Chief Justice Earl Warren at memorial services for assassinated President John F. Kennedy in the Rotunda of the Capitol, Washington, D.C., November 24, 1963.

PEACE
(See also Ideals, War)

1521. Peace upon any other basis than natural independence, peace purchased at the cost of any part of our national integrity, is fit only for slaves, and even when purchased at such a price it is a delusion, for it cannot last.

• Senator William E. Borah of Idaho, speech in the Senate, November 19, 1919, opposing ratification of the World War I peace treaty, the Treaty of Versailles, because it included provision for a League of Nations.

1522. An honorable peace is attainable only by an efficient war.

• Speaker Henry Clay of the House of Representatives, remark in the House, January 8, 1813. Clay was one of the principal leaders of the "war hawks" in the War of 1812.

1523. There never was a good war or a bad peace.

• Benjamin Franklin, letter to Josiah Quincy, September 11, 1783. In many American citations, the date of the letter is given as 1773, but the 1783 date was just a week after Franklin signed the Treaty of Versailles ending the American Revolutionary War, when there was an immediate point to his memorable remark; and authoritative sources regard the 1783 date as correct.

1524. Let us have peace.

• General Ulysses S. Grant, accepting Republican nomination for the Presidency, May 29, 1868.

1525. In this age when there can be no losers in peace and no victors in war, we must recognize the obligation to match national strength with national restraint.

• President Lyndon B. Johnson, speech to joint session of Congress, November 27, 1963, five days after he succeeded to the Presidency upon the assassination of John F. Kennedy.

1526. The mere absence of war is not peace.

• President John F. Kennedy, State of the Union message to Congress, January 14, 1963.

1527. Peace, like charity, begins at home.

• President Franklin D. Roosevelt, speech in Chautauqua, N.Y., August 14, 1936.

1528. We desire the peace which comes as of right to the just man armed; not the peace granted on terms of ignominy to the craven and the weakling.

• President Theodore Roosevelt, speech in Washington, D.C., December 3, 1901.

1529. True pacifism is not protest only. It is the presentation of a better way.

• The Very Reverend Francis B. Sayre, Dean of Washington Cathedral, sermon at St. Thomas Episcopal Church in New York City, February 14, 1971.

1530. The supreme need of our time is for men to learn to live together in peace and harmony.

• President Harry S Truman, inaugural address in Washington, D.C., January 20, 1949.

1531. Only a peace between equals can last . . .

• President Woodrow Wilson, speech to the Senate, January 22, 1917. Wilson was still attempting to bring peace to World War I, but instead the U.S. was in the war itself less than three months later.

1532. We came in peace for all mankind.

• Plaque on landing stage left on the moon by *Apollo 11* astronauts and bearing the signatures of Neil Armstrong, Michael Collins, Edwin Aldrin, Jr. and President Richard M. Nixon, July 1969.

PEOPLE

(See also Government, Gullibility)

1541. It is to the credit of human nature, that, except where its selfishness is brought into play, it loves more readily than it hates.

• Nathaniel Hawthorne, *The Scarlet Letter,* 1850.

1542. What the people want, they generally get.

• Chief Justice Charles Evans Hughes, address in Washington, D.C. at commemoration of 150th anniversary of first meeting of U.S. Congress, March 4, 1939.

1543. I am persuaded myself that the good sense of the people will always be found to be the best army.

• Thomas Jefferson, letter to Colonel Edward Carrington, January 16, 1787.

1544. . . . I am not among those who fear the people. They, and not the rich, are our dependence for continued freedom.

• Thomas Jefferson, letter to Samuel Kercheval, July 12, 1816.

1545. Let the word go forth from this time and place, to friend and foe alike, that the torch has been passed to a new generation of Americans—born in this century, tempered by war, disciplined by a hard and bitter peace, proud of our ancient heritage . . .

• President John F. Kennedy, inaugural address in Washington, D.C., January 20, 1961.

1546. This country, with its institutions, belongs to the people who inhabit it.

• President Abraham Lincoln, inaugural address in Washington, D.C., March 4, 1861.

1547. In this world a man must either be anvil or hammer.

• Henry Wadsworth Longfellow, *Hyperion,* 1839.

1548. . . . man is not an annual. He sees the annual plants wither.

• Henry D. Thoreau, *Journal,* January 14, 1853.

1549. The world is divided into two classes of people: the few people who make good on their promises (even if they don't promise as much), and the many who don't.

• Robert Townsend, *Up the Organization,* 1970.

1550. I've got a lot of people rooting for me, because there are more poor people than rich people.

• Lee Trevino, on winning the U.S. Open Golf Championship in Ardmore, Penna., June 22, 1971.

1551. The second, sober thought of the people is seldom wrong, and always efficient.

• Governor Martin Van Buren of New York, quoted in later years as having been written in an unidentified letter in 1829.

1552. We, the People of the United States, in order to form a more perfect union . . .

• Preamble to the Constitution of the United States, written in 1787.

PHILANTHROPY
(See also Charity)

1561. The only gift is a portion of thyself.

• Ralph Waldo Emerson, *Essays, Second Series:* Gifts, 1844.

1562. . . . the most acceptable service of God is the doing of good to man . . .

• Benjamin Franklin, *Autobiography,* section written in 1784.

1563. . . . nature hath implanted in our breasts a love of others, a sense of duty to them, a moral instinct, in short, which prompts us irresistibly to feel and to succor their distresses . . .

• Thomas Jefferson, letter to Thomas Law, June 13, 1814.

1564. He who gives himself entirely to his fellow-men appears to them useless and selfish; but he who gives himself partially to them is pronounced benefactor and philanthropist.

• Henry D. Thoreau, *Civil Disobedience,* 1849.

1565. Philanthropy is almost the only virtue which is sufficiently appreciated by mankind. Nay, it is greatly overrated; and it is our selfishness which overrates it.

• Henry D. Thoreau, *Walden:* Economy, 1854.

1566. Small gifts are charity; big gifts are philanthropy.

• Anonymous. Used by fund raisers at meetings with big givers.

PIONEERING
(See also Frontier, Neighbors)

1571. There are pioneer souls that blaze their paths / Where highways never ran . . .

• Sam Walter Foss, "The House by the Side of the Road," 1897.

1572. I, for one, do not believe that the era of the pioneer is at an end; I only believe that the area for pioneering has changed. The period of geographical pioneering is largely finished. But, my friends, the period of social pioneering is only at its beginning.

• President Franklin D. Roosevelt, speech in Baltimore, April 13, 1936.

1573. . . . venturing as we go the unknown ways, / Pioneers! O Pioneers!

• Walt Whitman, "Pioneers! O Pioneers!" 1865.

1574. A pioneer is a first who lasts.

• Said at the time in the 1930's when attempts were being made to popularize homesteading in the Matanuska Valley of Alaska.

1575. Pioneers are not interested in precedent.

• Anonymous. College saying of the 1930's.

PLACES
(See also New England)

1581. And this is good old Boston, / The home of the bean and the cod, / Where the Lowells talk only to Cabots / And the Cabots talk only to God.

• John C. Bossidy, "On the Aristocracy of Harvard," 1910.

1582. Washington, D.C. is no place for a civilized man to spend the summer.

• Attributed to President James Buchanan during his 1857–1861 term of office.

1583. East is East and West is San Francisco, according to Californians. Californians are a race of people; they are not merely inhabitants of a State. They are the Southerners of the West.

• O. Henry (William Sydney Porter), "A Municipal Report," 1910.

1584. In Boston they ask, How much does he know? In New York, How much is he worth? In Philadelphia, Who were his parents?

• Mark Twain (Samuel L. Clemens), "What Paul Bourget Thinks of Us," 1895.

1585. I'm from Missouri; you've got to show me.

• Representative Willard D. Vandiver of Missouri, speech in Philadelphia in 1899; but probably of much earlier derivation.

1586. Heaven is a Kentucky of a place.

• Anonymous, in *Kentucky Guide Book* in series of Guide Books sponsored by Federal Writers Project in the 1930's.

1587. New York City is a great place to visit, but I wouldn't want to live there.

• Anonymous and apparently eternal.

1588. Nineteen (sometimes seventeen) suburbs in search of a city.

• This anonymous description of Los Angeles was coined in the 1920's. It refers to the fact that the city of Los Angeles absorbed many different communities in order to unify such services as water supply, and also to the fact that many of these communities have their own "downtowns" and seem remote from the big city.

POLITICS

(See also Democrats, Republicans)

1591. Turn the rascals out.

• Attributed to Charles A. Dana, editor of *The New York Sun,* and used as the slogan of the Liberal Republican Party in 1872, when its candidate against President Grant was Horace Greeley. In that same year *The Sun* exposed the Credit Mobilier scandal involving members of the Grant Administration. The year before, *The New York Times* had exposed the Tweed Ring of corrupt city officials. The Liberal Republicans' slogan was an attempt to capitalize on a climate of scandal in public office, but the electorate did not respond.

1592. Of the two great parties, which at this hour almost share the nation between them, I should say that one has the best cause, and the other contains the best men.

• Ralph Waldo Emerson, *Essays, Second Series:* Politics, 1844. Based on an 1842 lecture, this essay referred to the Whig and Democratic parties.

1593. As Maine goes, so goes Vermont.

• Postmaster General James A. Farley, comment to reporters on November 4, 1936, after the Republican candidate, Governor Alfred M. Landon of Kansas, was able to win only these two states against President Franklin D. Roosevelt. Mr. Farley's comment was an updating of the old saw, originated when Maine voted weeks ahead of other states and seemed to be a bellwether of national sentiment, that "As Maine goes, so goes the nation."

1594. You cannot adopt politics as a profession and remain honest.

• Louis McHenry Howe, aide to President-elect Franklin D. Roosevelt, speech at Columbia University, New York, January 17, 1933.

1595. The same political parties which now agitate the United States have existed through all time.

• Thomas Jefferson, letter to John Adams, June 27, 1813. The two former Presidents had represented rivalries and differing points of view all their lives, but they had fought in the same battles for the same love of freedom.

1596. Politics is an astonishing profession. It has enabled me to go from an obscure member of the minor varsity at Harvard to being an honorary member of the Football Hall of Fame.

• President John F. Kennedy, at dinner of National Football Foundation in New York City, December 1961.

1597. Broadly speaking, any middle-of-the-road politician faces one of two prospects. He can allow himself to be torn in two by the forces he is attempting to conciliate. Or he can draw strength from both irreconcilable extremes by playing one off against the other.

• Samuel Lubell, *The Future of American Politics,* 1952.

1598. They see nothing wrong in the rule that to the victor belong the spoils of the enemy.

• Senator William L. Marcy of New York, speech in the Senate referring to the politicians of his state and defending the appointment of Martin Van Buren as U.S. Minister to Great Britain, January 21, 1832. It is sometimes supposed that because the spoils system was largely born in the Presidency of Andrew Jackson, President Jackson himself was the source of the familiar statement that "to the victor belong the spoils," but Senator Marcy was the man who put the policy so succinctly.

1599. The fact is that a reformer can't last in politics. He can make a show for a while, but he always comes down like a rocket. Politics is as much a regular business as the grocery or the dry-goods or the drug business.

• George Washington Plunkitt, quoted by William L. Riordon in *Plunkitt of Tammany Hall,* 1905.

1600. The best system is to have one party govern and the other party watch.

• Representative Thomas B. Reed of Maine, speech in House of Representatives, April 22, 1880.

1601. I'm as conservative as the Constitution, as liberal as Lincoln, and as progressive as Theodore Roosevelt.

• Governor George Romney of Michigan, a Republican, statement at a news conference in Hartford, Conn., February 23, 1965.

1602. Let's face it. Let's talk sense to the American people.

• Governor Adlai E. Stevenson of Illinois, acceptance speech at Democratic National Convention in Chicago which nominated him for the Presidency, July 26, 1952.

1603. When a leader is in the Democratic Party he's a boss; when he's in the Republican Party he's a leader.

• Harry S Truman, a Democrat, speech at Columbia University, April 28, 1959.

1604. A mugwump has his mug on one side of the political fence and his wump on the other.

• Saying in the Blaine-Cleveland Presidential election of 1884, aimed at the political independents who bolted the Republican party. The word "mugwump" was supposedly derived from the Algonquin Indian language, where it meant chief.

POPULARITY

1611. We thirst for approbation, yet cannot forgive the approver.

• Ralph Waldo Emerson, *Essays, First Series:* Circles, 1841.

1612. The actor's popularity is evanescent; applauded today, forgotten tomorrow.

• Edwin Forrest, American actor, mid-19th century.

1613. . . . nobody will care for him who cares for nobody.

• Thomas Jefferson, letter to Maria Cosway, October 12, 1786.

1614. All progress has resulted from people who took unpopular positions.

• Adlai E. Stevenson, speech at Princeton, N.J., March 22, 1954.

1615. Popularity is a matter of opinion.

• Anonymous comedian's comment about radio ratings in the 1930's.

1616. Such popularity must be deserved.

• Advertising slogan, source and time unknown.

POSTERITY

1621. Each generation is as independent of the one preceding, as that was of all which had gone before. It has then, like them, a right to choose for itself the form of government it believes most promotive of its own happiness . . .

• Thomas Jefferson, letter to Samuel Kercheval, July 12, 1816. Because of his ardent belief in the right of each generation to work out its own destiny, a whole book could probably be written of Jeffersonian quotations on the subject of future generations.

1622. Can one generation bind another and all others, in succession forever? I think not.

• Thomas Jefferson, letter to Major John Cartwright, June 5, 1824.

1623. . . . posterity is just around the corner.

• This Depression-time saying was one of the most popular lines in "Of Thee I Sing," the 1931 musical by George S. Kaufman, Morrie Ryskind and Ira Gershwin. It was, of course, a take-off on the Herbert Hoover Republicans' proclamation that "Prosperity is just around the corner."

1624. Few can be induced to labor exclusively for posterity. . . . Posterity has done nothing for us . . .

• Abraham Lincoln, speech in Springfield, Ill., February 22, 1842.

1625. What has posterity done for us?

• John Trumbull, *M'Fingal,* 1782.

POVERTY

1631. For poverty does survive.

• John K. Galbraith, *The Affluent Society,* 1958.

1632. Poverty is the open-mouthed, relentless hell which yawns beneath civilized society.

• Henry George, *Progress and Poverty,* 1878.

1633. This Administration today, here and now, declares unconditional war on poverty in America.

• President Lyndon B. Johnson, State of the Union message to Congress, January 8, 1964. Unfortunately, another war, in Vietnam, competed for attention.

1634. Poverty has many roots, but the tap root is ignorance.

• President Lyndon B. Johnson, message to Congress, January 12, 1965. By profession, before he went into politics, Mr. Johnson was a school teacher.

1635. If a free society cannot help the many who are poor, it cannot save the few who are rich.

• President John F. Kennedy, inaugural address in Washington, D.C., January 20, 1961.

1636. No men living are more worthy to be trusted than those who toil up from poverty . . .

• President Abraham Lincoln, first annual message to Congress, December 3, 1861.

1637. *How the Other Half Lives.*

• Jacob A. Riis, title of book studying the lives of the urban poor, 1890.

1638. . . . either wipe out the slum, or it wipes us out.

• Jacob A. Riis, *The Battle with the Slum,* 1902.

1639. I see one-third of a nation ill-housed, ill-clad, ill-nourished.

• President Franklin D. Roosevelt, second inaugural address, Washington, D.C., January 20, 1937. President Roosevelt's famous fraction became the familiar summary of poverty in the country—"one-third of a nation."

1640. Thinking this afternoon of the prospect of my writing lectures and going abroad to read them the next winter, I realized how incomparably great the advantage of obscurity and poverty which I have enjoyed so long (and may still perhaps enjoy).

• Henry D. Thoreau, *Journal,* September 19, 1854.

POWER
(See also Government, Rights)

1641. . . . power, whether vested in many or a few, is ever grasping, and like the grave, cries "Give, give!"

• Abigail Adams, letter to her husband, John Adams, November 27, 1775.

1642. Power is poison.

• Henry Adams, *The Education of Henry Adams,* 1907.

1643. I think all of our human experience shows that no one with absolute power can be trusted to give it up even in part.

• Louis D. Brandeis, testimony before U.S. Commission on Industrial Relations, January 23, 1915.

1644. In the councils of government, we must guard against the acquisition of unwarranted influence, whether sought or unsought, by the military-industrial complex. The potential for the disastrous rise of misplaced power exists and will persist.

• President Dwight D. Eisenhower, farewell address broadcast to the American people, January 17, 1961.

1645. Life is a search after power . . .

• Ralph Waldo Emerson, *The Conduct of Life:* Power, 1860.

1646. Absolute power does corrupt, and those who seek it must be suspect and must be opposed.

• Senator Barry M. Goldwater of Arizona, accepting Republican Presidential nomination in San Francisco, July 16, 1964.

1647. All power is inherent in the people.

• Thomas Jefferson, letter to John Cartwright, June 5, 1824. A century and a half later, the slogan "Power to the people" was considered a revolutionary watchword.

1648. . . . in the past, those who foolishly sought power by riding the back of the tiger ended up inside.

• President John F. Kennedy, inaugural address in Washington, D.C., January 20, 1961.

PREJUDICE
(See also Racism)

1651. Prejudice: A vagrant opinion without visible means of support.

• Ambrose Bierce, *The Devil's Dictionary,* 1906.

1652. For when you assemble a number of men to have the advantage of their joint wisdom, you inevitably assemble with those men all their prejudices, their passions, their errors of opinion, their local interests and their selfish views.

• Benjamin Franklin, speech to the Constitutional Convention in Philadelphia moving the unanimous adoption of the Constitution, September 17, 1787. The speech was read for Franklin by James Wilson of Pennsylvania and the Constitution was adopted that day for submission to the states for ratification.

1653. Irrational barriers and ancient prejudices fall quickly when the question of survival itself is at stake.

• Senator John F. Kennedy of Massachusetts, speech in Indianapolis, April 12, 1959.

1654. There is nothing stronger than human prejudice.

• Wendell Phillips, speech to Anti-Slavery Society in Boston, January 28, 1852.

1655. Ignorance is stubborn and prejudice dies hard.

• U.S. Ambassador to the U.N. Adlai E. Stevenson, speech at United Nations, October 1, 1963, on subject of race discrimination.

1656. It is never too late to give up our prejudices.

• Henry D. Thoreau, *Walden,* Economy, 1854.

PRESIDENCY

(See also Government, Ideals)

1661. A little over a week ago, I took a rather unusual step for a Vice President. I said something.

• Vice President Spiro T. Agnew, speech in Harrisburg, Penna., October 30, 1969.

1662. Roughly speaking, the President of the United States knows what his job is. Constitution and custom spell it out, for him as well as for us. His wife has no such luck. The First Ladyship has no rules; rather each new woman must make her own.

• Shana Alexander, "The Best First Lady," December 1968 (published in *The Feminine Eye,* 1970).

1663. I am acutely aware that you have not elected me as your President by your ballots. So I ask you to confirm me as your President with your prayers.

• President Gerald R. Ford, inaugural address in Washington, D.C., August 9, 1974.

1664. No man will ever bring out of the Presidency the reputation which carries him into it.

• Thomas Jefferson, letter to Edward Rutledge in 1796, the year in which Jefferson ran second to John Adams for the Presidency (thereby being elected Vice President).

1665. The second office of the government is honorable and easy; the first is but a splendid misery.

• Vice President Thomas Jefferson, letter to Elbridge Gerry, May 13, 1797. Jefferson was later to have eight years of that "splendid misery."

1666. A President's hardest task is not to do what is right, but to know what is right.

• President Lyndon B. Johnson, State of the Union message to Congress, January 4, 1965.

1667. The matter of executive privilege is one that it always depends on which side you're on.

• President Richard M. Nixon, remark at press conference, Washington, D.C., March 4, 1971.

1668. If nominated, I will not accept; if elected, I will not serve.

• General William T. Sherman, telegram to Republican National Convention in Chicago, June 5, 1884. Sometimes reported in similar but not exactly these words.

1669. The buck stops here.

• Sign on the White House desk of President Harry S Truman during the latter days of his presidency, from about 1950 on.

1670. The President gets a lot of hot potatoes from every direction . . . That makes me think of a saying that I used to hear from my old friend and colleague on the Jackson County Court. He said, "Harry, if you can't stand the heat you better get out of the kitchen."

• President Harry S Truman, speech in Washington, D.C., December 17, 1952. Mr. Truman was about to get out of the kitchen, to be succeeded by Dwight D. Eisenhower, but he had proven he could stand the heat.

1671. As the President came to be elected by the whole people, he became responsible to the whole people. I used to say the only lobbyist the whole people had in Washington was the President of the United States.

• Harry S Truman, at birthday dinner in New York City, May 8, 1954.

PRIDE

1681. The proud hate pride—in others.

• Benjamin Franklin, *Poor Richard's Almanac,* 1751.

1682. Idleness and pride tax with a heavier hand than kings and parliaments.

• Benjamin Franklin, letter on the Stamp Act, July 11, 1765. The following year, largely through Franklin's efforts in London, the Act was repealed.

1683. There is nothing so skillful in its own defense as imperious pride.

• Helen Hunt Jackson, *Ramona,* 1884. In this and other works, Mrs. Hunt spoke out against white take-overs of Indian land and colonial treatment of the Indians.

1684. What so proudly we hail . . .

• Francis Scott Key, "The Star-Spangled Banner," September 14, 1814.

1685. Land of the pilgrims' pride . . .

• Reverend Samuel F. Smith, "America," 1832. Sung for the first time at the Park Street Church in Boston on July 4, 1832 by a children's choir.

PRIVACY

1691. . . . the right to be let alone—the most comprehensive of rights, and the right most valued by civilized men.

• Associate Justice Louis D. Brandeis of Supreme Court, dissenting opinion in the wire-tapping case of Olmstead v. U.S., June 4, 1928.

1692. A man must ride alternately on the horses of his private and his public nature.

• Ralph Waldo Emerson, *The Conduct of Life:* Fate, 1860.

1693. I want to be alone.

• Attributed to Greta Garbo in the 1930's; if the words were never literally verified, the wish they represented was clearly understood. Miss Garbo's privacy was respected and legendary in Hollywood, and, after her retirement from motion picture stardom, in New York as well.

1694. A man has a right to pass through this world, if he wills, without having his picture published, his business enterprises discussed, his successful experiments written for the benefit of others, or his eccentricities commented upon, whether in handbills, circulars, catalogues, newspapers or periodicals.

• Chief Judge Alton B. Parker of the New York State Court of Appeals, decision in Roberson v. Rochester Folding Box Co., 1901. Judge Parker three years later was the Democratic Presidential nominee, in 1904.

1695. I feel the necessity of deepening the stream of my life; I must cultivate privacy. It is very dissipating to be with people too much.

• Henry D. Thoreau, *Journal,* August 2, 1854.

1696. The right to be let alone is becoming obsolete.

• Harriet Van Horne, *Never Go Anywhere Without a Pencil,* 1972.

PROHIBITION

1701. Our country has deliberately undertaken a great social and economic experiment, noble in motive and far-reaching in purpose.

• Secretary of Commerce Herbert Hoover, letter to Senator William E. Borah, February 28, 1928. His reference to prohibition was widely quoted as calling the 18th Amendment "a noble experiment."

1702. Whether or not the world would be vastly benefited by a total banishment from it of all intoxicating drinks seems not now an open question. Three-fourths of mankind confess the affirmative with their tongues, and I believe all the rest acknowledge it in their hearts.

• Abraham Lincoln, speech in Springfield, Ill., February 22, 1842. Lincoln was not totally consistent on the subject of prohibition. Two years earlier, as subsequently chronicled by H. L. Mencken, he had told his fellow members of the Illinois legislature on December 18, 1840 that "A Prohibition law strikes a blow at the very principles upon which our government was founded." Then, during the Civil War, when a complaint was made to him that General Grant was drinking heavily, he was reported to have said, "Find out what brand General Grant drinks. I'd like to send some to my other generals" (or words to that effect).

1703. I guess Prohibition is better than no liquor at all.

• Will Rogers, in the 1930's.

1704. All experience shows that temperance, like other virtues, is not produced by lawmakers, but by the influences of education, morality and religion. Men may be persuaded—they cannot be compelled to adopt habits of temperance.

• Governor Horatio Seymour of New York, statement on vetoing state Prohibition Act, 1854.

1705. Right off the boat . . .

• Expression used in the Prohibition era of the 1920's to describe supposedly authentic imported bootleg liquor.

PROSPERITY

1711. Prosperity is only an instrument to be used, not a deity to be worshipped.

• President Calvin Coolidge, speech the day before the Republican National Convention, June 11, 1928. The words were more prophetic than anybody knew at the time. The Depression came at the end of the following year.

1712. We are nearer today to the ideal of the abolition of poverty and fear from the lives of men and women than ever before in any land.

• Herbert Hoover, Speech in New York during 1928 Presidential campaign, October 22, 1928.

1713. Prosperity is just around the corner.

• President Herbert Hoover and his Republican Party adherents used this slogan beginning in 1931, operating to some extent on the theory that the Depression was simply a loss of confidence that could be cured by reassurances.

1714. The test of our progress is not whether we add more to the abundance of those who have much; it is whether we provide enough for those who have too little.

• President Franklin D. Roosevelt, second inaugural address, Washington, D.C., January 20, 1937.

1715. . . . it is a great deal better that some people should prosper too much than that no one should prosper enough.

• President Theodore Roosevelt, speech in Fitchburg, Mass., September 2, 1902. He was touring the country to explain and promote his anti-trust program, but also to reassure people he was not out to destroy the country's prosperous base.

PROTEST

1721. . . . what country can preserve its liberties, if its rulers are not warned from time to time, that this people preserve the spirit of resistance?

• Thomas Jefferson, letter to Col. William S. Smith, November 13, 1787. This was the letter in which Jefferson expressed approval of a revolution every 20 years. See quotation 816.

1722. . . . we will not accept the peace of stifled rights, or the order imposed by fear, or the unity that stifles protest.

• President Lyndon B. Johnson, address to joint session of Congress on voting rights, March 15, 1965.

1723. I want every American free to stand up for his rights, even if sometimes he has to sit down for them.

• Senator John F. Kennedy of Massachusetts, Democratic Presidential candidate, speech in Philadelphia, October 31, 1960.

1724. In these difficult years, America has suffered from a fever of words; from inflated rhetoric that promises more than it can deliver; from angry rhetoric that fans discontents into hatreds; from bombastic rhetoric that postures instead of persuading. We cannot learn from one another until we stop shouting at one another—until we speak quietly enough so that our words can be heard as well as our voices.

• President Richard M. Nixon, inaugural address in Washington, D.C., January 20, 1969.

1725. Severe truth is expressed with some bitterness.

• Henry D. Thoreau, *Journal,* March 15, 1854.

PUBLIC OPINION

1731. . . . what the growing chorus of voices is saying is that the quantity of goods and services produced is no longer acceptable as the measure of progress, that there is too much worship of quantity instead of quality in today's life.

• Stanley J. Goodman, chairman of May Department Stores Company of St. Louis, speech to National Retail Merchants Association in New York City, January 7, 1974.

1732. When public opinion changes, it is with the rapidity of thought.

• Thomas Jefferson, letter to Col. Charles Yancey, January 6, 1816.

1733. With public sentiment, nothing can fail; without it, nothing can succeed.

• Abraham Lincoln, speech in Ottawa, Ill., July 31, 1858.

1734. There is no group in America that can withstand the force of an aroused public opinion.

• President Franklin D. Roosevelt, remarks at signing of National Industrial Recovery Act, June 16, 1933. By the time the Act was declared unconstitutional by the Supreme Court on May 27, 1935, public opinion could not have cared less.

1735. Public opinion is a weak tyrant compared with our own private opinion.

• Henry D. Thoreau, *Walden:* Economy, 1854.

1736. Public opinion is stronger than the legislature, and nearly as strong as the ten commandments.

• Charles Dudley Warner, *My Summer in a Garden,* 1870.

1737. In proportion as the structure of a government gives force to public opinion, it is essential that public opinion should be enlightened.

• President George Washington, Farewell Address, dated September 17, 1796 and first published September 19, 1796. It was never delivered orally.

RACES

1741. Every man has pride of race, and under appropriate circumstances when the rights of others, his equals before the law, are not to be affected, it is his privilege to express such pride and to take such action based upon it as to him seems proper. . . . Our Constitution is color-blind, and neither knows nor tolerates classes among citizens.

• Associate Justice John Marshall Harlan of the Supreme Court, dissenting opinion in Plessy v. Ferguson, May 18, 1896. Justice Harlan's view in this famous "Jim Crow" case ultimately became law when a unanimous Supreme Court 58 years ago, almost to the day, made the first of a number of decisions banning the "Jim Crow" concept of separate facilities for blacks and whites. (See Warren quote below.)

1742. Men of different ancestries, men of different tongues, men of different colors, men of different environments, men of different geographies do not see everything alike. Even in our own country we do not see everything alike.

• President Lyndon B. Johnson, speech in Washington, D.C., February 11, 1964.

1743. We must learn to live together as brothers or perish together as fools.

• Reverend Dr. Martin Luther King, Jr., speech in St. Louis, March 23, 1964.

1744. I believe in the brotherhood of man, not merely the brotherhood of white men but the brotherhood of all men before the law.

• Senator Harry S Truman of Missouri, speech in Sedalia, Mo., June 15, 1940.

1745. We conclude that in the field of public education the doctrine of "separate but equal" has no place. Separate educational facilities are inherently unequal.

• Chief Justice Earl Warren, unanimous decision of the Supreme Court, May 17, 1954, in the case of Brown v. Board of Education of Topeka (reversing Plessy v. Ferguson decision noted in Harlan quote above). This was the first of a series of decisions outlawing discrimination of various kinds.

1746. Our nation is moving toward two societies, one black, one white—separate and unequal.

• Report of the National Advisory Commission on Civil Disorders, February 29, 1968. The Commission had been established July 28, 1967, after a series of race riots in American cities.

RADICALS
(See also Conservatives)

1751. We need not take shelter when someone cries "Radical!"

• Senator William E. Borah of Idaho, speech in the Senate, April 24, 1929.

1752. The spirit of our American radicalism is destructive and aimless: it is not loving; it has no ulterior and divine ends, but is destructive only out of hatred and selfishness.

• Ralph Waldo Emerson, *Essays, Second Series:* Politics, 1844.

1753. A radical is a man with both feet firmly planted in the air.

• President Franklin D. Roosevelt, radio address, October 26, 1939.

1754. By "radical" I understand one who goes too far; by "conservative" one who does not go far enough; by "reactionary" one who won't go at all.

• Governor Woodrow Wilson of New Jersey, speech in New York City, January 29, 1911.

1755. If conservative means small change, radical means large bills.

• Anonymous, widely used by conservative spokesmen in 1960's.

1756. Radicalism means exceeding the political speed limit.

• Anonymous, college campus saying of the 1930's.

REBELLION

(See also Dissent, Freedom, Government, Immigrants)

1761. . . . what do we mean by the American Revolution? Do we mean the American War? The Revolution was effected before the War commenced. The Revolution was in the minds and hearts of the people.

• John Adams, letter to editor Hezekiah Niles, February 13, 1818.

1762. A guy has to be a political idiot to say all power comes out of the barrel of a gun when the other side has the guns.

• Saul D. Alinsky, civic activist, comment on the Black Panther movement attributed to a "recent interview" with him by Israel Shenker in *The New York Times*, January 6, 1971.

1763. Here in America we are descended in blood and in spirit from revolutionists and rebels . . .

• President Dwight D. Eisenhower, speech in New York City, May 31, 1954, at a Columbia University Bicentennial Dinner.

1764. One hundred and eighty-one years ago, our forefathers started a revolution that still goes on.

• President Dwight D. Eisenhower, speech in Washington, D.C., April 19, 1956, the anniversary of the start of the American Revolutionary War.

1765. . . . a little rebellion, now and then, is a good thing, and as necessary in the political world as storms in the physical. . . . It is a medicine necessary for the sound health of government.

• Thomas Jefferson, letter to James Madison, January 30, 1787.

1766. . . . among free men there can be no successful appeal from the ballot to the bullet.

• President Abraham Lincoln, letter to James C. Conkling, August 26, 1863.

1767. The only justification of rebellion is success.

• Representative Thomas B. Reed of Maine, speech in the House of Representatives, April 12, 1878.

1768. . . . revolutions never go backwards.

• Senator William H. Seward of New York, speech in Rochester, N.Y., October 25, 1858.

RELIGION

1771. The First Amendment has erected a wall between Church and State which must be kept high and impregnable.

• Associate Justice Hugo L. Black of Supreme Court, decision in McCollum v. Board of Education of Champaign County District 71, March 8, 1948. This was the decision that outlawed released time in public schools for religious instruction.

1772. In God We Trust.

• Longtime motto of the United States, authorized by Secretary of the Treasury Salmon P. Chase to be imprinted on U.S. currency in 1864.

1773. All religions united with government are more or less inimical to liberty. All separated from government are compatible with liberty.

• Speaker Henry Clay, speech in the House of Representatives, March 24, 1818.

1774. . . . the most acceptable service of God is the doing good to man . . .

• Benjamin Franklin, *Autobiography*, 1784.

1775. Mine eyes have seen the glory of the coming of the Lord; / He is trampling out the vintage where the grapes of wrath are stored; / He hath loosed the fateful lightning of his terrible, swift sword; / His truth is marching on.

• Julia Ward Howe, "Battle Hymn of the Republic," February 1862, written to the tune of "John Brown's Body."

1776. An honest God is the noblest work of man.

• Robert G. Ingersoll, *The Gods*, 1872.

1777. . . . religion is a matter which lies solely between man and his God, that he owes account to none other for his faith or his worship . . .

• President Thomas Jefferson, letter to Danbury Baptist Association of Connecticut, January 1, 1802.

1778. I believe in an America where the separation of church and state is absolute . . . . where religious intolerance will someday end—where all men and all churches are treated as equal—where every man has the same right to attend or not attend the church of his choice. . . . I do not speak for my church on public matters—and the church does not speak for me.

• Senator John F. Kennedy of Massachusetts, speech to the Greater Houston Ministerial Association in Houston, Texas, September 12, 1960, during the Presidential election campaign. This speech is credited with having helped to elect the first Catholic President of the United States, John F. Kennedy.

1779. No people can be bound to acknowledge and adore the invisible hand, which conducts the affairs of men, more than the People of the United States.

• President George Washington, first inaugural address, in New York City, April 30, 1789.

1780. God requireth not any uniformity of religion to be enacted and enforced in any civil state; which enforced unanimity (sooner or later) is the greatest occasion of civil war, ravishment of conscience, persecution of Jesus Christ in His servants, and of the hypocrisy and destruction of millions of souls.

• Reverend Roger Williams, *The Bloudy Tenent of Persecution for the Cause of Conscience,* 1644. It was written in England, where the Reverend Williams had gone to receive a charter to Rhode Island; he had founded a settlement named Providence Plantation in Rhode Island, the first American settlement with full freedom of religion.

1781. Congress shall make no law respecting an establishment of religion, or prohibiting the free exercise thereof . . .

• Constitution of the United States, First Amendment, adopted December 15, 1791; these are the first words of the Bill of Rights.

1782. . . . we are bounde by the law of God and men to doe goode unto all men and evil to noe one.

• The Flushing Remonstrance, petition addressed by citizens of Flushing, N.Y., to Governor Peter Stuyvesant of New Amsterdam, December 27, 1657. The Flushing settlers were English, and had been ordered by the Dutch Governor not to extend their hospitality to Quakers. This was their reply.

REPUBLICANS

(See also Democrats, Politics)

1791. Republicans like to make things work. . . . The genius of Republican administrations has always rested with developing systems that genuinely deliver service to the people.

• Vice President Spiro T. Agnew, speech in Manchester, N.H., April 15, 1969.

1792. Any man who can carry a Republican primary is a Republican.

• Senator William E. Borah of Idaho, 1923. The Senator was objecting to "loyalty" or "dogma" tests for party membership. He was himself a Republican, and a rather unpredictably independent one.

1793. Fortunately, one of the most all-pervading principles of our Party—and one most important to us today—is the willingness to adapt our basic convictions imaginatively to current problems.

• President Dwight D. Eisenhower, address to Republican National Conference, June 7, 1957.

1794. . . . I don't want to see the Republican Party ride to political victory on the Four Horsemen of Calumny—Fear, Ignorance, Bigotry and Smear.

• Senator Margaret Chase Smith of Maine, "Declaration of Conscience" in the Senate, June 1, 1950. This sentence introduced the Declaration which was made on behalf of seven Republican Senators opposing the tactics of another Republican Senator, Joseph R. McCarthy of Wisconsin.

REPUTATION
(See also Fame)

1801. Glass, China, and Reputation, are easily cracked and never well mended.

• Benjamin Franklin, *Poor Richard's Almanac,* 1750.

1802. How many people live on the reputation of the reputation they might have made!

• Oliver Wendell Holmes, *The Autocrat of the Breakfast-Table,* 1858.

1803. One man lies in his words and gets a bad reputation; another in his manners, and enjoys a good one.

• Henry D. Thoreau, *Journal,* June 25, 1852.

1804. A man is judged by the company that keeps him.

• Attributed to many different wits of the 1920's and 1930's.

RETIREMENT
(See also Age)

1811. I have considered the pension list of the republic a role of honor.

• President Grover Cleveland, veto of a private pension bill, July 5, 1888.

1812. It is very grand to "die in harness," but it is very pleasant to have the tight straps unbuckled and the heavy collar lifted from the neck and shoulders.

• Oliver Wendell Holmes, *Over the Teacups,* 1891.

1813. There is a fulness of time when men should go, and not occupy too long the ground to which others have a right to advance.

• Thomas Jefferson, letter to Dr. Benjamin Rush, August 17, 1811.

1814. What are threescore years and ten hurriedly and coarsely lived to moments of divine leisure in which your life is coincident with the life of the universe?

• Henry D. Thoreau, *Journal,* December 28, 1852.

RIGHTS
(See also Freedom, Government)

1821. My individual freedom stops where your nose begins, as far as the swinging of my fist is concerned. My right to demonstrate my disagreement with a law does not give me the privilege of interfering with the rights of other people.

• Vice President Spiro T. Agnew, speech in Atlanta, Ga., February 21, 1970.

1822. The right of every person "to be let alone" must be placed in the scales with the right of others to communicate.

• Chief Justice Warren E. Burger in unanimous Supreme Court decision upholding a 1967 law to prevent the sending of erotic mail to people who don't want to receive it, May 4, 1970.

1823. . . . the earth belongs in usufruct to the living; . . . the dead have neither powers nor rights over it.

• Thomas Jefferson, letter to James Madison, September 6, 1789.

1824. The rights of one generation will scarcely be considered hereafter as depending on the paper transactions of another.

• Thomas Jefferson, letter to John Adams, April 25, 1794.

1825. Nothing then is unchangeable but the inherent and unalienable rights of man. . . .

• Thomas Jefferson, letter to Major John Cartwright, June 5, 1824.

1826. I want every American free to stand up for his rights, even if sometimes he has to sit down for them.

• Senator John F. Kennedy of Massachusetts, Presidential campaign speech in Philadelphia, October 31, 1960. The sit-in, begun as a labor strike tactic, was being used more as a political demonstration device, particularly for civil rights efforts.

1827. In giving rights to others which belong to them, we give rights to ourselves and to our country.

• President John F. Kennedy, message in note of 100th anniversary of Emancipation Proclamation, September 22, 1962.

1828. States have no rights—only people have rights. States have responsibilities.

• Governor George Romney of Michigan, statement to Republican Platform Committee in San Francisco, July 8, 1964.

SALESMANSHIP

1831. The greatest meliorator of the world is selfish, huckstering trade.

• Ralph Waldo Emerson, *Society and Solitude:* Works and Days, 1870.

1832. Our customers become our friends because of the money we save them.

• Sears, Roebuck & Co. catalogue, 1897.

1833. He could sell iceboxes to Eskimos.

• Believed to have originated in the Yukon during the gold rush to Alaska in the late 1890's; became popular in the 1920's during the era of frantic high pressure salesmanship.

1834. If you can sell someone something he doesn't want at a price he can't afford, that's salesmanship.

• Anonymous, believed to have originated in the 1920's.

SCIENCE

1841. Science has not yet mastered prophecy. We predict too much for the next year and yet far too little for the next ten.

• *Apollo 11* astronaut Neil A. Armstrong, address to joint session of Congress, September 16, 1969.

1842. The trouble with scientists is that they can't leave well enough alone.

• Art Buchwald, *Getting High in Government Circles,* 1971.

1843. Every great advance in science has issued from a new audacity of imagination.

• John Dewey, *The Quest for Certainty,* 1929.

1844. Men love to wonder, and that is the seed of our science.

• Ralph Waldo Emerson, *Society and Solitude:* Works and Days, 1870.

1845. . . . man is still the most extraordinary computer of all.

• President John F. Kennedy, speech in Washington honoring astronaut L. Gordon Cooper, Jr., May 21, 1963, after successful space flight.

1846. The language of science is universal, and perhaps scientists have been the most international of all professions in their outlook.

• President John F. Kennedy, speech in Washington, D.C., October 22, 1963.

1847. Science is nothing but developed perception, interpreted intent, common sense rounded out and minutely articulated.

• George Santayana, *The Life of Reason, Volume V, Reason in Science,* 1906.

1848. Our science and industry owe their strength to the spirit of free inquiry and the spirit of free enterprise that characterize our country.

• President Harry S Truman, letter to Senator Brien McMahon of Connecticut, February 1, 1946, supporting the Senator's bill to set up an Atomic Energy Commission of civilians to control man's most fearsome weapon.

1849. The Congress shall have Power . . . to promote the Progress of Science and useful Arts, by securing for limited Times to Authors and Inventors the exclusive Right to their respective Writings and Discoveries . . .

• Constitution of the United States, Article I, Section 8, adopted by the Constitutional Convention of 1787, ratified June 21, 1788 and put into effect March 4, 1789.

SEASONS

1851. The melancholy days are come, the saddest of the year, / Of wailing winds, and naked woods, and meadows brown and sere.

• William Cullen Bryant, "The Death of the Flowers," 1825.

1852. Hot midsummer's petted crone, / Sweet to me thy drowsy tone / Tells of countless sunny hours, / Long days, and solid banks of flowers . . .

• Ralph Waldo Emerson, "The Humblebee," 1839.

1853. Oh, the long and dreary Winter! / Oh, the cold and cruel Winter!

• Henry Wadsworth Longfellow, *The Song of Hiawatha,* 1855.

1854. Came the Spring with all its splendor, / All its birds and all its blossoms, / All its flowers and leaves and grasses.

• Henry Wadsworth Longfellow, *The Song of Hiawatha,* 1855.

1855. What is so rare as a day in June?

• James Russell Lowell, *The Vision of Sir Launfal,* 1848.

1856. No price is set on the lavish summer; / June may be had by the poorest comer.

• James Russell Lowell, *The Vision of Sir Launfal,* 1848.

1857. When the frost is on the punkin . . .

• James Whitcomb Riley, "When the Frost Is on the Punkin," 1883.

1858. We remember autumn to best advantage in the spring; the finest aroma of it reaches us then.

• Henry D. Thoreau, *Journal,* May 10, 1852.

SEX

1861. The Greeks Had a Word for It.

• Title of play by Zoe Akins, 1929.

1862. . . . men and women do not always love in accordance with the prayer . . .

• Sinclair Lewis, speech accepting the Nobel Prize for Literature in Stockholm, December 10, 1930, the first time this award had gone to an American writer.

1863. *Gentlemen Prefer Blondes.*

• Title of book by Anita Loos, 1925.

1864. There is probably no sensitive heterosexual alive who is not preoccupied with his latent homosexuality.

• Norman Mailer, *Advertisements for Myself,* "The Homosexual Villain," 1959.

1865. Adam's rib simply isn't the sedate sanctum that it once was. Eve's pill has changed all that.

• Senator Margaret Chase Smith, speech to a women's group in Washington, D.C., about the birth control pill, July 16, 1969.

1866. Whatever may befall me, I trust that I may never lose my respect for purity in others. . . . Can I walk with one who by his jests and by his habitual tone reduces the life of men and women to a level with that of cats and dogs?

• Henry D. Thoreau, *Journal,* April 12, 1852.

1867. Human sexuality is a gift of God, to be accepted with thanksgiving and used with reverence and joy.

• Interfaith Commission on Marriage and Family Life (National Council of Churches of Christ, U.S. Catholic Conference and Synagogue Council of America), disseminated in the 1960's.

SOCIETY

1871. There never has yet existed a wealthy and civilized society in which one portion of the community did not, in point of fact, live on the labor of the other.

• Senator John C. Calhoun of South Carolina, speech defending slavery, in the U.S. Senate, 1837.

1872. All men plume themselves on the improvement of society, and no man improves. Society never advances. It recedes as fast on one side as it gains on the other. It undergoes continual changes; it is barbarous, it is civilized, it is christianized, it is rich, it is scientific; but this change is not amelioration. For every thing that is given something is taken. Society acquires new arts and loses old instincts.

• Ralph Waldo Emerson, *Essays, First Series:* Self-Reliance, 1841.

1873. No society seems ever to have succumbed to boredom. Man has developed an obvious capacity for surviving the pompous reiteration of the commonplace.

• John K. Galbraith, *The Affluent Society,* 1958.

1874. . . . it is a good world on the whole; that it has been framed on a principle of benevolence, and more pleasure than pain dealt out to us.

• Thomas Jefferson, letter to John Adams, April 8, 1816.

1875. The great society is a place where men are more concerned with the quality of their goals than the quantity of their goods.

• President Lyndon B. Johnson, speech at Ann Arbor, Mich., May 22, 1964. The "great society" became the avowed goal of the Johnson administration, before increasing involvement in Vietnam disrupted this domestic objective.

1876. . . . we are a society on the move. We are in the early stages of the Second American Revolution. What began in part as the black revolution and the youth revolution has spread to some extent throughout virtually all elements of our society.

• John D. Rockefeller, III, lecture at University of Arkansas, Fayetteville, Ark., May 2, 1973.

1877. The men with the muckrakes are often indispensable to the well-being of society, but only if they know when to stop raking the muck.

• President Theodore Roosevelt, speech at the laying of the cornerstone for a new office building for the House of Representatives, Washington, D.C., April 14, 1906.

1878. The society of excess profits for some and small returns for others, the society in which a few prey upon the many, the society in which a few took great advantage and many took great disadvantage, must pass.

• Wendell L. Willkie, Republican Presidential nominee, speech in Springfield, Ill., October 18, 1940.

1879. High society is for those who have stopped working and no longer have anything important to do.

• President Woodrow Wilson, speech in Washington, D.C., February 24, 1915.

SPEED

1881. In skating over thin ice our safety is in our speed.

• Ralph Waldo Emerson, *Essays, First Series:* Prudence, 1841.

1882. Nothing is more vulgar than haste.

• Ralph Waldo Emerson, *The Conduct of Life:* Behavior, 1860.

1883. Lost time is never found again.

• Benjamin Franklin, *The Way to Wealth,* 1757.

1884. . . . with all deliberate speed . . .

• U.S. Supreme Court order, following up decision in Brown v. Board of Education of Topeka (May 17, 1954), used these words to describe how promptly they wanted schools desegregated, May 31, 1955.

1885. The hurrieder I go the behinder I get.

• Anonymous Pennsylvania Dutch saying.

1886. Speeders lose their licenses.

• Warning sign on highways in various states, mainly since World War II.

SPORT

(See also Baseball, Football, Golf)

1891. The bigger they come, the harder they fall.

• Bob Fitzsimmons, comment in San Francisco prior to his bout with heavyweight boxing champion Jim Jeffries, July 25, 1902. The remark has been widely quoted ever since, but the fact is that the bigger man, Jeffries, won the fight in eight rounds with a knockout. British-born Fitzsimmons had previously lost the title to Jeffries and was trying to regain it.

1892. A boxing match is like a cowboy movie. There's got to be good guys and there's got to be bad guys. That's what people pay for—to see the bad guys get beat.

• Attributed to ex-heavyweight champion Sonny Liston in his obituary in *The New York Times,* January 7, 1971.

1893. Winning isn't everything. It's the only thing.

• Attributed to Vincent Lombardi when he was coaching the Green Bay Packers football team in the 1960's.

1894. He can run but he can't hide.

• Heavyweight boxing champion Joe Louis, comment before bout with Billy Conn, which took place June 19, 1946 in New York City. Louis was right. He won by a knockout in eight rounds.

1895. . . . I do not in the least object to a sport because it is rough.

• President Theodore Roosevelt, speech in Cambridge, Mass., February 23, 1907. As the apostle of "the strenuous life" President Roosevelt, far from objecting, was much in favor of rough, combative sports.

1896. Week-end warriors.

• Anonymous, probably originated in the 1930's but not in common usage until the 1950's, referring to men who took all their sports exercise on Saturday and Sunday, particularly in competitive sports such as tennis and golf.

SUCCESS
(See also Achievement)

1901. *Treadmill to Oblivion.*

• Fred Allen, title of the comedian's autobiographical reminiscences, 1954.

1902. Success has ruined many a man.

• Benjamin Franklin, *Poor Richard's Almanac,* 1752.

1903. . . . happiness, I am sure from having known many successful men, cannot be won simply by being counsel for great corporations and having an income of fifty thousand dollars. An intellect great enough to win the prize needs other food besides success.

• Judge Oliver Wendell Holmes, Jr. of the Supreme Judicial Court of Massachusetts, "The Path of the Law," speech in Boston, January 8, 1897.

1904. The heights by great men reached and kept / Were not attained by sudden flight. / But they, while their companions slept, / Were toiling upward in the night.

• Henry Wadsworth Longfellow, "The Ladder of St. Augustine," 1850.

1905. . . . failure is not an American habit.

• Governor Franklin D. Roosevelt of New York, speech as Democratic Presidential candidate in San Francisco, September 23, 1932.

1906. Why should we be in such desperate haste to succeed, and in such desperate enterprises? If a man does not keep pace with his companions, perhaps it is because he hears a different drummer.

• Henry D. Thoreau, *Walden,* 1854.

1907. I have learned that success is to be measured not so much by the position that one has reached in life as by the obstacles which he has overcome while trying to succeed.

• Booker T. Washington, *Up from Slavery,* 1901.

SUPERSTITION

1911. Creditors are a superstitious sect; great observers of set days and times.

• Benjamin Franklin, *The Way to Wealth,* 1757.

1912. You cannot educate a man wholly out of the superstitious fears which were early implanted in his imagination . . .

• Oliver Wendell Holmes, *The Poet at the Breakfast-Table,* 1872.

1913. A superstition is something that has been left to stand over, like unfinished business, from one session of the world's witenagemot to the next.

• James Russell Lowell, *Among My Books,* 1870. The witenagemot, literally an Anglo-Saxon council, figuratively denotes a council of wise men.

1914. Men are probably nearer to the essential truth in their superstitions than in their science.

• Henry D. Thoreau, *Journal,* June 27, 1852.

1915. . . . the greatest minds yield in some degree to the superstitions of their age.

• Henry D. Thoreau, *Journal,* January 3, 1853.

SYMBOLS

1921. ". . . I lift my lamp beside the golden door!"

• Emma Lazarus, "The New Colossus," poem written in 1883 and later inscribed at the base of the Statue of Liberty.

1922. Don't tread on me.

• Used with drawing of a rattlesnake as a flag for the colonists early in the American Revolution, 1775 and 1776.

1923. Remember the Alamo!

• Battle cry of Texas in its war with Mexico after the fall of the Alamo and the death of its entire garrison in March, 1836. It became a triumphant motto at the Battle of San Jacinto, April 21, 1836, in which the Texans routed a Mexican Army and captured General Santa Anna.

1924. Remember the *Maine!*

• Slogan of the Spanish-American War in 1898, prompted by the blowing up of the U.S. battleship *Maine* mysteriously in the harbor of Havana, Cuba, February 15, 1898.

1925. Remember Pearl Harbor!

• Slogan of World War II, reminding people of Japanese surprise attack on Pearl Harbor, Hawaii, December 7, 1941, the event which brought the United States into World War II.

1926. The full dinner pail.

• Popularized in 1900 Presidential election by the motto of the McKinley-Roosevelt Republican ticket: "Four More Years of the Full Dinner Pail."

TACTICS

1931. Get there fustest with the mostest.

• Attributed to Confederate General Nathan Bedford Forrest as a description of his military tactics in the Civil War.

1932. I propose to fight it out on this line if it takes all summer.

• Lieutenant General U. S. Grant, dispatch to General Henry W. Halleck from Virginia, May 11, 1864, reporting on his plans in what was to be the long and bloody Battle of the Wilderness in the Civil War.

1933. Hit 'em where they ain't.

• Willie Keeler, great baseball placement hitter, summarized his approach at bat this way, around the turn of the century.

1934. Don't fire till you see the whites of their eyes.

• Generally credited to General Israel Putnam, though sometimes to Colonel William Prescott, at the Battle of Bunker Hill (actually took place on Breed's Hill) in Boston in the American Revolutionary War, June 17, 1775.

1935. Walk softly and carry a big stick.

• Inaccurate but popular version of statement by Vice President Theodore Roosevelt at Minnesota State Fair, September 2, 1901. See quotation 793 for correct text.

TAXES

1941. Everybody ought to pay some tax. It is wrong to have a democracy in which all the people don't contribute.

• Secretary of the Treasury-Designate John B. Connally, Jr., testimony before Senate Finance Committee, Washington, D.C., January 28, 1971.

1942. . . . in this world nothing is certain but death and taxes.

• Benjamin Franklin, letter to Jean-Baptiste Leroy, November 13, 1789.

1943. The wisdom of man never yet contrived a system of taxation that would operate with perfect equality.

• President Andrew Jackson, Proclamation to the People of South Carolina, December 10, 1832. President Jackson was delivering a warning against the doctrine of states' rights and secession. South Carolina had espoused the idea of nullification, seeking to nullify the Tariff of 1832; this was Jackson's reply. No state, he said, could nullify a Federal statute.

1944. Taxation is, in fact, the most difficult function of government—and that against which their citizens are most apt to be refractory.

• Thomas Jefferson, letter to bookdealer Joseph Milligan, April 6, 1816.

1945. The power to tax is the power to live, at least as far as local government is concerned.

• Mayor John V. Lindsay of New York City, at State commission hearing in New York City, April 26, 1971.

1946. . . . the power to tax involves the power to destroy . . .

• Chief Justice John Marshall, Supreme Court decision in McCulloch v. Maryland, March 6, 1819. This was a historic and precedental case in establishing the power of the Supreme Court to interpret the Constitution.

1947. Nothing brings home to a man the feeling that he personally has an interest in seeing that Government revenues are not squandered, but intelligently expended, as the fact that he contributes individually a direct tax, no matter how small, to his Government.

• Secretary of the Treasury Andrew Mellon, Annual Report, 1925.

1948. Taxation without representation is tyranny.

• Probably a paraphrase, used years later to describe what James Otis had said in arguing against writs of assistance before the Superior Court of Massachusetts in February 1761. The writs had been sought to enforce royal excise taxes.

1949. Taxes, after all, are the dues that we pay for the privilege of membership in an organized society.

• President Franklin D. Roosevelt, speech in Worcester, Mass., October 21, 1936.

1950. Our tax laws, as we who bear them know, are written to punish the poor and pardon the rich.

• Harriet Van Horne, *Never Go Anywhere Without a Pencil,* 1972.

TIME

(See also Advertising, Fame)

1951. Backward, turn backward, O Time, in your flight, / Make me a child again, just for tonight.

• Elizabeth Chase Akers, "Rock Me to Sleep, Mother," 1860.

1952. This time, like all times, is a very good one, if we but know what to do with it.

• Ralph Waldo Emerson, "The American Scholar," 1837.

1953. . . . time is money.

• Benjamin Franklin, *Advice to a Young Tradesman,* 1748.

1954. Lost Time is never found again . . .

• Benjamin Franklin, *The Way to Wealth,* 1757.

1955. Art is long, and Time is fleeting.

• Henry Wadsworth Longfellow, "A Psalm of Life," 1839.

1956. Time makes more converts than reason.

• Thomas Paine, "Common Sense," 1776.

1957. Never before have we had so little time in which to do so much.

• President Franklin D. Roosevelt, radio address, February 23, 1942.

1958. Time is but the stream I go a-fishing in.

• Henry D. Thoreau, *Walden,* 1854.

1959. That's what it was to be alive . . . to spend and to waste time, as though you had a million years.

• Thornton Wilder, "Our Town," 1938. Wilder combined careers as a novelist and a playwright, with "Our Town" as one of his great dramas.

1960. . . . time is the longest distance between two places.

• Tennessee Williams, "The Glass Menagerie," 1945.

TRADITION

(See also Custom)

1961. I am ashamed to think how easily we capitulate to badges and names, to large societies and dead institutions.

• Ralph Waldo Emerson, *Essays, First Series:* Self-Reliance, 1841.

1962. . . . I go (always other things being equal) for the man who inherits family traditions and the cumulative humanities of at least four or five generations.

• Oliver Wendell Holmes, *The Autocrat of the Breakfast-Table,* 1858.

1963. Look not mournfully into the Past. It comes not back again.

• Henry Wadsworth Longfellow, *Hyperion,* 1839.

1964. This American government, what is it but a tradition . . . endeavoring to transmit itself unimpaired to posterity. . . ?

• Henry D. Thoreau, *Civil Disobedience,* 1849.

1965. Tradition wears a snowy beard. Romance is always young.

• John Greenleaf Whittier, "Mary Garvin," mid-19th century.

TRAVEL

(See also Airplanes, Automobiles)

1971. Travelling is a fool's paradise.

• Ralph Waldo Emerson, *Essays, First Series:* Self-Reliance, 1841.

1972. . . . travellers change their guineas, but not their characters. The bore is the same, eating dates under the cedars of Lebanon, as over a plate of baked beans in Beacon Street.

• Oliver Wendell Holmes, *The Autocrat of the Breakfast-Table,* 1858.

1973. Travelling . . . makes men wiser, but less happy.

• Thomas Jefferson, letter to his nephew, Peter Carr, August 10, 1787. Jefferson had been in France for several years as the U.S. Minister when he made this observation.

1974. I love to sail forbidden seas, and land on barbarous coasts.

• Herman Melville, *Moby Dick,* 1851.

1975. We cannot learn to love other tourists—the laws of nature forbid it . . .

• Agnes Repplier, *Compromises,* 1904.

1976. . . . the swiftest traveller is he that goes afoot.

• Henry D. Thoreau, *Walden,* 1854.

1977. Strong and content I travel the open road.

• Walt Whitman, "Song of the Open Road," 1856.

TROUBLE

1981. If a man could have half his wishes, he would double his troubles.

• Benjamin Franklin, *Poor Richard's Almanac,* 1752.

1982. Trouble springs from idleness, and grievous toil from needless ease.

• Benjamin Franklin, *The Way to Wealth,* 1757.

1983. Women like to sit down with trouble as if it were knitting.

• Ellen Glasgow, *The Sheltered Life,* 1932.

1984. Now let none of us in any section look with prideful righteousness on the troubles in another section or the problems of our neighbors.

• President Lyndon B. Johnson, address to joint session of Congress on voting rights, March 15, 1965.

1985. . . . there are no gains without pains.

• Governor Adlai E. Stevenson of Illinois, acceptance speech at Democratic National Convention in Chicago upon receiving Presidential nomination, July 26, 1952. He was using a phrase from Benjamin Franklin.

1986. Nobody knows the trouble I've seen . . .

• Nineteenth century American Negro spiritual.

TRUTH

1991. . . . the deepest truths are best read between the lines . . .

• A. Bronson Alcott, *Concord Days:* "June," 1872.

1992. Truth, crushed to earth, shall rise again . . .

• William Cullen Bryant, "The Battle-Field," 1837.

1993. Truth brings the elements of liberty. . . . Truth makes man free.

• Mary Baker Eddy, *Science and Health,* 1875.

1994. No man thoroughly understands a truth until he has contended against it.

• Ralph Waldo Emerson, *Essays, First Series:* Compensation, 1841.

1995. Truth is tough. It will not break, like a bubble, at a touch; nay, you may kick it about all day like a football, and it will be round and full at evening.

• Oliver Wendell Holmes, *The Professor at the Breakfast-Table,* 1860.

1996. . . . the best test of truth is the power of the thought to get itself accepted in the competition of the marketplace . . .

• Associate Justice Oliver Wendell Holmes, Jr., dissenting opinion in Supreme Court, Abrams v. U.S., November 10, 1919. The case involved charges against proponents of Russian propaganda in this country.

1997. . . . His Truth is marching on.

• Julia Ward Howe, "Battle Hymn of the Republic," 1862. Written to the tune of "John Brown's Body," the song ascribed the truth that was marching on to the cause of the North in the Civil War. Only years later did it become accepted as a patriotic classic for the entire nation.

1998. . . . truth is stronger than error . . .

• Henry D. Thoreau, "Civil Disobedience," 1849.

1999. I never give them hell. I just tell the truth, and they think it is hell.

• President Harry S Truman, response during the 1948 Presidential campaign when greeted at campaign rallies with the cry from the crowd, "Give 'em hell, Harry!"

2000. There is nothing so powerful as truth—and often nothing so strange.

• Senator Daniel Webster, attributed to his argument on the murder of a Captain White, April 6, 1830.

UTOPIA

2001. Utopian expectations grow and make for a hard life; they stir up the resigned emotions and induce a perpetual futurism.

• Jacques Barzun, *Science: The Glorious Entertainment,* 1964.

2002. A human being always compares any action or object with somewhat he calls the Perfect: that is to say, not with any action or object now existing in nature, but with a certain Better existing in the mind.

• Ralph Waldo Emerson, "Human Culture," lecture in 1837.

2003. No human ideal is ever perfectly attained, since humanity itself is not perfect.

• Republican Presidential nominee Herbert Hoover, speech in Madison Square Garden, New York City, October 22, 1928.

2004. I please myself with imagining a State at last which can afford to be just to all men, and to treat the individual with respect as a neighbor; which even would not think it inconsistent with its own repose if a few were to live aloof from it, not meddling with it, nor embraced by it, who fulfilled all the duties of neighbors and fellow men. A State which bore this kind of fruit, and suffered it to drop off as fast as it ripened, would prepare the way for a still more perfect and glorious State, which also I have imagined, but not yet anywhere seen.

• Henry D. Thoreau, "Civil Disobedience," 1849.

VIOLENCE

2011. Of all the tasks of government, the most basic is to protect its citizens against violence.

• Secretary of State John Foster Dulles, speech in New York City, April 22, 1957. This speech came the month after Congress approved the Eisenhower Doctrine which authorized economic and military aid to stop Communist aggression in the middle east.

2012. It is organized violence on top which creates individual violence at the bottom.

• Emma Goldman, statement at her trial for working against military conscription during World War I, June 15, 1917. Miss Goldman was an anarchist leader. After two years in prison, she was deported.

2013. History shows us, demonstrates that nothing, nothing prepares the way for tyranny more than the failure of public officials to keep the streets safe from bullies and marauders.

• Senator Barry M. Goldwater of Arizona, accepting the Republican Pesidential nomination in San Francisco, July 16, 1964.

2014. When a fact can be demonstrated, force is unnecessary; when it cannot be demonstrated, force is infamous.

• Robert G. Ingersoll, *Prose-Poems and Selections,* 1884. Ingersoll was one of the great orators of his time and one of his time's most notable agnostics.

2015. Democracy will never solve its problems at the end of a billy club.

• President Lyndon B. Johnson, speech in Washington, D.C., July 28, 1964, referring to the rise of racial unrest and confrontation.

VOTING

2021. Voting is the first duty of democracy.

• President Lyndon B. Johnson, speech in Washington, D.C., August 11, 1964.

2022. The ignorance of one voter in a democracy impairs the security of all.

• President John F. Kennedy, speech in Nashville, Tenn., May 18, 1963.

2023. The ballot is stronger than the bullet.

• Abraham Lincoln, speech in May 1856 in Illinois. (History is not sure of the date, place or absolute correctness of the phraseology; some of Lincoln's speeches in this period were reported days later, without specific word-for-word texts. It is known, however, that he was speaking out strongly against the violence over the slavery issue in Kansas.) He used the comparison of the ballot and the bullet a number of times thereafter.

2024. Inside the polling booth every American man and woman stands as the equal of every other American man and woman. There they have no superiors. There they have no masters save their own minds and consciences.

• President Franklin D. Roosevelt, speech in Worcester, Mass., October 21, 1936.

2025. Nobody will ever deprive the American people of the right to vote except the American people themselves.

• President Franklin D. Roosevelt, radio speech, October 5, 1944. This campaign-time comment was not mere oratory. The fact is that not once in the twentieth century have even 65 percent of those eligible to vote actually cast their ballots in a Presidential election, up to and including 1972.

2026. Even *voting* for the right is *doing* nothing for it.

• Henry D. Thoreau, "Civil Disobedience," 1849.

WAR and WARS

(See also Armed Forces, Peace, Symbols)

2031. Boys are the cash of war. Whoever said / We're not free-spenders doesn't know our likes.

• John Ciardi, *This Strangest Everything,* "New Year's Eve," 1966.

2032. There is no greater pacifist than the regular officer. Any man who is forced to turn his attention to the horrors of the battlefield, to the grotesque shapes that are left there for the burying squads—he doesn't want war!

• General of the Army Dwight D. Eisenhower, speech in New York City, June 19, 1945.

2033. By the rude bridge that arched the flood, / Their flag to April's breeze unfurled, / Here once the embattled farmers stood, / And fired the shot heard round the world.

• Ralph Waldo Emerson, "Concord Hymn," written for the dedication of the Battle Monument at Concord, Mass., April 19, 1837 in memory of the Battle of Lexington and Concord that launched the American Revolutionary War on that date in 1775.

2034. There never was a good war or a bad peace.

• Benjamin Franklin, letter to Josiah Quincy, September 11, 1783. Many sources give the date as 1773, but Carl Van Doren's biography of Franklin confirms 1783 as the date. Since the Treaty of Paris that ended the American Revolutionary War was formally signed on

September 3, 1783 and Franklin was both a prime mover and a signer of the Treaty, the 1783 date seems particularly pertinent.

2035. Older men declare war. But it is youth that must fight and die.

• Herbert Hoover, speech at Republican National Convention in Chicago, June 27, 1944.

2036. It is well that war is so terrible—we would grow too fond of it.

• General Robert E. Lee, remark to General James Longstreet, Fredericksburg, Va., December 13, 1862. Lee's Confederate forces at the Battle of Fredericksburg that day inflicted 12,000 casualties on the Union Army as the Civil War raged.

2037. I know war as few other men now living know it, and nothing to me is more revolting. I have long advocated its complete abolition, as its very destructiveness on both friend and foe has rendered it useless as a means of settling international disputes. . . . In war there is no substitute for victory.

• General of the Army Douglas MacArthur, speech to joint session of Congress, April 19, 1951, after President Harry S. Truman had dismissed him from command in the Korean War.

2038. . . . if they mean to have a war, let it begin here.

• Captain John Parker, commander of the minute men at Lexington, Mass., as his forces confronted the British on April 19, 1775. He told his men on the Green to stand firm, not to fire unless fired upon and then added the instructions that sadly came true. The war did indeed begin there as the Battle of Lexington and Concord launched the American Revolution.

2039. There is many a boy here today who looks on war as all glory, but boys, it is all hell.

• General William T. Sherman, speech to convention of the Grand Army of the Republic, the organization of Union veterans of the Civil War, in Columbus, O., August 11, 1880. General Sherman's statement is often quoted in paraphrase as "War is hell."

2040. For it is all too obvious that if we do not abolish war on this earth, then surely, one day, war will abolish us from the earth.

• Harry S Truman, comment in Independence, Mo., January 25, 1966.

WASHINGTON, GEORGE

2041. The father of his country.

• Believed to have been used first by Francis Bailey in *The Lancaster Almanack,* 1779.

2042. To contemplate his unselfish devotion to duty, his courage, his patience, his genius, his statesmanship and his accomplishments for his country and the world, refreshes the spirit, the wisdom and the patriotism of our people.

• President Herbert Hoover, proclamation for Washington's 200th birthday, issued February 2, 1932.

2043. . . . never did nature and fortune combine more perfectly to make a man great . . .

• Thomas Jefferson, letter to Dr. Walter Jones, January 2, 1814.

2044. . . . first in war, first in peace, first in the hearts of his countrymen.

• Henry ("Light Horse Harry") Lee, text of resolution introduced in Congress by John Marshall December 19, 1799, five days after Washington's death. Representative Marshall introduced Representative Lee's resolution because Lee was absent from the House that day.

2045. Washington is the mightiest name on earth—long since mightiest in the cause of civil liberty; still mighticst in moral reformation.

• Abraham Lincoln, speech in Springfield, Ill., February 22, 1842. The subject of moral reformation was a timely one, because on this day Lincoln delivered the Washington's Birthday address to Springfield's Washingtonian Temperance Society, whose membership had been described as including a fair number of reformed drunkards.

2046. That nation has not lived in vain which has given the world Washington and Lincoln, the best great men and the greatest good men whom history can show.

• Senator Henry Cabot Lodge of Massachusetts, speech in Boston, February 12, 1909.

WEALTH
(See also Money)

2051. One of the troubles with an affluent society is that the more affluent everyone gets, the less anyone wants to do.

• Art Buchwald, *Getting High in Government Circles,* 1971.

2052. The problem of our age is the proper administration of wealth, so that the ties of brotherhood may still bind together the rich and poor in harmonious relationship.

• Andrew Carnegie, "Wealth," 1889. Carnegie, one of the wealthiest men of his time, had some very positive ideas about the way wealth should be used to do good.

2053. The man who dies thus rich dies disgraced.

• Andrew Carnegie, "Wealth," 1889. In a nutshell, this was Carnegie's call for putting money back to work in philanthropy from generation to generation.

2054. It requires a great deal of boldness and a great deal of caution to make a great fortune, and when you have got it, it requires ten times as much wit to keep it.

• Ralph Waldo Emerson, *The Conduct of Life:* Power, 1860.

2055. *The Affluent Society.*

• John K. Galbraith, title of his book on what was described as "the economics of opulence," 1958.

2056. Put not your trust in money, but put your money in trust.

• Oliver Wendell Holmes, *The Autocrat of the Breakfast-Table,* 1858.

2057. Few rich men own their own property. The property owns them.

• Robert G. Ingersoll, speech in New York City, October 29, 1896. The son of a midwestern minister, Ingersoll was the most prominent agnostic of his day, but despite his preeminence as an orator and lecturer he was not a rich man; he was not owned by his property.

2058. The loved and the rich need no protection—they have many friends and few enemies.

• Wendell Phillips, speech in Boston, December 21, 1860.

2059. I don't want to be a millionaire. I just want to live like one.

• Attributed to Toots Shor, originally in the 1940's, when he opened his own restaurant in New York and became the favorite "character" of a group of New York sports writers and columnists.

2060. . . . a man is rich in proportion to the number of things he can afford to let alone.

• Henry D. Thoreau, *Walden,* "Where I Lived and What I Lived for," 1854.

WEATHER

2061. Everybody talks about the weather but the only people who do anything about it are hotelkeepers. They pray.

• Gertrude Berg, *Molly and Me,* 1961.

2062. The hard soil and four months of snow make the inhabitant of the northern temperate zones wiser and abler than his fellow who enjoys the fixed smile of the tropics.

• Ralph Waldo Emerson, *Essays, First Series:* Prudence, 1841.

2063. The changes between wet and dry are much more frequent and sudden in Europe than in America. Though we have double the rain, it falls in half the time.

• President Thomas Jefferson, letter to his friend Constantin F. C. de Volney, February 8, 1805.

2064. Into each life some rain must fall, / Some days must be dark and dreary.

• Henry Wadsworth Longfellow, "The Rainy Day," 1841.

2065. There is a sumptuous variety about the New England weather that compels the stranger's admiration—and regret. . . . In the spring I have counted one hundred and thirty-six different kinds of weather inside of four-and-twenty hours.

• Mark Twain (Samuel L. Clemens), speech in New York City, December 22, 1876. He was addressing the New England Society of New York.

2066. Everybody talks about the weather, but nobody does anything about it.

• Probably written by Charles Dudley Warner, it appeared anonymously in the *Hartford Courant* about 1890. Warner was the Connecticut newspaper's editor. It has been wrongly attributed many times to the authorship of Mark Twain.

WELFARE

2071. . . . the toughest proposition ever faced by believers in the free-enterprise system: the need for a frontal attack against Santa Claus . . . the Santa Claus of the free lunch, the government handout, the Santa Claus of something-for-nothing and something-for-everyone.

• Senator Barry M. Goldwater of Arizona, speech in New York City, January 15, 1964.

2072. . . . our American experiment in human welfare has yielded a degree of well-being unparalleled in the world.

• Republican Presidential nominee Herbert Hoover, speech in New York City, October 22, 1928.

2073. One thousand dollars invested in salvaging an unemployable youth today can return forty thousand dollars in his lifetime.

• President Lyndon B. Johnson, State of the Union message to Congress, January 8, 1964.

WEST

2081. Out where the handclasp's a little stronger, / Out where the smile dwells a little longer, / That's where the West begins.

• Arthur Chapman, "Out Where the West Begins," 1917.

2082. Go West, young man, go West and grow up with the country.

• Horace Greeley, *New York Tribune,* July 13, 1865. Used by both Greeley and others at earlier times as well, but generally deriving its popularity from this particular phraseology.

2083. I come . . . from the West where we have always seen the backs of our enemies.

• Major General John Pope of the Union Army, address to his troops in Virginia, July 14, 1862.

2084. We go eastward to realize history and study the works of art and literature, retracing the steps of the race; we go westward as into the future, with a spirit of enterprise and adventure.

• Henry D. Thoreau, "Walking," 1862. Published in *The Atlantic* after his death.

WOMEN

2091. Men are much the same as they were a generation or two ago, but women are changing very fast, in ways we cannot yet see.

• Shana Alexander, *The Feminine Eye,* 1970.

2092. I do not like to see American girls in this generation give up their own individualities in order to attract men, for if men can be attracted by such behavior, then it is alarming.

• Pearl Buck, *My Several Worlds,* 1954.

2093. A sufficient measure of civilization is the influence of good women.

• Ralph Waldo Emerson, *Society and Solitude:* Civilization, 1870.

2094. Man has his will—but woman has her way.

• Oliver Wendell Holmes, *The Autocrat of the Breakfast-Table,* 1858.

2095. It is a good time to be a woman because your country, more now than at any time in its history, is utilizing your abilities and intelligence.

• Claudia Taylor (Mrs. Lyndon B.) Johnson, speech at Texas Women's University, Denton, Texas, March 31, 1964. The basic laws banning discrimination against women in employment were enacted during her husband's administration.

2096. Too often the great decisions are originated and given form in bodies made up wholly of men, or so completely dominated by them that whatever of special value women have to offer is shunted aside without expression.

• Mrs. Eleanor Roosevelt, U.S. Delegate to the United Nations, speech at the U.N. in December 1952.

2097. We hold these truths to be self-evident: that all men and women are created equal . . .

• (For authorship see quotation number 2099.)

2098. The history of mankind is a history of repeated injuries and usurpations on the part of man toward woman, having in direct object the establishment of an absolute tyranny over her.

• (For authorship see quotation number 2099.)

2099. Resolved, that woman is man's equal—was intended to be so by the Creator, and the highest good of the race demands that she should be recognized as such.

• All three quotations above are from the Seneca Falls Declaration of Sentiments and Resolutions, Seneca Falls, N.Y., July 19, 1848. The historic first woman's rights convention there dramatized the demands of women for equality, but the reform was a long time coming.

2100. Woman's virtue is man's greatest invention.

• Cornelia Otis Skinner, "Paris '90," one-woman sketch, 1952.

2101. . . . women are now in an age of unprecedented power in which they are more openly, more candidly, and more honestly pursuing rather than pretending to be pursued—in which they are more openly, candidly, and honestly pursuing whether it be for economic security, personal achievement, or men.

• Senator Margaret Chase Smith of Maine, *Declaration of Conscience,* 1972. In a sardonic footnote, Senator Smith was defeated for re-election in the very year this book was published, leaving the Senate without a single woman member.

2102. The trouble with women, men used to be fond of saying, is that they just don't know how to be gentlemen. Men were fond of saying this a good many years ago. Now they're more likely to complain that women—some women—simply don't know how to be ladies.

• Harriet Van Horne, *Never Go Anywhere Without a Pencil,* 1972.

WORK

2111. Do the day's work.

• Calvin Coolidge, speech as President of Massachusetts state Senate, January 7, 1914.

2112. The right to work, I had assumed, was the most precious liberty that man possesses.

• Associate Justice William O. Douglas of Supreme Court, dissenting opinion in Barsky v. Regents, April 26, 1954.

2113. . . . the time is never lost that is devoted to work.

• Ralph Waldo Emerson, *Society and Solitude:* Success, 1870.

2114. It's hard to grow up when there isn't enough man's work.

• Paul Goodman, *Growing Up Absurd,* 1960.

2115. Wanting to work is so rare a merit that it should be encouraged.

• President Abraham Lincoln, letter to Major Ramsey, October 17, 1861. Mr. Lincoln was commending the case of two young men whose mother had written to him saying her sons wanted to work.

2116. No man is born into the world whose work / Is not born with him . . .

• James Russell Lowell, "A Glance Behind the Curtain," 1843.

2117. Far and away the best prize that life offers is the chance to work hard at work worth doing.

• President Theodore Roosevelt, speech in Syracuse, N.Y., September 7, 1903.

WORRIES

2121. There are two days in the week about which and upon which I never worry. . . . One . . . is Yesterday. . . . And the other day I do not worry about is Tomorrow.

• Robert J. Burdette, "The Golden Day," late 19th century.

2122. How much pain have cost us the evils which have never happened.

• Thomas Jefferson, letter to Thomas Jefferson Smith (no relation), February 21, 1825.

2123. . . . the misfortunes hardest to bear are those which never come.

• James Russell Lowell, *Democracy and Other Addresses,* 1887.

2124. Deep into that darkness peering, long I stood there wondering, fearing, / Doubting, dreaming dreams no mortal ever dared to dream before.

• Edgar Allan Poe, "The Raven," 1845. Worry was a mild word for the state of mind which tormented and inspired Poe.

2125. Worry doesn't pay the rent.

• Widely used during the 1930's; authorship unknown.

YOUTH

(See also Age)

2131. These kids are not going for a revolution, they're going for a revelation. . . . It's a wonder they don't insist on reinventing the wheel because it came out of a bourgeois, decadent society.

• Saul D. Alinsky, quoted in article by Israel Shenker in *The New York Times,* January 6, 1971.

2132. . . . I have been terribly impressed by the youth of America, black and white.

• Eldridge Cleaver, *Soul on Ice,* 1968. Somewhat less impressed with other aspects of U.S. life, the Black revolutionary became a fugitive from American justice as an exile in Algeria.*

2133. America is a country of young men.

• Ralph Waldo Emerson, *Society and Solitude:* Old Age, 1870.

2134. A boy becomes an adult three years before his parents think he does, and about two years after he thinks he does.

• Major General Lewis B. Hershey, Director of Selective Service, December 30, 1951. The ultimate authority on when a boy became a man was, in many instances, the Selective Service System General Hershey headed.

2135. I do not find it easy to send the flower of our youth, our finest young men, into battle. I have spoken to you today of the divisions and the forces and battalions and the units, but I know them all, every one. I have seen them in a thousand streets, of a hundred towns, in every state in this Union—working and laughing and building, and filled with hope and life. I think I know to how much their mothers weep and how their families sorrow.

• President Lyndon B. Johnson, announcing further troop commitments to the war in Vietnam to a Washington press conference, July 28, 1965. At this juncture the U.S. was still fairly optimistic about an early victory in Indochina.

2136. How beautiful is youth! How bright it gleams / With its illusions, aspirations, dreams!

• Henry Wadsworth Longfellow, "Morituri Salutamus," 1875.

2137. If youth be a defect, it is one that we outgrow only too soon.

• James Russell Lowell, speech in Cambridge, Mass., November 8, 1886.

2138. Certainly the time when the young are to be seen and not heard is gone in America—and gone for good.

• President Richard M. Nixon, speech to National 4-H Congress in Chicago, December 1, 1971.

2139. We cannot always build the future for our youth, but we can build our youth for the future.

• President Franklin D. Roosevelt, speech in Philadelphia, September 20, 1940.

INDEXES

KEY WORD INDEX

(Note: Quotation number follows each entry.)

Approaches—old . . . many times do not speak to problems we face today—575, 791
Approbation—We thirst for . . . yet cannot forgive the approver—1611
Aquarius—the next twenty years, the age of . . . of the great year—702
Architects—All are . . . of Fate—1201
Archives—Language is the . . . of history—1201
Areas—how tremendous the . . . are that are as yet unexplored—704
Aristocracy—is always cruel—95
Aristocracy—There is also an artificial . . . founded on wealth and birth—94
Aristocracy—there is a natural . . . among men—94
Aristocracy—This is the harmless, inoffensive, untitled . . . —93
Aristocrat—is the democrat ripe and gone to seed—91
Arm—A shot in the . . . can be fatal—623
Armed—the peace which comes as of right to the just man . . . —1528
Armed—in the holy cause of liberty—809
Armies—banking establishments are more dangerous than standing . . . —642
Armor—the . . . of a righteous cause—281
Arms—the . . . we have been compelled by our enemies to assume —815
Army—and navy are the sword and the shield this nation must carry—103
Army—and Navy forever—104
Army—good sense of the people will always be found to be the best . . . —533, 1543
Army—If the . . . and the Navy ever look on Heaven's scenes—1334
Army—No nation ever had an . . . large enough to guarantee against attack—112
Army—the right way, the wrong way and the . . . way—664
Arrests—Police officers should be judged by quality, not quantity of . . . —1164
Arsenal—We must be the great . . . of democracy—792
Art—civilization without culture and . . . is no civilization—486
Art—displacing religion, has become the justification—121
Art—In free society . . . is not a weapon—126
Art—is a jealous mistress—123
Art—is long and Time is fleeting—127, 1955
Art—it cannot be maintained that dressing has risen to the dignity of an . . . —344, 603
Art—the real . . . of living—1096
Art—We must never forget that . . . is not a form of propaganda—125
Artists—and bohemians have always gravitated to the bottom of the income pyramid—124

Bread—Man does not live by . . . alone—762
Bread—Take not from the mouth of labor the . . . it has earned—1185
Bread—the man who cannot live on . . . and water is not fit to live—761
Breakfast cereal—The idea that you can merchandise candidates like . . . —274
Breakfast table—Life has few pleasanter prospects than a well-provisioned . . . —765
Bridge—By the rude . . . that arched the flood—2033
Broadcasting—has consistently demonstrated a remarkable capacity—252
Broadcasting—The fact that the government licenses . . . —253
Broadcasting—the most powerful social force—251
Brother—of iniquity, father of mischief—874
Brotherhood—crown thy good with . . . —51, 1511
Brotherhood—I believe in the . . . of man, not merely the . . . of white men—1744
Brotherhood—so that the ties of . . . may still bind together the rich and poor—2052
Buck—The . . . stops here—1669
Build—thee more stately mansions, O my soul—133
Build—We cannot always . . . the future for our youth, but we can . . . our youth for the future—2139
Builds—a builder who . . . best when called upon to build greatly —1484
Bullet—ballot is stronger than the . . . —2023
Bullet—no successful appeal from the ballot to the . . . —1766
Bureaucracy—Liberalism should be found not striving to spread . . . —1232
Buried—All men are partially . . . in the grave of custom—493
Burned—many a martyr has been . . . at the stake while the votes were being counted—1374
Business—For the ordinary . . . of life, an ounce of habit is worth a pound of intellect—953
Business—has to prosper before anybody can get any benefit from it—265
Business—It is just as important that . . . keep out of government as that government keep out of . . . —263
Business—The . . . of America is . . . —262
Business—underlies everything in our national life—268
Business—This world is a place of . . . —266
Buy—Never . . . what you do not want because it is cheap—943
Buy—Would you . . . a used car from this man?—190

Cabots—Where the Lowells talk only to . . . —1581
Californians—are a race of people—1583

Choice—between the quick and the dead—141
Choice—Citizens by birth or . . . of a common country—325
Choice—Destiny is a matter of . . . —551
Choosing—freedom to work at jobs of their own . . . —1
Christmas—A good conscience is a continual . . . —405
Church—I do not speak for my . . . on public matters and the . . . does not speak for me—1778
Church—a wall between . . . and state which must be kept high—1771
Church—where every man has the same right to attend or not attend the . . . of his choice—1778
Cigar—What this country really needs is a good five-cent . . . —1413
Circles—Blessed are they who go around in . . . —695
Cities—Burn down your . . . and leave our farms—331
Cities—monuments to man—336
Cities—Thine alabaster . . . gleam—1511
Cities—We will neglect our . . . to our peril—334
Citizen—first requisite of a good . . . —322
Citizen—humblest . . . of all the land—281
Citizen—Political action is the highest responsibility of a . . . —321
Citizen—strict observance of the written laws is doubtless one of the high duties of a good . . . —1214
Citizen—When we assumed the soldier, we did not lay aside the . . . —117, 324
Citizens—by birth or choice of a common country—325
Citizens—that against which their . . . are most apt to be refractory—1944
Citizenship—is man's basic right—323
City—A baseball club is part of the chemistry of the . . . —191
City—A great . . . is that which has the greatest men and women—340
City—in any . . . there are true wildernesses—1262
City—is recruited from the country—332
City—no American . . . has been able to solve its own traffic problem—184
City—No . . . government can make any suburb do anything—334
City—suburbs in search of a . . . —1588
Civil—Be . . . to all—204
Civilization—and profits go hand in hand—261
Civilization—fundamental premise of our American . . . is a belief in the dignity of the individual—52
Civilization—In the . . . of today, literature dominates—1257
Civilization—Law and order lie at the foundations of . . . —1219
Civilization—saving grace of an ugly . . . —121
Civilization—sufficient measure of . . . is the influence of good women—2093

Civilization—without culture and art is no . . . —486
Civilized—Washington, D.C. is no place for a . . . man to spend the summer—1582
Classes—Our Constitution neither knows nor tolerates . . . among citizens—1741
Classes—ultimate extinction of all privileged . . . —906
Clean—an America in which we can have the . . . air, the . . . water—264
Cleaners—a man can be taken to the . . . —467
Clergy—New England, where the . . . long held a monopoly of what passed for learning—1445
Clever—Nothing is always a . . . thing to say—202
Climate—New England has a harsh . . . —1443
Clothe—a land that can feed and . . . the world—1191
Clothes—and manners do not make the man—341
Clothes—Beware of all enterprises that require new . . . —345
Clothes—how far men would retain their relative rank if divested of their . . . —96
Clothes—new . . . are often won and worn after a most painful birth—343
Club—Democracy will never solve its problems at the end of a billy . . . —2015
Club—I won't want to belong to any . . . that will accept me as a member—351
Club—If you want to be a member of the . . . , you have to pay your dues—353
Clubhouse—the players lie in the . . . —894
Coat—a patch on your . . . is better than a writ on your back—511
Coat—a respectable Republican cloth . . . —342
Coerce—Government cannot . . . individual conscience—401
Coin—Peace and justice are two sides of the same . . . —1162
College—Administering a . . . today is playing chess on the *Titanic*—361
College—A . . . diploma is a license to look for a job—367
College—The ideal . . . for me is Mark Hopkins on one end of a log—362
College—The most conservative persons I ever met are . . . undergraduates—365
Colonization—not be considered as subjects for future . . . by any European powers—788
Color-blind—Our Constitution is . . . —1741
Colored—There are no white or . . . signs on the foxholes or graveyards—229
Colored man—is no longer subject to be bought and sold—225
Colors—men of different . . . do not see everything alike—1742

Conservative—It . . . means small change, radical means large bills—1755
Conservative—I'm as . . . as the Constitution, as liberal as Lincoln—1601
Conservative—is a man with two good legs who has never learned to walk—416
Conservative—is an old democrat—413
Conservative—one who does not go far enough—1754
Conservative—The most . . . persons I ever met are college undergraduates—365
Conservative—The true . . . seeks to protect the system of private enterprise—415
Conservatives—Men are . . . when they are least vigorous or most luxurious—412
Conservatives—We expect old men to be . . . —411
Conservatism—What is . . . ?—414
Conservator—The family, that great . . . of national virtue and strength—729
Consolation—freedom seems to me the chief . . . of old age—23
Constitution—chart and compass is the . . . —432
Constitution—conservative as the . . . —1601
Constitution—follows the flag—797
Constitution—has proven itself the most marvelously elastic compilation—427
Constitution—I have taken an oath to do impartial justice according to the . . . —394
Constitution—If there is any principle of the . . . that more imperatively calls for attachment—813
Constitution—is color-blind—1741
Constitution—is what the judges say it is—424
Constitution—I will support and defend the . . . of the United States—1293
Constitution—Keep your eye on the . . . —428
Constitution—laws, when made in pursuance of the . . . , form the supreme law of the land—426
Constitution—Let us then stand by the . . . —431
Constitution—No matter whether the . . . follows the flag or not—461
Constitution—of the United States is a law for rulers and people—422
Constitution—of the United States was made not merely for the generation that then existed, but for posterity—421
Constitution—Our . . . works—423
Constitution—Our peculiar security is the possession of a written . . . —425
Constitution—the people's . . . , the people's government—922

Damn—the torpedoes, full speed ahead—443
Dancer—we need the musician and the . . . to bring beauty and meaning—485
Danger—the role of defending freedom in its hour of maximum . . . —821
Dangerous—banking establishments are more . . . than standing armies—642
Dangerous—The most . . . animal in the U.S.A. is the road hog—188
Dare—Far better it is to . . . mighty things—180
Dare—Those who . . . , do; those who . . . not, do not—8
Dared—men and women who . . . to dissent—581
Darkness—Deep into that . . . peering—2124
Darkness—help the ones in . . . up—317
Day—What is so rare as a . . . in June—1855
Days—Happy . . . are here again—970
Days—There are two . . . in the week about which I never worry—2121
Dead—choice between the quick and the . . . —141
Dead—have neither powers nor rights—1823
Dead—literature clear and cold and pure and very . . . —1254
Dear—John letter—1312
Death—Give me liberty or give me . . . —810
Death—He brought . . . into the world—505
Death—I have a rendezvous with . . . —504
Death—Nothing can happen more beautiful than . . . —507
Death—nothing is certain but . . . and taxes—501
Death—The report of my . . . was an exaggeration—506
Death—Why fear . . . —502
Debate—Let us not be afraid of . . . or dissent—584
Debate—this home of legislative . . . represents human liberty—392
Debt—A national . . . if not excessive will be to us a national blessing—512
Debt—No nation ought to be without a . . . —514
Debt—Oh . . . where is thy sting—516
Debts—It is incumbent on every generation to pay its own . . . —513
Decisions—All . . . should be made as low as possible in the organization—693
Decisions—of the courts on economic and social questions—466
Decisions—Too often the great . . . are originated and given form in bodies made up wholly of men—2096
Declaration—placed in the . . . for future use—526
Decorum—There are few things that so touch us with instinctive revulsion as a breach of . . . —1326
Defeat—gray twilight that knows not victory nor . . . —180
Defeat—is a fact—1171
Defect—If youth be a . . . , it is one that we outgrow—2137

Defense—Millions for . . . but not a cent for tribute—164, 783
Defense—of freedom, like freedom itself, to be one and indivisible—671
Defiance—in . . . of every hazard—815
Defiance—of the law is the surest road to tyranny—1215
Degree—the best of both worlds: a Harvard education and a Yale . . . —363
Degrees—mainly a matter of . . . —1464
Deity—Prosperity is not a . . . to be worshipped—1711
Delayed—Justice . . . is democracy denied—1166
Delayed—Justice . . . is not only justice denied—1167
Delusion—Peace purchased at such a price it is a . . . —1521
Democracy—All the ills of . . . can be cured by more . . . —536
Democracy—arsenal of . . . —792
Democracy—in a republic—56
Democracy—It is wrong to have a . . . in which all the people don't contribute—1941
Democracy—I've never known a country to be starved into . . . —1081
Democracy—Justice delayed is . . . denied—1166
Democracy—most important effect of the frontier has been in promotion of . . . —853
Democracy—No . . . can long survive which does not accept recognition of the right of minorities—1375
Democracy—Not only will we fight for . . . , we will make it more worth fighting for—532
Democracy—that is, a government of all the people—535
Democracy—Voting is the first duty of . . . —2021
Democracy—will never solve its problems at the end of a billy club—2015
Democracy—works only when the people are informed—538
Democrat—aristocrat is the . . . ripe and gone to seed—91
Democrat—conservative is an old . . . —413
Democrat—I am not a member of any organized political party. I am a . . . —544
Democratic—convention is always a political party—545
Democratic—driving force behind our progress is our faith in our . . . institutions—60
Democratic—if the . . . Party cannot be helped by the many who are poor—543
Democratic—In a . . . society like ours—404
Democratic—party is like a mule—81, 541
Democratic—not all people in this world are ready for . . . processes—531
Democratic—sense of what is . . . —1504
Democratic—the ultimate indignity to the . . . process—274
Democratic—When a leader is in the . . . Party he's a boss—1603

Dissent—we may never confuse honest . . . with disloyal subversion—581
Dissipated—It is the luxurious and . . . who set the fashions—605
Distance—Time is the longest . . . between two places—1960
Distinctions—Wit levels all . . . —1072
Distributed—The American system has produced more goods, more widely . . . —1, 301
Divide—the false accusations that . . . us—1520
Divided—A house . . . against itself cannot stand—585
Divided—United we stand, . . . we fall—171
Dividing—By uniting we stand, by . . . we fall—156
Divisiveness—heal the scars of . . . —160
Dixie—To live and die in . . . —383
Do—ask not what your country can . . . for you—1516
Do—ask what you can . . . for your country—1516
Do—difficult we . . . immediately; impossible takes a little longer—6
Do—How . . . you . . . is a lot more friendly than what . . . you . . . —1465
Do—I have taken an oath to . . . impartial justice—394
Do—it is easier to . . . evil than it is to . . . good—4
Do—It's not what you . . . , it's how you . . . it—1156
Do—so little time in which to . . . so much—1957
Do—the day's work—2111
Do—Those who dare, . . . ; those who dare not, . . . not—8
Do—Whenever you are to . . . a thing, ask yourself how you would act—686
Do—you can't . . . anything every day—21
Doctor—God heals and the . . . takes the fees—1352
Doctor—I would not think of having a . . . I didn't like—1351
Doctor—Just what the . . . ordered—1356
Doctor—My liking him won't make him a better . . . —1351
Doctors—are enabling us to live longer and healthier—485
Doctors—cure all kinds of ills except the shock of . . . bills—1357
Doctor's—Health that mocks the . . . rules—976
Doctrine—men and women who dared to dissent from accepted . . . —581
Does—What a man . . . , compared with what he is, is but a small part—1144
Dog—keeps him from broodin' over bein' a . . . —84
Dog—A man's . . . stands by him—83
Dog—a reasonable amount o' fleas is good for a . . . —84
Dog—it is better to be a dead lion than a living . . . —442
Dog—The one absolutely unselfish friend that man can have is his . . . —83

Dreams—There's a long, long trail awinding into the land of my . . . —596
Dreams—We are merchants of . . . —17
Dress—Fond pride of . . . is sure a very curse—602
Dress—to please others—601
Dressing—it cannot be maintained that . . . has risen to the dignity of an art—344, 603
Drink—I'll . . . to that—616
Drink—I would rather forget to . . . than . . . to forget—617
Drinks—are on the house—615
Drinks—He that . . . fast pays slow—612
Drinks—Whether the world would be benefited by banishment of all intoxicating . . . —1702
Drive—carefully; the life you save may be your own—185
Drive—Too many used car buyers . . . a hard bargain—189
Drummer—because he hears a different . . . —1145, 1906
Dues—If you want to be a member of the club, you have to pay your . . . —353
Dull—It is not all books that are as . . . as their readers—1255
Duties—I will well and truthfully discharge the . . . of the office on which I am about to enter—1293
Duties—strict observance of the written laws is doubtless one of the high . . . of a good citizen—1214
Duty—determines destiny—554
Duty—dare to do our . . . as we understand it—1097
Duty—honor, country—116
Duty—of the government itself to find new remedies—1234
Duty—sense of . . . prompts us irresistibly—1563
Duty—those who think they know what is your . . . better than you know it—402
Duty—Voting is the first . . . of democracy—2021
Duty—When . . . whispers low, "Thou must"—403

Eagle—I wish the bald . . . had not been chosen as the representative of our country—82
Ear—Music is invaluable where a person has an . . . —1391
Earlier—the more or less fossilized productions of his . . . years—1252
Early—to bed and . . . to rise—973
Earned—Take not from the mouth of labor the bread it has . . . —1185
Earnest—I am in . . . —562
Earns—Any government, like any family, can for a year spend a little more than it . . . —643
Earth—belongs in usufruct to the living—1823
Earth—is given as common stock for man to labor and live on—1194
Earth—Geography can be defined as "What on . . . "—885

Earth—laughs in flowers—752
Earth—nature's wealth deep under the . . . —637
Earth—these stars of . . . , these golden flowers—753
Earth—We in America have from the beginning been cleaving and baring the . . . —1196
Ease—grievous toil from needless . . . —1982
Easier—to do evil than it is to do good—4
East—is East and West is San Francisco—1583
Eastward—We go . . . to realize history and study—2084
Eat—Kill no more pigeons than you can . . . —764
Eat—to live and not live to . . . —763
Eat—to please thyself, but dress to please others—601
Eccentric—the unorthodox and the . . . —820
Economic—decisions of the court on . . . and social questions depend on their . . . and social philosophy—466
Economy—I am confident that our free and vigorous American . . . can more than hold its own—790
Economy—is always a guarantee of peace—641
Economy—is one of the highest essentials of a free government—641
Editorial—advertisements in a newspaper are more full of knowledge than the . . . columns are—11
Educate—You cannot . . . a man wholly out of superstitious fears—1912
Educating—establish and improve the law for . . . the common people—653
Education—best of both possible worlds: Harvard . . . and Yale degree—363
Education—child's . . . should begin at least one hundred years before he was born—73
Education—consequences of foreign . . . are alarming—652
Education—eating soul food will not solve a single problem of . . . —231
Education—in the field of public . . . the doctrine of "separate but equal" has no place—1745
Education—is perhaps the most important function of state and local government—657
Education—Next in importance to freedom and justice is popular . . . —651
Educational—Our . . . system teaches us not to think—655
Egg—always a best way of doing everything, if it be to boil an . . . —661
Elastic—Constitution has proven itself the most marvelously . . . —427
Elderly—A man of ninety is a great comfort to all his . . . neighbors—503
Elected—If . . . , I will not serve—1668
Elected—you have not . . . me as your President by your ballots—1663
Election Day—Democrats always disagree until . . . —546

Geography—still remains a fact—881
Geritol—Protocol, . . . and alcohol—577
Get—it first and . . . it right—663
Get—there fustest with the mostest—662, 1931
Get—To . . . along, go along—207
Get—What the people want, they generally . . . —1542
Ghetto—the needs of the . . . people are so much clearer to the people—222
Gift—Language was the immediate . . . of God—1204
Gift—The only . . . is a portion of thyself—1561
Girl—every . . . who came along / was sure to come your way—1306
Girls—I do not like to see American . . . give up their individualities—2092
Give—it back to the Indians—1133
Give—up money rather than do an immoral act—206
Giver—We do not quite forgive a . . . —313
Gives—He who . . . himself entirely to his fellow-men—1564
Giving—Thanksgiving is the only kind of . . . some people know—935
Glory—Mine eyes have seen the . . . of the coming of the Lord—1775
Glory—of our institutions—1363
Go—To get along . . . along—207
Go—We . . . eastward to realize history—2084
Go—We . . . westward as into the future—2084
Go—West, young man, . . . West and grow up with the country—2082
Goal—riders in a race do not stop short when they reach the . . . —27
Goals—great society is a place where men are more concerned with the quality of their . . . —1875
Goals—traditional . . . of earning a great deal of money—132
God—bless our mortgaged home—244
God—grants liberty only to those who love it—833
God—heals and the doctor takes the fee—1352
God—helps those who help themselves—1471
God—honest . . . is the noblest work of man—1776
God—In . . . We Trust—1772
God—It is a noble land that . . . has given us—1191
God—Language, as well as the faculty of speech, was the immediate gift of . . . —1204
God—most acceptable service of . . . is doing good to man—1562, 1774
God—one nation, under . . . —741
God—One, with . . . , is always a majority, but—1374
God—putting our trust in . . . —381
God—reigns and the government at Washington still lives—909
God—shed his grace on thee—51
God—So help me . . . —1293
God—So near is . . . to man—403

God—that this nation, under . . . , shall have a new birth of freedom—825
God—Trees are monuments to . . . —336
God—the unseen hand of . . . —742
God—What . . . hath wrought—1154
God's—One on . . . side is a majority—1372
Going—When the . . . gets tough, the tough get . . . —449
Gold—No people in a great emergency ever found a faithful ally in . . . —1385
Gold—you shall not crucify mankind upon a cross of . . . —1182, 1381
Golden—I lift my lamp beside the . . . door—1113
Good—highest . . . of the race demands that woman be recognized as man's equal—2099
Good—If men be . . . , government cannot be bad—918
Good—it is easier to do evil than it is to do . . . —4
Good—man who insists he is as . . . as anybody believes he is better—168, 672
Good—most acceptable service of God is doing . . . to man—1774
Good—No one ever thought they were . . . at the time—1501
Good—old days were a myth—1501
Good—There's got to be . . . guys and there's got to be bad guys—1892
Good—what was . . . for the country was . . . for General Motors—267
Goode—we are bounde by the law of God and men to doe . . . unto all—1782
Good-nature—is worth more than knowledge—151
Goodness—greatness of real . . . and the . . . of real greatness —1241
Goodness—is the only investment that never fails—687
Goods—Advertising moves the . . . —13
Goods—American system has produced more . . . , more widely distributed—1, 301
Goods—place where men are more concerned with quality of goals than the quantity of their . . . —1875
Good will—How cheap a price for the . . . of another—454
Gourmet—anybody who's cut his second molars considers himself a . . . —769
Govern—best system is to have one party . . . and the other party watch—1600
Govern—No man is good enough to . . . another man without that other's consent—915
Government—All religions separated from . . . are compatible with liberty—1773
Government—All religions united with . . . are more or less inimical to liberty—1773

Government—American . . . , what is it but a tradition—1964
Government—Any . . . , like any family, can for a year spend a little more than it earns--643
Government—as a . . . of the people—56
Government—at Washington still lives—909
Government—basis of effective . . . is public confidence—914
Government—best protection against bigger . . . in Washington is better . . . in the states—908
Government—cannot coerce individual conscience—401
Government—Constitution has proven itself the most marvelously elastic compilation of rules of . . . —427
Government—duty of the . . . itself to find new remedies—1234
Government—economy is one of the highest essentials of a free . . . —641
Government—education is perhaps the most important function of state and local . . . —657
Government—Even to observe neutrality you must have a strong . . . —1431
Government—freedom of the press can never be restrained but by despotic . . . —828
Government—free press stands as one of the great interpreters between . . . and people—832
Government—happiness of the people is the sole end of . . . —901
Government—If men be good, . . . cannot be bad—918
Government—If the . . . becomes a law-breaker—471
Government—impersonal hand of . . . can never replace the helping hand of a neighbor—1423
Government—in proportion as the structure of a . . . gives force to public opinion—1180
Government—In the councils of . . . , we must guard against unwarranted influence—101
Government—is a trust—904
Government—is not an exact science—903
Government—is us—920
Government—just as important that business keep out of . . . as that . . . keep out of business—263
Government—labor gathers with loyalty to its . . . —1186
Government—little rebellion now and then is a medicine necessary for the health of . . . —1765
Government—natural progress of things for liberty to yield and . . . to gain ground—912
Government—newspapers without a . . . —1451
Government—night watchman of democratic representative . . . —428
Government—No city . . . can make any suburb do anything—337

Happened—How much pain have cost us the evils which have never . . . —2122
Happiness—cannot be won simply by being counsel for great corporations—1903
Happiness—is speechless—962
Happiness—is the only good—965
Happiness—Man is the artificer of his own . . . —969
Happiness—men's . . . depends upon their expectations—964
Happiness—labors which promote the . . . of mankind—716
Happiness—life, liberty and the pursuit of . . . —521
Happiness—No other sure foundation can be devised for the preservation of freedom and . . . —1178
Happiness—of man, as well as his dignity, consists in virtue—961
Happiness—of the domestic fireside—1014
Happiness—of the people is the sole end of government—901
Happiness—pursuit of . . . —521, 966
Happiness—To fill the hour, that is . . . —963
Happy—Hail, Columbia! . . . land—982
Happy—days are here again—970
Happy—inalienable right of all to be . . . —968
Happy—place to be . . . is here—965
Happy—Thrice . . . is the nation that has a glorious history—994
Happy—time to be . . . is now—965
Happy—Travelling makes men wiser but less . . . —1973
Happy—way to be . . . is to make others so—965
Harder—The bigger they come, the . . . they fall—1891
Hardest—misfortunes . . . to bear are those which never come—2123
Harvard—best of both worlds: a . . . education and a Yale degree—363
Haste—Nothing is more vulgar than . . . —1882
Haste—Why should we be in such desperate . . . to succeed—1906
Hate—Dr. Freud invented mothers and fathers for their children to . . . —721
Hate—next to love the sweetest thing is . . . —1284
Hates—human nature loves more readily than it . . . —1541
Hating—price of . . . other human beings is loving oneself less—153
Hatred—abjure the . . . that consumes people—1520
Head—America cannot be an ostrich with its . . . in the sand—796
Head—Shoot if you must this old, gray . . . —745
Heal—the scars of divisiveness—160
Heals—God . . . , and the doctor takes the fee—1352
Health—first wealth is . . . —972
Health—is not a condition of matter, but of mind—971
Health—is worth more than learning—974
Health—that mocks the doctor's rules—976

Home—Your . . . away from . . . —1054
Homeless—Send these, the . . . , tempest-tossed to me—1113
Homes—As the . . . , so the state—1011
Homosexuality—no sensitive heterosexual alive who is not preoccupied with his latent . . . —1864
Honest—When knaves fall out, . . . men get their goods—1022
Honest—You cannot adopt politics as a profession and remain . . . —1594
Honor—base prosperity which is bought at the price of national . . . —1032
Honor—Duty, . . . , country—116
Honor—First to fight for right and freedom / And to keep our . . . clean—1334
Honor—louder he talked of his . . . , the faster we counted our spoons—1021
Honor—we hold all continents and peoples in equal . . . —671
Honor—we mutually pledge to each other our lives, our fortunes and our sacred . . . —523
Honor—When faith is lost, when . . . dies—1033
Honored—Nor . . . less than he who heirs / Is he who founds a line—75
Honors—A nation reveals itself by the men it . . . —1031
Hope—flatteries of . . . are as cheap and pleasanter than the gloom of despair—1483
Hope—While there's . . . , there's life—138
Hopes—frontier of unfulfilled . . . and threats—851
Hopes—Humanity with all its fears / With all the . . . of future years—865
Hopes—Our hearts, our . . . , our prayers, our tears—735
Hopes—We should not let our fears hold us back from pursuing our . . . —733
Hopes—Whatever America . . . to bring to pass in the world—43, 158
Horsemen—Four . . . of Calumny—1794
Horse-races—difference of opinion that makes . . . —586
Horses—best not to swap . . . while crossing the river—306
Hospitality—consists in a little fire, a little food, an immense quiet—1041
Host—The thoughtful . . . puts the first stain on the dinner tablecloth—1045
Hotel—It used to be a good . . . , but that proves nothing—1051
Hotelkeepers—only people who do anything about the weather are . . . —2061
Hour—To fill the . . . , that is happiness—963
House—A . . . divided against itself cannot stand—585
House—Let me live in my . . . by the side of the road—1062

House—man builds a fine . . . and now he has a master, a task for life—1061
House—ornament of a . . . is the friends who frequent it—1042
Houses—Our . . . are such unwieldy property—1065
Housing—eating soul food will not solve a single problem of . . . —231
How—It's not what you do, it's . . . you do it—1156
Huckstering—greatest meliorator of the world is selfish, . . . trade—1831
Human nature—It is to the credit of . . . that it loves more readily than it hates—1541
Humanity—Be ashamed to die until you have won some victory for . . . —135
Humanity—for which American patriots sacrificed their lives—56
Humanity—itself is not perfect—2003
Humanity—with all its fears / With all the hopes of future years—865
Humble—Be it ever so . . . , there's no place like home—1015
Humble—To be . . . to superiors is duty, to equals courtesy—453
Hunger—does not breed reform; it breeds madness and distempers that make an ordered life impossible—1086
Hunger—Our policy is not directed against any country but against . . . —787
Hungry—A . . . man is not a free man—108
Hungry—People who are . . . are the stuff of which dictatorships are made—1083
Hungry—we feed the . . . because we receive pleasure from these acts—315
Hunter's—limits too narrow for the . . . state—1131
Hurrieder—The . . . I go the behinder I get—1885
Hyphens—Some Americans need . . . in their names because only part of them has come over—1116

Ice—In skating over thin . . . our safety is in our speed—1881
Iceboxes—He could sell . . . to Eskimos—1833
Idea—If the . . . is good, it will survive defeat—1171
Ideal—No human . . . is ever perfectly attained—2003
Idealism—those who have tried to establish a monopoly of . . . —1099
Idealist—America is the only . . . nation in the world—1103
Ideals—of youth are fine, clear and unencumbered—1096
Ideals—we, too, have our . . . —1099
Ideas—individual . . . —820
Ideas—The enemy of the conventional wisdom is not . . . but the march of events—1175

Jails—not enough . . . to enforce a law not supported by the people—1213
Jealous—Art is a . . . mistress—123
Jeanie—I dream of . . . with the light brown hair—593
Jefferson—when Thomas . . . dined alone—1179
Jew—premise of Catholic, Protestant and . . . alike is a belief in the dignity of the individual—52
Job—A college diploma is a license to look for a . . . —364
Job—People who are hungry and out of a . . . are the stuff of which dictatorships are made—1083
Joke—Thou canst not . . . an enemy into a friend, but thou may'st a friend into an enemy—1073
Joke—With Congress, every time they make a . . . it's a law, and every time they make a law it's a . . . —393
Joy—But there is no . . . in Mudville, mighty Casey has struck out—195
Judge—of your natural character by what you do in your dreams—592
Judged—A man is . . . by the company that keeps him—1804
Judged—The way you behave is the way you be . . . —208
Judges—are apt to be naive, simple-minded men—462
Judges—Constitution is what the . . . say it is—424
Judging—I know of no way of . . . the future but by the past—862
Judgment—at 40 the . . . reigns—25
Judgment—independent . . . —820
Judgment—Nothing strengthens the . . . like individual responsibility—407
Judgment—town life makes one more tolerant and liberal in one's . . . —335
Judgment—vote according to the dictates of my . . . —394
Judicial—province and duty of the . . . department—464
Judiciary—an ignorant, a corrupt, or a dependent . . . —465
June—may be had by the poorest comer—1856
June—What is so rare as a day in . . . —1855
Justice—charity must be built on . . . —314
Justice—delayed is democracy denied—1166
Justice—delayed is not only . . . denied, it is also . . . circumvented, . . . mocked and the system of . . . undermined—1167
Justice—Equal and exact . . . for all men—1165
Justice—Expedience and . . . frequently are not even on speaking terms—1168
Justice—has nothing to do with expediency—1170
Justice—He who treats his friends and enemies alike has neither love nor . . . —143
Justice—is always in jeopardy—1169
Justice—Law and order enforced with . . . and by strength—1219

Manners—Fine . . . need the support of fine . . . in others—1322
Manners—Good . . . are the traffic rules for society—1325
Manners—Without good . . . , living would be chaotic—1325
Manners—Your . . . are always under examination—1321
Man's—One . . . cuss is another . . . custom—495
Man's—woman is . . . equal, was intended so by the Creator—2099
Man's—Woman's virtue is . . . greatest invention—2100
Mansions—Build thee more stately . . . , O my soul—133
Manure—It is its natural . . . —816
Many—All communities divide themselves into the few and the . . . —92
Marching—His Truth is . . . on—1997
Mare—The old gray . . . she ain't what she used to be—85
Marines—have landed—1331
Marines—proud to claim the title of United States . . . —1334
Marines—streets are guarded by United States . . . —1334
Marines—Tell it to the . . . —1335
Mark—If you would hit the . . . aim a little above it—134
Markets—artificial rigging and distortion of world commodity . . . —782
Marketplace—competition of the . . . —1996
Mark Hopkins—ideal college for me is . . . on one end of a log—362
Marriage—Is not . . . an open question?—1342
Marriage—should be an equal and permanent partnership—1345
Marriage—community consisting of master, mistress and two slaves, in all two—1341
Marriage—there will be love without . . . —1343
Marriage—Where there's . . . without love—1343
Married—women they . . . when they were young—1344
Martyr—many a . . . has been burned at the stake—1374
Marvel—Yet do I . . . at this curious thing—223
Masses—Your huddled . . . yearning to be free—1113
Master—community consisting of a . . . , a mistress and two slaves, making in all two—1341
Master—now he has a . . . and a task for life—1061
Masters—they have no . . . save their own minds and consciences—2024
Masters—We know no . . . —395
Materialism—no people on earth so relentlessly denounce . . . —492
Materials—strives so hard to share its . . . —492
Materia medica—if the whole . . . could be sunk to the bottom of the sea—1354
Matter—Health is not a condition of . . . but of mind—971
May—every month was . . . —1306
Mayflower—My folks didn't come over on the . . . —1114

Mountains—over our land are protected—637
Mousetrap—build a better . . . —713
Mouth—If I don't open my . . . —24
Mouth—Put your money where your . . . is—877
Much—so little time in which to do so . . . —1957
Muck—if they know when to stop raking the . . . —1455, 1877
Muckrakes—The men with the . . . —1455, 1877
Mugwump—has his mug on one side of the political fence—1604
Mule—Democratic Party is like a . . . —81
Music—is invaluable where a person has an ear—1391
Music—is perpetual—1395
Music—is the universal language of mankind—1392
Music—Let him step to the . . . which he hears—1145
Music—Let . . . swell the breeze—1394
Music—Mind the . . . and the step—1397
Music—the night shall be filled with . . . —1393
Musician—we need the . . . and the dancer—485
Myth—"good old days" were a . . . —1501

Naked—clothe the . . . —315
Names—Some Americans need hyphens in their . . . —1116
Nation—America is the only idealist . . . —1103
Nation—Any . . . can be our friend—789
Nation—As Maine goes, so goes the . . . —1593
Nation—is moving toward two societies—1746
Nation—make this . . . better for those who are to follow us—1520
Nation—neglecting cities we neglect the . . . —334
Nation—new . . . conceived in liberty—674, 824, 992
Nation—No . . . ought to be without a debt—514
Nation—of many nationalities—58
Nation—one . . . under God—744
Nation—one-third of a . . . —1639
Nation—Our . . . is founded on observance of law—1215
Nation—people of the whole . . . doing just as they please—173
Nation—reveals itself—1031
Nation—sovereign . . . of many sovereign states—56
Nation—that destroys its soil—636
Nation—That . . . has not lived in vain—1243
Nation—that this . . . , under God, shall have a new birth of freedom—825
Nation—This . . . will survive—835
Nation—Thrice happy is the . . . that has a glorious history—994
National debt—if not excessive, will be to us a national blessing—512

Old—How do you grow . . . so easily—1271
Old—New arts destroy the . . . —122
Old—none would be . . . —1274
Old—organizations and . . . approaches do not speak to problems we face today—575, 791
Old—Tranquility is the . . . man's milk—28
Old—We expect . . . men to be conservatives—411
Older—men declare war—2035
Oldest—consideration enjoyed by the . . . inhabitant—1272
One—on God's side—1372
One—with God—1374
One-third—of a nation—1064, 1082, 1639
Opiate—621
Opinion—difference of . . . makes horse-races—586
Opinion—error of . . . may be tolerated—534
Opinion—essential that public . . . be enlightened—1180, 1737
Opinion—force of an aroused public . . . —1734
Opinion—Popularity is a matter of . . . —1615
Opinion—Public . . . is a weak tyrant—1735
Opinion—Public . . . is stronger than the legislature—1736
Opinion—structure of a government gives force to public . . . —1180, 1737
Opinion—vagrant . . . without visible means of support—1651
Opinion—weak tyrant compared with our own private . . . —1735
Opinion—When public . . . changes—1732
Opinions—fear the . . . of others and hesitate—294
Opinions—mothball his . . . —111
Opium—sorceries of . . . or wine—622
Opportunities—frontier of unknown . . . —851
Opportunity—age is . . . —30, 1275
Opportunity—another name for . . . —1475
Opportunity—equal . . . to develop our talents—673
Opportunity—I seen my . . . and I took it—1474
Opportunity—land of . . . —1472
Opposition—silencing the voice of . . . —295
Optimist—says the bottle is half full—1485
Oratory—Amplification is the vice of modern . . . —1494
Order—After . . . and liberty—641
Order—breeds habit—951
Order—imposed by fear—1722
Organization—decisions should be made as low as possible in the . . —693
Organizations—old . . . do not speak to the problems—575, 791
Organizes—man is known by the company he . . . —691

Origin—was involved in obscurity—726
Orphans—Late children, early . . . —724
Orthodoxy—heresy of one age becomes the . . . of the next—583
Ostrich—America cannot be an . . . —796
Other—*How the . . . Half Lives*—1637
Out—Three strikes you're . . . —198
Outgrow—one that we . . . only too soon—2137
Outstretched—It only takes an . . . hand—844
Overcome—We shall . . . —1094
Own—Few rich men . . . their . . . property—2057
Owns—If a man . . . land, the land . . . him—1192
Owns—property . . . them—2057

Pace—If a man does not keep . . . with his companions—1906
Pacifism—is not protest only—1529
Pacifist—no greater . . . than the regular officer—2032
Paid—no hard times when labor is well . . . —1183
Pain—How much . . . have cost us the evils which never happened—2122
Pains—no gains without . . . —5, 1985
Painter—we need the poet or the . . . —485
Paleface—speak with forked tongue—1134
Panaceas—History can contribute nothing in the way of . . . —1504
Panic—shouting fire in a theatre and causing a . . . —812
Papers—All I know is what I read in the . . . —1454
Par—finishing under . . . is considered a big success—895
Paradise—Travelling is a fool's . . . —1971
Parents—boy becomes an adult three years before his . . . think he does—2134
Park—part . . . —352
Parking—for the faculty—364
Parking—part . . . lot—352
Parties—Of the two great . . . —1592
Partners—married . . . should provide against injustice of present laws—1345
Partnership—marriage should be an equal and permanent . . . —1345
Party—convention is always a political . . . —545
Party—Democratic . . . is like a mule—81, 541
Party—have one . . . govern—1600
Party—have the other . . . watch—1600
Party—He serves his . . . best—1515
Party—I am not a member of any organized political . . . —544
Party—one of the most all-pervading principles of our . . . —1793
Party-pooper—Better a . . . —624

Peace—promise for the . . . of the world—147
Peace—purchased at the cost of our national integrity—1123, 1521
Peace—soldier above all prays for . . . —115
Peace—upon any other basis than national independence—1123, 1521
Peace—We came in . . . for all mankind—1532
Peace—which comes as of right—1528
Pearl Harbor—Remember . . . —1925
Penalty—Whoever violates laws of nature must pay the . . . —639
Pension—considered the . . . list of the republic a roll of honor—1811
People—abridgement of the freedom of the . . . —826
People—answerable to the . . . —922
People—consent of the . . . —901
People—Constitution is a law for rulers and . . . —422
People—created for the benefit of the . . . —904
People—dissipating to be with . . . too much—1695
People—educating the common . . . —653
People—fool all of the . . . some of the time—944
People—fool some of the . . . all of the time—944
People—given more . . . more true freedom—1
People—good sense of the . . . the best army—533, 1543
People—Government functions do not include the support of the . . . —905
People—government of all the . . ., by all the . . ., for all the . . . —917
People—government of the . . ., by the . . ., for the . . . whose just powers—56
People—government of the . . ., by the . . ., for the . . ., shall not perish—916
People—happiness of the . . . is the sole end of government—901
People—heritage of all the . . . —637
People—insinuation that one . . . or another is inferior—671
People—interpreters between the government and the . . . —832
People—law not supported by the . . . —1213
People—made by the . . . —922
People—made for the . . . —922
People—maintaining in perpetuity the rights of the . . . —906
People—Nobody will ever deprive the American . . . of the right to vote except—2025
People—No . . . can be bound to acknowledge the invisible hand—1779
People—not all . . . in this world are ready for democratic processes—531
People—of the whole nation doing just as they please—173
People—only . . . have rights—1828
People—power is inherent in the . . . —1647

People—really great . . . , proud and high spirited—1032
People—Revolution was in the minds and hearts of the . . . —1761
People--right of the . . . to make and alter their constitutions—430, 921
People—rooting for me—1550
People—second, sober thought of the . . . is seldom wrong—1551
People—should patriotically and cheerfully support their government—905
People—Some . . . get ulcers—696
People—the . . . rule—423
People—that values its privileges above its principles—682
People—themselves choose—1
People—things . . . cannot do for themselves—919
People—This country belongs to the . . . who inhabit it—1546
People—those who fear the . . . —1544
People—turn a free . . . back into hateful paths of despotism—526
People—ungrateful and sinning . . . —465
People—We the . . . of the United States—1552
People—What the . . .want—1542
People—when the . . . are informed—538
People—who make good on their promises—1549
People—who push other . . . around—169
People—who were afraid of risks—996
People—who will try anything once—625
People's choice—275
People's Constitution—922
People's government—922
People's habits—Nothing needs reforming as other . . . —955
Perception—Science is nothing but developed . . . —1847
Perfect—equality affords no temptation—675
Perfect—Humanity itself is not . . . —2003
Perfect—somewhat he calls the . . . —2002
Perils—frontier of unknown opportunities and . . . —851
Period—first . . . of American history—998
Perish—survive or . . . with my country—561
Perish—together as fools—1743
Perpetual—music is . . . —1395
Perpetual Youth—elixir of . . . called alcohol—614
Person—because we are not the . . . involved—214
Perspective—When seen in the . . . of half-a-dozen years or more—606
Perspiration—Genius is one percent inspiration and 99 percent . . . —1151
Persuaded—Men may be . . . —1704
Pessimist—says it is half empty—1485

Race—competition is best for the . . . —371
Race—Every man has pride of . . . —1741
Race—highest good of the . . . —2099
Race—insinuation that one . . . or another is inferior—671
Race—riders in a . . . do not stop short when they reach the goal—27
Race—set one . . . against another—58
Races—enslave all . . . —58
Races—nation of many nationalities, many . . . —58
Radical—By . . . I understand one who goes too far—1754
Radical—is a man with both feet firmly planted in the air—1753
Radical—means large bills—1755
Radical—when someone cries . . . —1751
Radicalism—American . . . is destructive and aimless—1752
Radicalism—means exceeding the political speed limit—1756
Radio—fact that government licenses broadcasting does not make . . . and television instrumentalities of government—253
Rain—double the . . . in half the time—2063
Rain—Into each life some . . . must fall—2064
Range—Home, home on the . . . —1013
Rank—how far men would retain their relative . . . if—96
Rare—Wanting to work is so . . . —2115
Rare—What is so . . . as a day in June—1855
Rascals—Turn the . . . out—1591
Rat race—is run desperately by bright fellows—374
Reactionary—one who won't go at all—1754
Readers—not all books are as dull as their . . . —1255
Reading—dated a new era in his life from . . . a book—1256
Reading public—mature and sophisticated . . . —291
Real estate—What we call . . . —1193
Reality—Their life lacks . . . —488
Really—What this country . . . needs is a good five-cent cigar—1413
Reason—Time makes more converts than . . . —1956
Reason—where . . . is left free to combat it—534
Rebellion—a little . . . now and then—1765
Rebellion—The only justification of . . . is success—1767
Rebels—descended in blood and spirit from revolutionists and . . . —72, 581, 1763
Reconciliation—calls for an act of mercy—160
Recruited—city is . . . from the country—332
Red—Badge of Courage—441
Red—Three cheers for the . . . , white and blue—104
Rediscovering—An old author is constantly . . . himself—1252
Reform—Hunger does not breed . . . —1086
Reformation—mightiest in moral . . . —2045
Reformer—can't last in politics—1599
Reforming—Nothing so needs . . . as other people's habits—955

Rich—need no protection—1373, 2058
Rich—pardon the . . . —1950
Rich—there are more poor people than . . . people—1550
Rich—They and not the . . . are our dependence for continued freedom—1544
Riches—alone attract less awe and public merit—492
Richest—country on the globe—492
Richest—That man is the . . . —645
Riders—in a race do not stop short when they reach the goal—27
Right—as God gives us to see the . . . —316, 1098
Right—Citizenship is man's basic . . . —323
Right—firmness in the . . . —316, 1098
Right—first medical . . . of all Americans—975
Right—First to fight for . . . and freedom—1334
Right—get it . . . —663
Right—hardest task is not to do what is . . . —1666
Right—hew to the line of . . . —154
Right—I had rather be . . . than President—1093
Right—know what is . . . —1666
Right—makes might—174, 1097
Right—no . . . to strike against the public safety—1184
Right—of all to be happy—968
Right—of every person "to be let alone"—1822
Right—of the people to alter or abolish—521
Right—of the people to make and to alter their constitutions—430, 921
Right—Our country, may she always be in the . . . —1513
Right—our country, . . . or wrong—1513
Right—peace which comes as of . . . —1528
Right—to advance—1813
Right—to be alone—1691
Right—to be let alone—1696
Right—to choose for itself the form of government—1621
Right—to demonstrate my disagreement with a law—801, 1821
Right—to have rights—323
Right—to pass through this world—1694
Right—vindicate the . . . as best we may—381
Right—voting for the . . . is doing nothing for it—2026
Right—way, wrong way and Army way—664
Rights—can never be forfeited—1345
Rights—certain unalienable . . . —521
Rights—exclusive . . . to their respective writings and discoveries—1849
Rights—free to stand up for his . . . —1723, 1826
Rights—Governments exist to protect the . . . of minorities—1373

Starved—into democracy—1081
State—As the home, so the . . . —1011
State—cannot get a cent from any man—644
State—education is perhaps the most important function of . . . and local government—657
State—still more perfect and glorious . . . —2004
State—which can afford to be just to all men—2004
States—better government in the . . . —908
States—free and independent . . . —522
States—have no rights—1828
States—have responsibilities—1828
Status—The . . . Seekers—136
Stein—With a . . . on the table—613
Step—one small . . . for a man—701
Stick—Speak softly and carry a big . . . —793
Stick—Walk softly and carry a big . . . —1935
Sting—Oh debt, where is thy . . . —516
Stomach—way to a man's heart is through his . . . —768
Stomach—worship God on an empty . . . —1085
Strange—nothing so . . . as truth—2000
Streams—America whose . . . are protected—637
Streets—keep the . . . safe from bullies and marauders—2013
Streets—seen them in a thousand . . . of a hundred towns—2135
Strength—and progress and peaceful change—820
Strength—disorderly and unscrupulous . . . —1219
Strength—Law and order enforced with justice and by . . . —1219
Strike—no right to . . . against the public safety—1184
Strikes—Three . . . you're out—198
Struck out—mighty Casey has . . . —195
Struggle—real hero of this . . . is the American Negro—227
Students—sex for the . . . —364
Styles—liberals change as the . . . change—1235
Sub—Sighted . . . , sank same—1403
Subject—being a bad . . . —1426
Subjugation—by armed minorities—794
Substitute—no . . . for victory—2037
Suburb—make any . . . do anything—337
Suburbs—in search of a city—1588
Subversion—never confuse honest dissent with disloyal . . . —581
Succeed—man cannot be said to . . . —846
Succeed—Most people would . . . in small things—47
Succeed—Nations . . . only as they are able to respond to challenge—308
Success—finishing under par is considered a big . . . —895

Why—Some men see things as they are and say . . . —1095
Why not—I dream things that never were and say, ". . ." —1095
Wife—old . . . , old dog and ready money—843
Wife—proud . . . and a surprised mother-in-law—725
Wild—blue yonder—36
Will—its own sweet . . . —1286
Will—at 20 years of age the . . . reigns—25
Wine—eloquent if you give him good . . . —611
Wine—instead of water—488
Wine—sorceries of opium or . . . —622
Wing—coming in on a . . . and a prayer—33
Wings—of man—37
Winner—take all—878
Winning—isn't everything—1893
Wins—Somebody loses whenever somebody . . . —872
Winter—cold and cruel . . . —1853
Winter—long and dreary . . . —1853
Wisdom—conventional . . . —1175
Wisdom—of age—24
Wisdom—privilege of . . . to listen—1177
Wise—healthy, wealthy and . . . —973
Wiser—makes men . . . but less happy—1973
Wiser—We are . . . than we know—1172
Wish—I . . . to live—166
Wish—I sincerely . . . ingratitude was not so natural—932
Wish—Men who . . . to live—166
Wish—Nothing is so commonplace as to . . . to be remarkable—46
Wishes—If a man could have half his . . . —1981
Wit—at thirty the . . . reigns—25
Wit—makes its own welcome—1072
Witenagemot—one session of the world's . . . to the next—1913
Woman—good time to be a . . . —2095
Woman—has her way—2094
Woman—is man's equal—2098
Woman—usurpations on the part of man toward . . . —2098
Woman's—virtue is man's greatest invention—2100
Women—great city is that which has the greatest men and . . . —340
Women—all men and . . . are created equal—2097
Women—are changing very fast—2091
Women—are now in an age of unprecedented power—2101
Women—Diplomats, . . . and crabs—573
Women—men and . . . do not always love in accordance with the prayer—1862
Women—influence of good . . . —2093

AUTHOR INDEX

(Note: Quotation number follows each entry.)

Aaron, Henry (Hank) (1934–   ) baseball player
21
Adams, Abigail (Smith) (1744–1818) wife of John Adams
1361, 1641
Adams, Franklin P(ierce) (1881–1960) columnist and radio personality
1411
Adams, Henry B(rooks) (1838–1918) writer-historian
951, 1642
Adams, John (1735–1826) writer, statesman, second President
561, 901, 961, 1002, 1121, 1761
Adams, John Quincy (1767–1848) statesman, sixth President, son of John Adams
311, 1091
Adams, Samuel (1722–1803) pamphleteer, Revolutionary War leader
1122
Addams, Jane (1860–1935) social worker
1092
Agnew, Spiro T(heodore) (1918–   ) resigned Vice President
1, 301, 401, 801, 1371, 1661, 1791, 1821
Aiken, George D(avid) (1892–   ) statesman
1081
Akers, Elizabeth Chase (1832–1911) journalist, poet
1951
Akins, Zoe (1886–1958) playwright
1861
Alcott, A(mos) Bronson (1799–1888) educator, writer
1011, 1991
Aldrin, Edwin E(ugene) Jr. (1930–   ) astronaut
1532
Alexander, Shana (Ager) (1925–   ) writer
1351, 1662, 2091
Alinsky, Saul D(avid) (1909–1972) social activist
1762, 2131
Allen, Fred (John F. Sullivan) (1894–1956) comedian
1901

INDEX OF SUBJECT HEADINGS

(Note: Quotation numbers follow each entry.)

Past • 1501–1504
Patriotism • 1511–1520
Peace • 1521–1532
People • 1541–1552
Philanthropy • 1561–1566
Pioneering • 1571–1575
Places • 1581–1588
Politics • 1591–1604
Popularity • 1611–1616
Posterity • 1621–1625
Poverty • 1631–1640
Power • 1641–1648
Prejudice • 1651–1656
Presidency • 1661–1671
Pride • 1681–1685
Privacy • 1691–1696
Prohibition • 1701–1705
Prosperity • 1711–1715
Protest • 1721–1725
Public Opinion • 1731–1737

Races • 1741–1746
Radicals • 1751–1756
Rebellion • 1761–1768
Religion • 1771–1782
Republicans • 1791–1794
Reputation • 1801–1804
Retirement • 1811–1814
Rights • 1821–1828

Salesmanship • 1831–1834
Science • 1841–1849
Seasons • 1851–1858
Sex • 1861–1867
Society • 1871–1879
Speed • 1881–1886
Sport • 1891–1896
Success • 1901–1907
Superstition • 1911–1915
Symbols • 1921–1926

Tactics • 1931–1935
Taxes • 1941–1950
Time • 1951–1960
Tradition • 1961–1965
Travel • 1971–1977
Trouble • 1981–1986
Truth • 1991–2000

Utopia • 2001–2004

Violence • 2011–2015
Voting • 2021–2026

War and Wars • 2031–2040
Washington, George • 2041–2046
Wealth • 2051–2060
Weather • 2061–2066
Welfare • 2071–2073
West • 2081–2084
Women • 2091–2102
Work • 2111–2117
Worries • 2121–2125

Youth • 2131–2139